FEN TIGER

To Jeff

FEN TIGER

The Success of Dave 'Boy' Green

Happy Birthday 2010

Bob Lonkhurst

David 'Boy' Green MBE

Published by
BL Associates

Published by BL Associates
6 Drayton Avenue
Potters Bar
Hertfordshire

First published 2004
© Bob Lonkhurst and Dave 'Boy' Green 2004

Typeset and designed by
Typecast (Artwork & Design)
Yeovil, Somerset
Cover and illustrations by
PDQ, Digital Media Solutions Ltd.

Printed in Great Britain by
Clays Ltd. St Ives plc.

A catalogue record for this book is
available from the British Library

ISBN 0-9540271-2-4

DEDICATION

FOR
ANDY SMITH

A remarkable man who had such
an impact on Dave's life.

… and for Dave's parents, Ken and
Mary, his loyal and loving wife
Kay, and their three children
David, Suzanne and Emma.

Also by Bob Lonkhurst

MAN OF COURAGE: *The Life and*
                        Career of Tommy Farr

GENTLEMAN OF THE RING: *The Life and*
                        Career of Jack Petersen

EAST END IDOL: *The Amazing Story*
                        of Terry Spinks MBE

CONTENTS

FOREWORD

I was proud and also extremely flattered when Dave 'Boy' Green asked me to write the foreword to his biography. And I agreed without a moment's hesitation. There is always a special bond between boxers who fight each other.

Though I fought 36 opponents, I've had a special rapport with Dave ever since he challenged me for my world welterweight title 24 years ago.

People who don't know or understand boxing genuinely believe the hype that surrounds most big fights. The public are led to presume fighters develop a bitter hatred towards each other as the battle gets nearer.

Promoters, aided and abetted by the media, have been selling fights on that premise since boxing began. Yet nothing could be further from the truth. There are always exceptions, but in most cases there is mutual respect between fighters.

We are all involved in a very dangerous business – risking our lives every time we step through the ropes. How can anyone, therefore, not honour and admire a man who is prepared to reach the top of his profession?

But I must admit I wasn't too pleased with Dave when we first met in Landover, Maryland, in March 1980. When we were introduced at the pre-fight press conference I didn't take kindly to his attitude. He appeared to be sneering contemptuously at me – at least I thought he was.

As it turned out, Dave was particularly unlucky the night we clashed. I threw thousands of punches in my career, but nothing compared with the flawless left hook I crashed against his chin in the fourth round.

That was unquestionably my most devastating knockout win. But I am delighted to say from the moment Dave recovered from that blow we have remained the best of friends.

When he retired, Dave came out to Las Vegas several times to see me defend my title. He was my guest at ringside when I beat Tommy Hearns and Marvellous Marvin Hagler.

I shall never forget when I came to England a couple of years after our fight and visited Dave, his charming wife Kay and son in Chatteris. We had a wonderful day together, and the name of the village pub where we had lunch will stick in my mind for ever – it was called the Pike & Eel.

Dave was a brave fighting man who never gave less than one hundred per cent whenever he put on the gloves. He is a warm human being who does tremendous work for charity, and I'm thrilled he has made such a success in business.

It would give me great pleasure if Dave were to visit me and my family at my home in California because he will always have a special place in my heart.

SUGAR RAY LEONARD
California, USA – 2004

ACKNOWLEDGEMENTS

The foreword is an extremely important section of any biography, especially if it is in the form of a moving tribute to the subject provided by a well known celebrity. I did, however, wonder if we were aiming too high when I suggested to Dave that Sugar Ray Leonard would be the ideal person to provide such for this book.

Although Dave received an initial response to an e-mail, I still had reservations because Sugar Ray is a very busy man and often difficult to locate. Colin Hart of *The Sun*, however, offered to take the idea on board, made contact with Leonard, and obtained what is the ultimate tribute to one of Britain's most exciting fighters.

My sincere thanks therefore go to Sugar Ray for kindly devoting time to his former opponent, and to Colin for doing all the leg-work.

Many people have made important contributions by relating stories about Dave's schooldays, boxing career, family and business life, and his work for charity. I make special mention of Dave Cole, who first introduced him to boxing, Jim Moore who trained Green as an amateur, Gordon Palmer, secretary of his fan club, and Rod Marriner, his greatest fan who not only saw all his fights, but still spends a lot of time in his company.

I had the benefit of speaking at length with Pat Ringham, former Sports Editor of the *Cambridgeshire Times*, who gave vivid accounts of the impact Dave had on people living in the Fens. His contribution was essential.

Special thanks go to Brian Asplin, Editor of *Cambridgeshire Times Group*, who kindly gave authority to reproduce extracts from his paper which are so crucial to Dave's story. Wendy Nottage, a journalist with the same group, wrote an article advising readers that the book was being written. Her request for people with stories about Green prompted a good response.

Bob Emerson, Dave's long term business partner, devoted a great deal of time to enlighten me about their business relationship. That information has never been in the public domain, and therefore forms a crucial part of the book.

I am extremely appreciative of the contribution of Robert Smith, Assistant General Secretary of the British Boxing Board of Control, whose father guided Green so successfully throughout his boxing career and into business. He loaned me newspaper cuttings, documents and photographs from his father's study thereby giving a much wider insight into Dave's life.

Although it was not possible to interview Andy Smith, who now suffers from ill health, I acknowledge the tremendous part he has played in the Dave Green story. He was an eloquent and passionate speaker who could have written this book far better than me. I have therefore quoted him throughout because he knew Dave better than anyone.

Former schoolteachers, Dennis Hall and Rita Goodger, provided interesting stories about Green as a pupil, and I acknowledge information given by local people, including John Salisbury, Alice Hanlon, Peter and Frances Aspinall.

Boxing personalities Jimmy Harrington, John Bibby and Marcus McDonnell related amusing anecdotes, whilst Gil Boyd provided massive information about Dave's tireless work for charity, as did John Tucker. My son Phil assisted me considerably during last minute preparations for which I am grateful.

I thank my good friend Barry Hugman for his continued guidance towards publication, and his wife Jennifer who kindly read the manuscript. I am also indebted to my dear friend Maureen Cox whose advice I frequently called upon when the going got tough.

Once again, I extend special thanks to Jean Bastin of Typecast (Artwork & Design), for her professionalism regarding typeset and design of the book.

ACKNOWLEDGEMENTS

Although much of what is contained in this biography was obtained during interviews and research, I acknowledge the following publications which I consulted: *Chatteris Advertiser, Cambridgeshire Times, Cambridge Evening News, Peterborough Evening Telegraph, Boxing News, Daily Mail, Daily Mirror, Daily Telegraph, The Sun, Sunday People, Sunday Times, Jersey Evening Post,* and *Sport & Showbiz.*

All photographs reproduced in this book are from Dave's private collection, and whilst every effort has been made to trace original sources, this has not been possible in some cases. I do, however, acknowledge permission kindly given by the *Cambridgeshire Times, Peterborough Evening Telegraph,* and Dumbleton Studios, Cambridge.

Finally, I thank members of Dave's family for their patience and massive contributions. Brother, Michael, described their lives as children, while David, Suzanne and Emma enlightened me about his warmth and support as a father. Loyal and loving wife Kay related instances that only a woman could. This was particularly rewarding because during our first meeting she remarked: "I don't know why you want to interview me because you won't be able to print anything I tell you."

INTRODUCTION

I regard myself as fortunate to have seen all of Dave 'Boy' Green's professional fights in London. It was therefore an honour and privilege when he asked me to write his biography.

Green was without doubt, one of the most exciting British fighters of the last 30 years. Raw aggression rather than dazzling skill made him an internationally known figure. He was good for boxing, and one of the few men capable of selling out major arenas such as Wembley and the Royal Albert Hall.

Like so many other fans, I was thrilled by his performances in the ring. A Dave Green fight-night conjured up a special kind of excitement because his aggression and determination created an atmosphere rarely seen in modern times.

Boxing fans always know when a fighter has a big heart, and that is why we loved Green from the moment he turned professional. A stocky, broad-shouldered young man, he was loaded with a do-or-die spirit, and brought to the ring superb physical condition, strength and punching power in both hands. He was also a rarity among modern-day fighters – an excellent body puncher.

The fans always got value for money, and I vividly recall sitting on the edge of my seat every time I watched him fight. I never took my eyes off the ring from the moment he climbed through the ropes clad in his tiger-skin dressing-gown. His snarling aggression and baring of the gum shield added to the excitement. Dave Green was that kind of fighter – he held his audience.

Shrewdly guided by the astute Andy Smith, Green seemed unbeatable as a young light-welterweight, smashing a string of opponents to defeat with apparent ease. He ripped the British title from Joey Singleton with an awesome display of aggression, and six months later stopped experienced Frenchman, Jean-Baptiste Piedvache, to capture the European crown.

The same brand of excitement was served up when he moved up to welterweight. He halted former world champion, John H. Stracey, in one of the most eagerly awaited all-British pairings for many years. He then gave a truly memorable display against world champion, Carlos Palomino, before being knocked out in the 11th round with the fight very much in the balance. In less than three years as champion, Palomino went on to become one of the highest ever money-earners in the welterweight division, yet Dave came so close to beating him.

Putting the Palomino defeat firmly behind him, Dave re-grouped, and 18 months later brutally destroyed Henry Rhiney to capture his second European championship. Although he lost it to Jorgen Hansen in what was expected to be a routine defence, Green had good connections. In less than a year he received a massive purse to challenge Sugar Ray Leonard for the world title in the United States. The champion, however, was too smart, and knocked Dave cold in the fourth round with one of the best punches of his career.

Despite repeated calls for him to quit, Green boxed on for another 20 months until Andy Smith pulled him out of a fight against lowly-rated Reg Ford at the Royal Albert Hall. The sparkle had gone, and it was a compassionate move by the man, who apart from being his manager, was also his closest friend. Had he not acted as he did, Dave would have fought on, not for the money, but because he loved the sport.

Green had a simple philosophy about being a fighter: "It's just a matter of when two fellows meet in the ring, it's got to be one or the other. That's what I believe. When they were gloving me up before a fight, I would look across the ring and say to myself; 'It's him or me.' I liked it to be me."

Andy Smith once compared Dave to Carmen Basilio, and also said there were similarities with Rocky Marciano. They were reasonable comparisons because like the two former world champions, Green was a quiet, home-loving man outside the ring. He remained polite and reserved, with a warm sense of humour which endeared him to people wherever he went. Once he stripped off his dressing-gown, however, he became a mean and ruthless fighting machine, and made it clear from the start that he fought without compromise.

Dave would never claim to have been a great technical boxer, but his surging aggression and relentless body attacks certainly made him one of the country's great crowd-pleasers. He was also one of the most courageous, and opponents had to knock him out to win. Only men of the highest calibre succeeded in doing so. With Dave Green, action of the highest quality was always guaranteed.

"When Dave's in the ring, it's always pure excitement," Andy Smith once remarked. "If you haven't got the punches to put him down, then you are in terrible trouble."

Without Smith, it is unlikely that Dave would have reached the heights he did because apart from being his boxing manager, he was also his financial and business advisor. He was an eloquent speaker, who at his many press conferences, described every issue with passion and in great detail. Nobody knew Green better, and for that reason I have quoted him throughout the book because his comments are so important in giving a better understanding of Dave's personality and ability.

Sponsored for much of his career by Adidas, boxing dramatically changed Dave's life. When he turned professional he was working on a carrot farm, but on Smith's advice, stuck at the job for several years and lived off his meagre earnings. Purse money from his fights went in to a savings account, and 12 months later he was able to purchase his first property.

Within a few years, he had a luxury Georgian-style house built, and took stylish holidays abroad. From a second-hand mini motor car, he upgraded to a gleaming white sponsored Chrysler Alpine, and over the last two decades has always driven a top of the range Mercedes with a personalised index plate.

Andy Smith was also instrumental in easing Dave into business some months before he quit boxing. Starting as a sales representative with Chatteris based company, Renoak Limited, he rapidly progressed to Managing Director, and 23 years later is joint owner of what is a substantial and highly respected packaging and distribution operation.

Despite the transformation in his life, Dave never lost contact with boxing. He held a trainer's licence for three years before becoming a member of the Southern Area Council of the British Boxing Board of Control, a position he held for 14 years. He maintained close contact with Sugar Ray Leonard, who on a filming trip to Britain in 1982, insisted on visiting his former opponent at his Chatteris home. In return, Green travelled to America for many of Sugar Ray's big fights, and was given the red carpet treatment. Testimony of the respect which exists between the two is reflected in the fact that the American superstar readily agreed to provide the foreword for this book.

Fame and wealth have never affected Dave. His personality has never changed, and he has the respect of everyone who knows him. Having never left his roots, he is just as happy playing dominoes with his mates in the bar of his local pub as he is attending prestigious functions at plush hotels in the big city centres. He loves presenting prizes to youngsters at small amateur boxing shows, and does a massive amount of work for charity. Nothing is too much trouble for him.

Green's story is not just about boxing. It is one of incredible success achieved by a boy born into a Cambridgeshire farming community whose determination and courage have taken him to the top in sport and business. Appreciative of his good fortune, he is committed to putting something back into society.

Unlike many great fighters, Dave invested his ring earnings wisely and provided a wonderful life-style for his family. Supported by his loyal and hard-working wife Kay, he has fulfilled most of his dreams.

Writing Dave's book has been a thoroughly enjoyable

experience. The task was made easier by the fact that he has retained numerous scrapbooks bulging with cuttings of his fights. An old school exercise book contains meticulous details of all his junior and senior amateur contests which are reproduced in the appendix.

I have deliberately referred to Dave's entire professional career, as well as many contests when he was a junior and senior amateur. Not to have done so would have detracted from the true picture I wanted to portray. His exciting style conjured up memories of another Chatteris legend, Eric Boon, who took a genuine, yet unobtrusive interest in his career.

Dave 'Boy' Green is a role model for sport, in particular boxing, and I sincerely hope I have been able to give readers an accurate insight of a truly remarkable man. It is a privilege to know him.

Bob Lonkhurst
Potters Bar – 2004

✦ 1 ✦

SCHOOLDAYS

A cloud of sadness and deep emotion descended over the Royal Albert Hall in London late on a cold November evening during 1981. The audience were stunned because the career of one of Britain's most popular and exciting fighters had come to an abrupt and unexpected end.

For decades, top quality boxing promotions had been staged at the great arena. Champions had come and gone, and the ring had been the work-place for thousands of fighters of all levels. Yet the drama of this particular evening will live in the memories of those present for a very long time.

As the bell rang to end round five of a light-middleweight contest, a small white-haired manager climbed through the ropes, put a hand on his fighter's shoulder and said: "That's it son – I'm pulling you out." Without another word, he strode to the centre of the ring, took the MC's microphone and uttered the chilling words: "Ladies and gentlemen, that is the last time you will see the Fen Tiger."

Dave 'Boy' Green was devastated as he stood in his corner. A cocktail of blood, sweat and tears streamed down his face as the reality set in. His career as a professional fighter was over. He couldn't understand it because having just had his best round of the fight, he believed victory was only minutes away.

The manager, however, saw it differently. The sparkle had gone, and Green was struggling against a second-rate fighter he would have beaten with ease a couple of years earlier. It was time to say goodbye.

Everyone in the audience knew of his massive contribution to British boxing over recent years. Memories of the thrills and excitement he generated, the atmosphere of the packed houses and the antics of his wonderful Fenland supporters, all came flooding back.

The spontaneous ovation they gave him as he left the ring for the last time was a moving salute. "A wonderful response for a wonderful man," said his manager and friend, Andy Smith. There would never be any talk of a comeback.

* * *

David Robert Green was born on Coronation Day, 2 June 1953, at 5 High Street, Chatteris, the small terraced house home of his parents, Ken and Mary. He had a brother, Michael, two years his elder.

Situated amid the flat, fertile Fenland region of Cambridgeshire, about 12 miles west of Ely, Chatteris is a small market town steeped in history. It appears in the Doomsday Book as Cetriz to signify its woodland region. Until the mid-17th century, however, it was situated on a Fen Island completely surrounded by water separating it from surrounding settlements. Modern-day Fenland was created by an amazing feat of engineering which transformed huge areas of swampland into one of the most profitable farming regions in Britain.

Gradually, over hundreds of years, the town increased in size with the development of industry and transport. In 1847, a railway line was opened from Cambridge through St Ives, Chatteris and March. The estimated population during this time was 5,000. There were 15 inns and hotels, a further 43 beer houses, and by the early part of the 20th century, the town had two breweries.

Served by the Forty Foot drain, Chatteris Docks were constructed, and barges became an important transport link. In the late 1800's, Chatteris Engineering Works was created, and specialised in manufacturing equipment for the South African gold mining industry. After the company changed its name midway through the 20th century, goods manufactured included gearboxes for use on ships including the HMS Ark Royal. Another local company made hangmans' nooses.

Between the wars, Chatteris firmly established itself as the centre of the country's rapidly growing carrot industry. Rich in vitamin C, carrots, which had for many years been grown mainly as animal feed, suddenly became a nutritious and popular ingredient of the human diet. Consequently, after the second world war, it became the main crop of the Fens, providing work for thousands of agricultural labourers.

Modernisation in farming methods, however, meant that hundreds of jobs were gradually lost. The horse drawn plough became a thing of the past, and complicated machinery replaced individuals to wash and grade carrots. Many therefore moved away from agriculture into jobs involving manufacturing and commerce.

The Greens were a farming family, Ken and his brother Fred having bought some land adjacent to their father's farm between Sutton Gault and Manea when they were in their 20's. Together, they worked the two farms until their father, Ernest Green, died in 1965. Ken and Fred then amalgamated the two properties into one 92 acre arable farm.

They grew sugar beet, potatoes, wheat and barley, and also reared about 100 pigs and some cattle. They had three working horses named 'Pink', 'Punch' and 'Blossom', which were used for ploughing the fields and general work around the farm before the introduction of a tractor.

Ken Green worked from 8am until dark, usually seven days a week, while his wife kept house and cared for the children. Almost from when they were toddlers, Dave and his brother spent hours at the farm especially during harvesting time. As soon as they were big enough they started doing jobs around the buildings and in the fields. Most school holidays were spent on the farm, and Dave was 13 when they first went away for a real holiday – one week at Great Yarmouth. They had plenty of days out to places such as Hunstanton, Skegness, Yarmouth and Wickstead Park, Kettering, but Ken's life was usually tied up on the farm.

With no sophisticated machinery as in modern times, everything was done by hand. Sugar beet was chopped from the ground and thrown into heaps to await collection.

After the crops had been removed from the ground by a 'spinner', potato picking was done by gangs of casual labourers. They filled baskets, tossed them into the back of a trailer where Dave and Michael emptied them and threw the baskets back into the fields.

Wheat and barley was cut by a reaping machine, bound into sheaves and tossed to the ground. The boys then helped stand the sheaves into blocks of 16 to dry. It was a laborious task called shocking. A week or so later, the sheaves were collected and stacked to await threshing.

One of their smaller tasks was mucking out the pigsties and filling them with new litter which they carried from nearby stacks. They also fed the horses, Dave's favourite being a chestnut called 'Punch'.

* * *

At the age of five, Dave started school at Burnsfield Infants. Two years later he moved to the adjacent King Edward County Primary, a mixed school with 10 classes catering for children aged seven to 11. He was happy there, and received good attendance certificates in 1961, '62 and '63 during which time he missed only 10 days.

He was a polite and co-operative pupil who did his best in the classroom, although he found games and sport more to his liking than subjects such as English, maths and history. For him, sports day was the highlight of the school year, and in his final term won the high jump and long distance events.

4

He loved football, and was only eight when he first played in the school team. Most of his team-mates, including his brother, were at least two years older and in their final year. Despite this, Dave quickly developed into a creative naturally left-sided player. He soon became the star of the team, and the following year was selected to play for Isle of Ely Schools. At the age of 11 he was captain of Cambridgeshire County Schools team.

The headmaster at King Edward was Dennis Hall, himself a talented footballer, who in his younger days played for March Town. There being a strong emphasis on sport within the school, he was personally involved both during school hours and on Saturdays which were match days. He quickly recognised Green's talent and took a particular interest in him, always believing he had the ability to play at the highest level.

Matches were played most Saturday mornings between September and Easter against junior schools from March, Ely, Littleport, Soham, Haddenham and surrounding areas. A bus was provided to take the boys to all away games.

There was also an annual local derby match against Cromwell Secondary School first year team who were aged between 11 and 12. Being younger boys, King Edward was usually beaten, often by a wide margin. In Dave's final year, however, they secured a draw which was regarded locally as an outstanding achievement.

Dave's childhood was a happy one, and apart from football he loved other sports including cricket, table tennis and running. He was an aggressive batsman at cricket and played for the school in his final year, but lacked the patience to stay at the wicket and build a big score.

He also liked fishing. There were lots of small drains around his father's farm which were full of fish such as roach, chub, pike and eels. Three miles from Chatteris was the Forty Foot, a huge waterway frequently used for competition fishing.

Dave received tremendous support from his parents in everything he did. They were a hard working, yet happy and

5

contented family living in a gentle and relaxed environment. Much of his determination and enthusiasm stemmed from encouragement given to him by his father who loved sport and was always trying to help him.

As a boy, Ken Green had not been allowed to play football on Saturdays because he had to work on his father's farm. Yet despite being restricted he became a good footballer, and before the war played regularly for Chatteris Horsway. He always said that if he had children he would encourage them to play as much sport as possible. Consequently, whether Dave was playing football, cricket, running cross-country or in mile races, Ken was there to cheer him on. They had a wonderful father and son relationship.

At the age of 11, Dave moved to Cromwell County Secondary School at Wenny Road, Chatteris. Whilst there were a wider range of subjects to study, sport continued to dominate his life, and this was reflected in his school reports.

At the age of 12 he was described as a promising classroom student, particularly at mathematics. Over the next three years, however, those reports became littered with comments such as: *"must pay more attention; fidgety during lessons; has difficulty in concentrating – it tends to interrupt his private conversations."*

His English teacher frequently remarked that he found it difficult to concentrate. In science, it was claimed that he was easily distracted, whist another teacher made the comment: *"he must bear in mind that sport isn't everything in life."*

Whilst mathematics was the only educational subject in which Dave showed particular interest, gymnastics, games and athletics were those at which he really excelled. Most terms, favourable remarks appeared on his school reports regarding his prowess at football and athletics. He brought great pride to the school by being a member of the County teams at both.

His development at football was incredible, and during his first term at Cromwell progressed from being a member of the County Under 12 team to the Under 13 side made up of second year boys.

Dave also developed into an outstanding wicket keeper at cricket. The position suited him because it required concentration on every ball bowled. Being a hyperactive boy, he needed to be involved all the time. Had be been put in a position of little activity, he would have quickly lost interest and stopped playing the game.

Although he enjoyed running and won races at his junior school, Dave first came to prominence as an athlete in 1964. He entered a three-lap race for 10-11 year olds at a big sports event staged annually on Whit Monday by Chatteris Town Committee at Manor Field, and finished well ahead of his rivals.

At Cromwell School, he developed a keen interest in cross-country running. With his close friend and rival, David Smalley, he trained every day, doing five laps around the school playing field between 12 noon and 12.30pm before they went to lunch. He won a Cambridgeshire Schools County championship in consecutive years when aged 13 and 14. Smalley was runner-up each year.

Both also represented Cambridgeshire in the All-England schools championships the same years. At Derby in 1966, Green finished 127th and Smalley 128th in a field of 500 of the best young runners in the country. The following year, Dave improved to 89th. These were incredible performances for a lad who had no steep hills on which to build his stamina. He had to make do with small humpback bridges and flat lonely Fenland lanes on which to prepare. Determination, however, made up for the loss of important facilities, and he always had an abundance of that.

Dave loved running, and while some boys took notes to school from their mothers claiming backache or some other excuse, he would run three miles or more and thoroughly enjoy it. By this stage, however, he was starting to develop as a promising schoolboy boxer. Although running remained an essential part of his training, he stopped taking part in competitions, but always believed that had he continued he would have eventually won a major cross-country championship.

Apart from his love of sport, Dave was involved in many other things as a youngster, all of which helped give him a good start in life. He attended Sunday school at Zion Baptist Chapel, East Park Street, for a number of years, and between 1963 and 1965 was awarded certificates of merit for scripture. When brother Michael first started at the age of five, Dave cried because he was too young to go. He cried again when he had to leave.

He obtained a National Cycling Proficiency Certificate, and was a boy scout with the 2nd Chatteris Troop. In 1966, he won a three-day competition at the Easter training camp. At March & District Scouting Association sports day in July the same year, his sporting prowess helped secure victories in the sack-race, high jump and relay events.

* * *

For a number of years, Chatteris Amateur Boxing Club, formed in the 1940's and originally based at the George Hotel, operated from Slade End School, Bridge Street. The premises, which had been unoccupied for some years, were leased from Cambridgeshire County Council and converted into a well equipped gym.

Green was introduced to boxing early in 1967 when a schoolmate, Dave Cole, asked him to join the club. Cole had taken up boxing 12 months earlier after he and his brother went to a tournament organised by Chatteris ABC at Manea Village Hall. The club was short of junior boxers, and when secretary, Dick Leader, asked if he could persuade some more youngsters to join, he immediately thought of Dave.

The two were close friends because both were keen on sport and in the same class. Loving a challenge, Green agreed to go to a club training night as did half a dozen other sport-minded youngsters from their class.

Dave became the youngest of 35 club members up to the age of 20. Juniors trained from 6pm to 7pm, and seniors 7pm to 8pm or later. The gym had a floor-level ring at one end with punch-bags and a speedball, while further punch-bags hung from the ceiling at the opposite end.

Green's first trainer was Arthur Binder, a legend in Chatteris, who for years had been a highly respected football and boxing coach. Born in 1898, he was an amateur boxer during the first world war, then began his association with soccer in 1920 as trainer for Chatteris Engineers, at the time one of the finest teams for miles around. He remained with the club until the outbreak of the second world war, and later gave valuable service to Chatteris Town.

Arthur's connection with boxing was even more illustrious both at amateur and professional level. His greatest success was with local boy, Eric Boon, whom he taught to box at the age of 11. They formed a formidable partnership for over 70 fights before London promoter, Jack Solomons, took over Boon's management.

Chatteris Boxing Club flourished under Binder, who for a couple of years, was also instructor to the Army Cadet Force. In 1949, his team had one All-England champion and three runners-up, all from Chatteris.

Dave trained on Tuesday and Thursday evenings, and adapted well to his new venture. His determination for success at everything he did made him a natural, and because of his involvement in other sports he was already extremely fit. Binder liked the way he fought because his raw style was similar to that of Boon when he first put the gloves on.

Despite his inexperience, Dave was ready for his first contest within a month or so of joining the club. Although his parents were somewhat surprised when he told them, they gave him their blessing. "If that's what you want to do son, it's alright by us," his father told him.

As Dave weighed less than six stone, it was difficult for the organisers to find him an opponent for his first contest scheduled to take place at the Dorothy Ballroom, Cambridge, on 31 March 1967. The only available boy of his age was Mario Stango from Bedford, an established schoolboy boxer who two weeks earlier had won a national championship at 6st 8.

Although it was a difficult decision, Chatteris secretary, Dick Leader, agreed to the contest even though he knew Stango would be several pounds heavier. Green had shown remarkable ability in the gym, so Dick, an excellent matchmaker who knew every boxer's ability, was confident he could look after himself.

Because he had never been to a boxing show, Dave wasn't overwhelmed at the prospect of his first fight. Even when he reached the venue he was still unaware of the quality of the opponent he was to face. It was only when he was actually in the dressing-room that the details unfolded.

Dave Cole, who was boxing on the same bill, stayed with Green all the time. He did his best to familiarise him with the set-up by pointing out some of the lads from other boxing clubs and explaining what they had achieved. Thinking nothing of it, he indicated Mario Stango. "See that lad over there," he remarked. "He's just won a schoolboy championship."

Cole only realised the significance of what he had said when Dick Leader walked into the dressing-room an hour or so later and said: "Come on Greeny, get yourself ready, you're on in a few minutes." Curious to see who his schoolmate was boxing, Cole peered at the secretary's list and was horrified when he read that he had been matched with Stango. Leader was furious with Cole and asked why he had mentioned to Green that Stango was a schoolboy champion. Cole, who immediately regretted what he had done, explained that he had no idea that Mario was Green's opponent because there was no reference to it in the programme. What he said was in complete innocence.

Green was somewhat bewildered when he understood the situation, but being the confident boy he was, soon relished the challenge of fighting such an experienced opponent. Not once did he contemplate the possibility of getting beaten.

As was to be expected, Stango was always in control and won comfortably on points, but Dave was far from disgraced. He had the dinner-jacketed crowd roaring him on as he

10

nipped in and out, and bounced back and forth as though he had springs in his heels. Every so often he even had the cheek and confidence to stand and trade punches with the schoolboy champion. Yet in the main he gave the classic example of following his trainer's instructions of keeping on the move.

The bout ended to tremendous applause, and Dave not only won the prize for the best loser of the night, but received congratulations from more total strangers than any of his club officials could ever remember. He had gone into the ring wearing a pair of baggy shorts which were rolled over at the top because the elastic was broken, his red Emmanuel House school vest and a pair of grubby frayed white plimsoles which he had scrubbed after using them for cross-country running.

As he left the ring, a woman from the audience walked up and congratulated him for putting up such a wonderful display. "You were magnificent," she said with a warm smile and thrusting a five pound note into his hand. "Take this and buy yourself a nice new pair of boxing boots."

Another admirer gave him 10 shillings, and a few days later Dave bought himself a complete new outfit – vest, shorts and a pair of boxing boots. "It was amazing what you could buy for a fiver in those days," he remarked when recalling the event. "I just wish I could have found out who that woman was. I would loved to have met her again and thanked her properly."

It was an amazing debut because weighing only 5st 12, Green gave away about half a stone in weight to an extremely talented young boxer who had lost only twice in his three year career. Stango, a southpaw, had also won on points at Leicester the previous evening, and on his path to the schoolboy championship had won quarter-final, semi and final within the space of five weeks between mid-February and 18 March. He would progress to win a National Federation of Boys' Clubs championship in 1969, and a Southern Area title as a professional in 1974.

Joint guests of honour at the Cambridge show were British

11

and Empire bantamweight champion, Alan Rudkin, and national hunt jockey, Josh Gifford. In presenting Dave with a travelling rug as his prize, Rudkin gave him warm words of encouragement which thrilled the youngster. He also signed his programme. The previous year, Alan had put up a magnificent display against Fighting Harada for the world title in Tokyo only to lose narrowly on points. He became Green's idol, and from the day he met him, Dave followed all of his fights until he retired from the ring in 1972.

Despite being disappointed at not winning his first contest, Dave was convinced he had a future as a boxer. Everyone at the club heaped praise upon him because, what had on paper looked to be a ridiculous match, turned out to be close and exciting. Showing great courage and determination, he convinced everyone he had exactly the right attitude to become successful. He trained hard in the gym, and maintained his fitness by running and playing football.

Dave's first success in the ring came in his next contest on a show at St Ives two weeks later. Although he was far less experienced than local boy, C. Thompson, he was full of confidence and attacked from the opening bell. Showing exceptional promise for a raw novice, he had his opponent in all sorts of trouble, and boxing at his own pace, stayed in front throughout each round to take a good points decision. He impressed everyone, including a local newspaper reporter who, in his column in the *Cambridgeshire Times* the following week, made the comment: "the Chatteris boy is a fighter if ever there was one."

The victory was a tremendous spur for Dave. Showing great punching power he scored three more within the space of two weeks on shows at Boston, Leicester and Chatteris, all inside two rounds. The Chatteris show, staged at The Palace, was the club's last of the season, and featured 17 year old heavyweight sensation, Joe Bugner (Bedford Boys), who the previous month had won the London North West Divisional championship.

Bugner and Green were the stars on what was described as

another sensational evening of boxing. Because of travel difficulties, many boxers arrived late, and the start had to be delayed for more than half an hour, but it was well worth the wait. Green thrilled the locals as he blasted Ray McLean, from the London-based Lynn Club, to defeat in just 42 seconds of the opening round. Bugner also scored a first round success when his opponent, Dave Hallinan, retired after taking two counts.

After close back-to-back contests against experienced Kelvin Kelly of Coventry Irish, in which he lost the first and won the return, Green endured an eventful two days at the end of May. On the evening of the 25th, he was placed in two finals of the Isle of Ely Schools sports competition. Early the next morning, a lorry crashed into his house, and that evening he was outpointed by Andy Cunningham (Bingham ABC) on a Chatteris club junior show at Slade End School.

The crash occurred at about 5am on 26 May when an articulated refrigerator lorry travelling along Chatteris High Street, left the road as the driver negotiated a double bend. The lorry, laden with 12 tons of frozen vegetables, and belonging to March Cold Stores Ltd, went out of control and crashed through one end of wooden facia in front of the gas showrooms. After colliding with the front of 7 High Street, severing a television aerial in the process, sheer weight carried the vehicle into the Green household at number five before the cab became firmly embedded into the wall of number three.

Diesel oil gushed from the lorry fuel tanks and spilled along the road as the driver climbed out unhurt apart from a slightly grazed leg, and walked to the nearby Police Station. Emergency services, including the fire brigade, were quickly on the scene, and the oil was washed away and the roadway covered with sawdust.

The most serious damage was done to Ken Green's house, and it was amazing that nobody was hurt. There was a gaping hole in the front bedroom wall just four feet from where he and his wife were sleeping. The window and frame were

13

completely shattered, and the wall beneath it cracked and bowed. Dave and his brother were fast asleep in their room at the back of the house and not in any danger. The cottage, however, was severely damaged from front to back, and the roof completely moved. The financial extent of the damage was substantial.

The accident quickly attracted photographers and reporters from local newspapers. The following week a report appeared on the front page of the *Cambridgeshire Times* together with photographs of Dave's parents surveying the damage.

"There was such a blast that it threw the whole wardrobe door open," Mary Green told reporters. "We got up, dressed and went to see if the children were alright. We've moved most of the furniture out, but we don't know what's going to be done with it."

Ken Green's brother Fred lived next door at number seven with his wife Margaret. They had just woken up when they heard the massive bump. One of their front bedroom walls moved, and plaster scattered all over the floor.

Local residents described the scene as looking like bomb damage in the war. That particular area of the High Street was described as dangerous, and locals insisted that drivers often negotiated it too quickly. It was just a matter of time before a serious accident occurred.

As it was no longer possible to live at the house, Ken Green and his family went to stay with his wife's father, George Palmer, round the corner at Station Street. Their furniture was put into storage and they remained there until they were able to get a council house at Tithe Road three months later. The damaged houses at 5 and 7 High Street, were owned by Ken's brother Fred who eventually had them repaired and converted into a large single property.

The same evening, Chatteris Amateur Boxing Club wound up the season by staging an excellent junior tournament at the Slade End School headquarters. The main aim was to get contests for local boys who had still not made their ring debuts, but the bill also included novice juniors including

14

Dave. There were 12 close competitive bouts all ending in points decisions, and as a result of Dick Leader's astute match-making, a number of Chatteris youngsters gained valuable experience against good opposition.

Putting the terrible shock of the crash behind him, Green showed real potential against Andy Cunningham from Bingham by using an excellent left jab and producing plenty of power in the right. Despite his efforts, however, he lost a majority decision because the Bingham youngster had the edge in ringcraft.

Dave was fortunate to be a member of a club as popular and well-run as Chatteris. Even before the new season commenced in September 1967, invitations were received for members to box on tournaments up and down the country. It was a clear indication of the high regard officials from other clubs had for Chatteris and the reliability of it's boxers. Even when the club was very small, they were always in demand, and quite often there were lads boxing at different venues on the same night. Travel was usually by car or van, and on a busy night five or six youngsters would crowd into the backs of vehicles. Discipline at the club was strict, and no lad who was due to box ever failed to turn up.

By this stage, membership had risen steeply. Most juniors who were with the club the previous season, rejoined. Experienced seniors, Matty Payne, Bernie Wing and Robin Laud, a national schoolboy champion in 1962 who won 50 of 55 schoolboy and junior bouts, were joined by lightweight, Joe Canham, and Trevor Pearson, a flyweight who had boxed for the club a few years earlier.

Testimony of the club's popularity came from the fact that a number of promising juniors including Pasquali Adamante and Carlo Caparaso transferred from St Ives which was more or less in the doldrums. Both had been in championship class the previous season, and together with their trainer, Johnny Rout, who had been recruited to assist Arthur Binder and Jimmy Allen, recognised the potential of Chatteris.

Dave started the new season by winning an excellent

rubber contest at six stone against Kelvin Kelly (Coventry Irish) on his club's tournament at The Palace, Chatteris, on 20 October. By the end of the year he had won three more within the space of six weeks.

With his raw aggressive style of fighting, he quickly became a real crowd-pleaser. At Huntingdon on 7 December, he and Frankie Wagstaff from Bedford, a year his elder, gave the larger than usual crowd a fistic treat. Although they were the youngest boxers on the bill, it was by far the best contest of the evening, producing three rounds of scintillating boxing which drew great applause at the end of each session. At the final bell, officials, cornermen and other boxers joined in the ovation.

They had met a few weeks earlier at Ely with Green winning on points. Determined to gain revenge, Frankie, who would progress to become an NABC semi-finalist in 1969 and '70, was more aggressive, throwing hooks and uppercuts like a veteran. Yet it only served to spur Dave on.

The fight swung one way and then the other as both boys attacked furiously. Despite being several pounds lighter, Green began to look the stronger towards the end of round two as time and again he rocked the Bedford lad with thumping left and right swings.

In the third, they stood toe-to-toe and punched it out throughout the entire session. Neither gave an inch, but Dave's shots were the more accurate and gained him a unanimous decision. The two were due to meet again on a Chatteris show on 2 February, but after the contest the Bedford and Chatteris club secretaries agreed on the spot not to let them face each other again in the meantime.

Boxing at venues throughout Cambridgeshire and beyond, Dave developed into a promising junior. He was extremely enthusiastic and listened carefully to everything Arthur Binder and the other trainers told him. He also had great respect for Bernie Wing one of the club's most experienced seniors who frequently gave him advice.

One of his biggest disappointments as a junior was the lack

16

of fights. Quite often, he and other club members travelled to shows only to find that it had not been possible to match them for one reason or another. In early December 1967, he and Wing, together with club officials, completed a 140 mile round trip to Hemel Hempstead to box on a Markyate club show only to find that their opponents from Finchley had failed to turn up. There were plenty of other occasions when Dave experienced similar disappointment and frustration.

By this time, Green was firmly established in the school and county football teams, but to the disappointment of his headmaster, Donald Cooper, he decided to give it up to concentrate on boxing. "I didn't miss football a bit," he recalled. "I made up my mind to give everything I had to boxing. It was the only way really. Even in a kick-around I could have done some damage, be out of boxing for months and then I'd regret it."

Early in 1968, Green and Dave Cole were entered for the national schoolboy championships. Both got a bye in the first stage at Wroxham in January, but Green was eliminated in the next round at Dereham on 17 February when he was outpointed by T. Bines (Colchester).

Despite his disappointment, Dave returned to winning ways at Littleport four days later, outpointing old foe, Frankie Wagstaff. Both boys again gave a wonderful display of boxing, but Green, who won comfortably, appeared to have made the better progress since their previous meeting. Their proposed contest at Chatteris on 2 February had been postponed because of Dave's schoolboy championship commitments.

In the ensuing weeks, Green's boxing career was one of success and disappointment. At Somersham, he gave a highly impressive performance to cut down his older opponent, M. Malone, in just two minutes of the opening round. In a report in the *Cambridgeshire Times*, the reporter wrote: "For a boy of his age, David has a very hard punch." A week earlier he had boxed extremely well to outpoint a very classy boxer, D. O'Connor (Birmingham).

There were plenty of disappointments as well, particularly

when trips to shows at Boston and Huntingdon were to no avail because either opponents failed to turn up or matches couldn't be made. In the ring, Dave was outpointed by classy Joey Chapman (West Ham) who was taller and heavier. Against Graham Hills at Harold Hill on 29 April, he was considered very unlucky not to get the decision. Despite damaging both hands, he still gave an aggressive display which thrilled the Essex crowd.

Although the results of his last two contests were disappointing, Dave had every reason to be satisfied with his first complete season as a boxer. For a lad who had never been involved in a street or playground fight, he had shown tremendous natural ability scoring 12 victories from 18 contests. As well as aggression he also displayed great toughness, and as a result his defeats were all on points.

His performances were the basis for what would develop into an outstanding ring career. He was learning his trade amid a sound environment in a club operated by people who cared. There were plenty of role-models as well, and the highlight of the Chatteris club's season occurred in April when Pasquali Adamante won the senior 9st 2 championship in the national schoolboy finals at RAF Stanmore. Dave Cole, meanwhile, failed by the narrowest of margins to win a North East London junior ABA championship.

2

FARMWORK AND FIGHTING

Dave left school in July 1968 at the age of 15. During his final days at Cromwell he won the inter-house mile race for senior boys. In the 880 yards event later the same day, however, he didn't have the pace over the shorter distance, and was narrowly beaten by an older and much taller boy. It was at the time when secondary school pupils were starting to stay on until they were 16, which meant he was often competing against boys a year his elder.

Despite the difference in age, Dave was disgusted with himself because even from a young age he worked extremely hard to achieve perfection in all his sporting activities. He hated being beaten, and his competitive spirit was highlighted minutes after the end of the race when he sat down and cried.

Dave's first job after leaving school was at Alan Wool's chicken and pig farm situated at New Road about two miles outside Chatteris on the way to Manea. He had originally hoped to work on his father's farm, but there was insufficient work because his brother Michael had started there two years earlier.

Wool was a local man who Dave knew, so needing work he went and saw him, and was offered a job looking after day old red chicks until they reached 20 weeks. At three to four days old, they were moved into a large shed containing a number of gas heaters to keep them warm.

It was a responsible job, and Dave's tasks included feeding the chicks, keeping them clean and maintaining correct temperature levels. Together with a female worker he also gave them injections required to prevent disease.

At any one time there were as many as 5,000 chicks crowded inside the building, and therefore a great deal of care and caution was needed. Any sudden movement made them panic and rush to one side which could have resulted in many being smothered to death.

At the age of 20 weeks, the young hens were moved into batteries in another bigger shed to prepare them for laying eggs at 22 or 23 weeks. In a batch of 5,000 there could be as many as 50 young cockerels which were only identified as they developed. As they were unable to lay eggs, it was Dave's job to destroy them.

Dave thoroughly enjoyed the work for which he was paid £8.25 per week. He cycled from home early each morning in all weathers except for a few days at the peak of winter when the roads were blocked by deep snowdrifts. Instead, he walked and still got there on time.

The job, however, was not without certain drawbacks and an element of danger. One day the youngster was trying to catch some chicks to put into boxes for transfer to another building. He switched off the heaters which hung from the ceiling, but forgot to shut down the gas supply. Completely unaware of the danger, he continued working inside the shed until he began to lose consciousness. Fortunately, he was near to a door, and probably on instinct, managed to stumble outside before he was completely overcome.

The work was also very messy. Consequently, whenever Dave went to a local youth club in the evenings, his mates used to laugh and tell him he smelt of chickens. It also created a problem when he tried to get a girl-friend.

After about a year, Green joined Laws Brothers, a carrot farming and washing company doing contract work at farms throughout the Fens. Situated on the outskirts of Chatteris, it was operated by Ron, David and Gordon Laws, all of whom had been amateur boxers. Dave knew Ron who lived locally, and whilst talking to him one day, was offered a job. He stayed with the company for about a year and learned a great deal about the carrot industry which was a massive source of revenue in the region.

Dave was about 18 when he was offered a job with F.J. Feast & Son, a massive carrot farming and washing business at Southery near Downham Market, Norfolk. It arose because he had been at school at the same time as the owner's son, Greg Feast, who knew he worked for Laws Brothers.

The farm was situated about 20 miles from Chatteris meaning that Green had to leave home by 6.30am each morning to be at work by 7.15am. At the beginning, he drove there in his blue mini motor car which he had bought when he was 17, but after about a year was given a works van. Each day he picked up workmates at Littleport and other places on route. He took them home again at 3.30pm, then returned to the farm and cleared up before going home.

The carrot season, which involved cultivation and harvesting, operated for 10 months of the year, from July through until May. Apart from fields in which the crops were grown, the business at Southery also had a huge carrot-washer in the form of two cubic drums covering an area of 10,000 square feet.

Machinery was used to remove carrots from the ground after which teams of workers packed them into bags to await collection. Harvesting was very regimented, with three sub-contracted bulker lorries taking crops from the fields to the washer. Whilst one vehicle was at the farm being unloaded, another would be collecting carrots from the fields, and a third on route to or from the washing plant.

Dave's job was extremely strenuous, and much of it involved unloading the lorries, which on arrival at the farm, were manoeuvred into position over a conveyor belt. Slats were then removed from the back of the vehicle to allow the carrots to drop steadily onto the belt which carried them to the washer.

As the carrots dropped out of the washer, a team of 10

women removed any surplus debris before they were carried through to the bagging room. There, they were fed into 28lb bags which were then sewn up.

Once the washer was full, the conveyor belt automatically stopped, whereupon Dave would run inside and start throwing the bags onto contract lorries for transportation to vegetable markets all over the country. The whole process was then repeated, and by the end of each day, 80 tons of carrots had been washed, bagged and loaded.

It was a massive operation, and apart from growing carrots in their own fields, F.J. Feast & Son also had contracts to cultivate the crop on land throughout Norfolk and Cambridgeshire. Loads of carrots were taken to the washing plant from fields up to 30 miles away.

Dave got on well with his employer, and learned all aspects of the business. One winter, the ground was so wet that for several months it was not possible to get machines into the fields, and crops therefore had to be removed by hand. Groups of travellers were taken on and paid by the number of 28lb bags they filled. Knowing all the dodges that were likely to occur, Jack Feast paid Green an extra £5 a week to supervise their work. It was shrewd judgement because Dave was well respected by the Fen travellers, and a good working relationship developed.

Dave worked, Monday to Friday, and from 7.30am to 12 noon on Saturdays, his wages being £12 per week when he started. He was on the go all the time, and although the work was very demanding, he was dramatically building up his strength, particularly in his back, arms and shoulders. It was ideal additional preparation for his fights.

* * *

As his boxing career progressed, Dave continued to face good quality opponents. At the start of the new season in September 1968, however, he again became extremely frustrated over the lack of contests. Despite training since mid-

August, he didn't get a fight until November. Before that he had travelled to Kettering, but was not matched, and later when he was due to box at Bedford, they had to turn back due to heavy fog.

During the 1968-69 season, Green fought national schoolboy finalist, David Sayell from Aylesbury on four occasions, winning twice. On his club's show at The Palace on 14 February 1969, he produced an outstanding performance, intelligently switching his attack from head to body to take a good points decision. According to a local newspaper report, he threw the punch of the night – a perfect right to the stomach. It floored Sayell, but came too late because the final bell sounded before the referee could take up the count. Dave was noticeably annoyed at being denied a knockout victory.

The Chatteris show was unique in that for the first time a sponsorship scheme was introduced whereby supporters were invited to provide prizes for contests. It was a situation which had been created some months earlier by Ely Amateur Boxing Club with outstanding success. Before the show, the Ely club sportingly offered to sponsor one of the Chatteris bouts.

Despite Dave's continued good form, living in Cambridgeshire did have drawbacks regarding major championships. To pursue a junior ABA title he had to enter the North East London divisional championships which generally attracted some of the best young boxers in the country.

Nevertheless, he was full of confidence having scored two consecutive victories within the space of three weeks during March. At York Hall, Bethnal Green, on 17 April, however, he was unfortunate to be drawn against Joey Chapman (West Ham) who had outpointed him at Littleport the previous year. In the semi-final of Class A for boys aged 15-16 years at 7st, Chapman was again too good for Green, and won a unanimous decision.

Dave Cole was more fortunate than Green as he reached the London junior finals without throwing a punch. At the

North East London junior championships he came in too heavy for his group in Class B, but was given a walk-over in the 11st section, and with it a divisional title.

Although Green was bitterly disappointed, it was no disgrace to lose to Chapman who came from one of the finest clubs in the country. West Ham ABC had a fine record of producing a succession of top class youngsters, including the 1956 Olympic gold medallist, Terry Spinks.

Had the draw been kinder to Green, things may well have turned out differently. Chapman went on to win the North East London title, and reached the final of the London championships where he lost to Gary Evans.

In the semi-final on 16 May, Joey beat David Sayell (Aylesbury) whom Green had already defeated twice that season. The second occasion was at Chatteris just 24 hours after Dave had lost to Chapman. Aggressively determined, Green quickly put the previous night's defeat at the back of his mind and battered Sayell to a second round defeat. After taking one count, a left hook to the head toppled the Aylesbury man again forcing the referee to stop the contest.

One of the great things about Dave was his mature attitude in being able to put defeats to the back of his mind. Late in 1969, he was outpointed in consecutive contests by Junior ABA champion, Gary Evans. At Ely on 10 October they were involved in one of the best contests of the evening. After the opening round, Green realised there was no point in trying to box Gary at distance. He therefore put everything into attack over the final two rounds, but found his opponent just too clever for him.

In their second bout at Manor Place Baths, Walworth, on 17 November, Dave was representing an Eastern Counties team against Fitzroy Lodge. Although he lost by a majority decision, he almost pulled off a shock victory when he floored Evans just seconds before the final bell, but time ran out before he could finish it. "David was very unlucky, but we are delighted with his performance," said Jim Moore the Eastern Counties team manager.

The defeat did Green no harm whatsoever. His good form continued three days later at Corby when he was awarded a unanimous decision over talented Kirkland Laing. It was the start of a successful run which would take him to his first boxing championship.

By March 1970, the success of Chatteris ABC was incredible. Within the space of a few days, members boxed on tournaments at Ely, Beccles, March and Thetford. The previous month, three boys fought at Somersham, and all won, Green outpointing local lad, James Scott, in the best bout of the evening. Five days later at Corby, he and Pasquali Adamante scored a credible double, beating boxers from the Midland club, Clifton.

The contests were perfect preparation for Dave's entry into the North East London junior championships at York Hall, Bethnal Green, on 28 April. Jim Moore had high hopes of his chances, and Green didn't let him down, winning the Class B title at 7st 7. He scored a great victory over Stephen Sloane (Garden City Club) who was stopped in the second round at the request of his corner after Dave had sent him to the canvas with a combination of vicious body punches followed by a left and right to the head.

Victory took Green forward to the London Junior ABA semi-finals at Liardet Hall, Finchley, two weeks later. In what was also the national Junior ABA quarter-final, he lost a majority decision to Keith Hussey (Battersea). It was extremely close with Green edging the opening round, the second being even, and Hussey winning the third in which he got through with good quality punches to sway it in his favour.

It was Dave's final contest as a junior because he would attain the age of 17 five weeks later. He had won 23 of 35 contests between 1967 and 1970, 12 of those victories coming inside the distance. All of his defeats were on points. Although he failed to win a major junior championship, he was only beaten by good quality opponents. Hussey was a national schoolboy champion in 1968, and Joey Chapman went on to win an NABC title in 1970.

* * *

The 1969-70 season was a very successful one for the Chatteris club. Apart from Dave winning the North East London Junior title and reaching the semi-finals of the London ABA championships, Bernie Wing was Eastern Counties, Grade 1, middleweight champion and Brian Goodenough, Eastern Counties Grade 3 champion at 9st 7. It was estimated that during the season members travelled more than 5,000 miles to attend tournaments.

Although the club was flourishing under Arthur Binder, he was getting on in years and badly needed help with training. In 1969, Johnny Rout took over as the main coach, and was later assisted by Jim Moore, a former Army physical training instructor.

Originally from Lincolnshire, Jim moved to Chatteris after being demobbed. He attended most of the local boxing shows, got to know Binder, and was eventually asked to help out at the club on training nights. Having been attached to the 5th Physical Training Corps between 1948 and 1951, he was a good man to have around. He had a sound knowledge of boxing, his tough upbringing having included competing in the Army Suez Canal championships.

With the passing of time, Jim got more involved in club activities by taking boys, including Dave Green, to shows in his car, and working as a cornerman. When Dick Leader retired in 1968, he took over as matchmaker and secretary. His skills were soon recognised by clubs further afield, and the following year he was appointed Eastern Counties team manager, taking boxers to West Germany, Jersey and London. He was a great organiser, and in March 1970 put together an excellent 16 fight programme for the Chatteris club at Cromwell School.

Green was still a junior when Moore joined the club, and although Jim watched him box on many occasions they had very little to do with each other. One night at Thurmaston, however, Arthur Binder suddenly felt he wasn't up to it and asked Jim to take Dave to the ring. Within a short time he became his trainer.

Once Dave moved up to senior level at the beginning of the 1970-71 season, he trained on Tuesday and Friday evenings, and also Sunday mornings. He got on well with Moore who worked him hard. He did three rounds of skipping, three on the heavy bag together with stints of shadow boxing and speed-work.

His determination to succeed was reflected in his attitude towards the vigorous training routine Moore set him. He was dedicated, reliable, and always did as he was told. There was never any shirking, and Jim soon realised that Dave could be left alone to do most of his exercises. When he had finished, he would remain at the gym and help the trainers to look after some of the other lads.

Green made an impressive start in the senior ranks, outpointing Dave Smith of Eltham & District ABC at Norwich on 1 October 1970. Smith was another good class opponent who as a professional would become Southern Area bantamweight champion, and challenge for the British fly and bantamweight titles.

In his next contest at Cromwell School, Chatteris, four weeks later, Dave showed his immense power and aggression in beating John Scott of Somersham in two rounds. He drove John around the ring with solid jabs and hard rights, floored him twice in the second round before the Somersham lad's corner asked the referee to stop it. It was an impressive display by Green whose potential reached a wider audience because the fight was featured on the Anglia TV programme *"About Anglia"*.

Five days later, Green, the Chatteris club's youngest senior, and Bernie Wing, the most experienced, produced outstanding performances on a dinner-show at the Windmill Club, Rushden. Dave won a unanimous decision over experienced Ian 'Bronco' Ramage from Newmarket, renown for his strength and toughness. The following week, the *Cambridgeshire Times* ran a headline on the sports page: "GREEN AND WING SPARKLE AT RUSHDEN."

Boxing to instructions, Dave settled quickly in a close, skilful contest. Both boys scored with straight jabs and hooks to the body, but when Green shortened his punches he looked close to a stoppage victory. Ramage, however, lived up to his reputation and weathered the storm, fighting bravely until the final bell. Both boys received tremendous ovations at the end of what was a magnificent fight.

Jim Moore had previously twice refused offers for Green to fight Ramage because he didn't want to overmatch him. Even at this stage of his career the Chatteris youngster feared nobody, and when Jim asked if he felt ready for it, he insisted the match was accepted. "I had to find out if David was ready to meet such a strong lad as Ramage," Moore told the *Cambridgeshire Times*, "but last week the offer was accepted, and David didn't let the club down."

Ramage, who was being strongly tipped to cause upsets in the flyweight division that season, gained revenge three weeks later on Kings Lynn ABC dinner show at the Dukes Head Hotel. It was another very close affair, but Ramage, who since their last contest had won a National Stable Lads championship, easily won the opening round. Although Dave improved during the remaining two, he was unable to make up the leeway. Both were presented with their prizes by 1956 Olympic gold medal winner, Terry Spinks, himself a former Stable Lads champion.

At Bedford on 14 December, Green boxed brilliantly to outpoint old foe, Frankie Wagstaff, for the fourth time in a real crowd-pleaser. Jim Moore was ecstatic over his performance and told a local reporter: "In my opinion he is developing into one of the best flyweights in the country."

Although he had been a senior for just a matter of months, club matchmakers knew Dave could be relied upon to provide excitement. Consequently, he frequently found himself facing good quality opponents who were often more experienced.

After impressively winning five of his first six senior contests, he was due to face Frankie Wagstaff in a return contest on Chatteris ABC's show at Cromwell School. When Frankie was declared unfit, club-mate, Mario Stango stepped in.

Although Dave relished the chance to gain revenge over the lad who beat him in his first schoolboy contest, the outcome was disastrous. He was beaten in the opening round because he reacted to the referee's order to stop boxing a split-second faster than his opponent.

At the official's command, he immediately dropped his guard, but a heavy right from Stango was already on its way. It landed flush on the chin sending Dave crashing to the floor, his head striking the canvas heavily as he fell. As there was no chance of him being able to continue, the referee immediately called a halt. It was the first time in 42 contests that he had been beaten inside the distance.

A section of the crowd called for the bout to be ruled a "no-contest", but the referee had acted within the rules because he considered the punch to be an accident. Had he deemed it to be a deliberate foul, Stango would have been disqualified.

Green suffered no ill-effects from the defeat, and five days later turned in a fine performance to take a unanimous decision over D. Gaffney on a charity show at Watford Town Hall. His performance won him the Callowland Youth Cup awarded annually for the best boxer of the night. It was the first time the trophy had been won by a boxer from outside the London area. "It is something we are very proud of," Jim Moore told the *Chatteris Advertiser*. "David did exceptionally well."

On 11 March 1971, Dave suffered another set-back in the bantamweight semi-final of the North East London divisional championships at York Hall, Bethnal Green. Against full England international, Billy Taylor of Repton, he was too inexperienced, and was stopped in the second round.

It was no disgrace to lose to Taylor who went all the way to the ABA final only to lose to George Turpin. He was a quality fighter who won a junior ABA title in 1969 and an NABC championship the following year. He would go on to win a silver medal at a multi-national tournament in Holland in May 1972, represent Great Britain at the Munich Olympics the same year, and remain an England international until 1973.

Despite being only 17, Dave was made of stern stuff and quickly put the Stango and Taylor defeats behind him. Just four days after the disappointment against Taylor, he took another decision from Frankie Wagstaff. Four days later he beat his first overseas opponent.

Green and Chatteris club mates, Dave Cole and Bernie Wing, were included in an Eastern Counties team against Bremen in the second Anglo-German match staged at Beccles on 19 March. Boxing at featherweight, Dave scored an excellent victory over H. Humrick who was at least six inches taller and consequently exposed much of his lower body. Both boys scored with good left jabs in the opening stages, but once an opening appeared Dave was quick to take advantage. Two hard shots to the stomach brought the German's guard down, whereupon the Chatteris boy quickly switched to the head and sent Humrick to the floor for a count of six. On rising he was subjected to another vicious onslaught causing the referee to intervene after two minutes 10 seconds of the opening round.

The following week at Hunstanton, again representing Eastern Counties, Green destroyed another German, 19 year old H. Stroh of Wesel after just two minutes 25 seconds of the first round. After sizing his man up, he got through with hard lefts to head and body. When Stroh dropped his guard, Dave crashed a powerful right hook to the jaw. The German's legs shook and he immediately appealed to the referee that he had taken enough.

Dave was extremely fit, and since becoming a senior just six months earlier, his strength and physique had developed immensely. The following evening he was in action at Newmarket where he won a majority decision over D. Waldock of Luton Irish who had recently beaten Chatteris club-mate, Pasquali Adamante.

All his hard work and enterprise during the season was

rewarded at Norwich on 5 June when he won the Eastern Counties featherweight championship, albeit without throwing a punch. His opponent, Peter Senni, of Norwich Lads Club, was two pounds over the 9st limit at the weigh in. In accordance with the ABA rules, Jim Moore promptly claimed the title on Green's behalf.

The two boxers did, however, meet in a special contest the same evening with Dave taking a unanimous decision. Boxing brilliantly, he opened a cut over Senni's right eye, and scored well with left jabs. "I was sorry we didn't actually fight for the title," he told a local reporter, "but at least I got the satisfaction of knowing I could beat him."

In his final bout of the season, Dave stopped Kent champion and Southern Counties finalist, Peter Sutcliffe, in three rounds before a crowd of 3,000 at an open-air show at Ipswich. It was his 15th victory of the season against four losses. He had matured considerably since the Taylor defeat in March, scoring seven victories against a points defeat to Mickey Spencer of Fitzroy Lodge, another top class boxer. Mickey had won junior ABA titles in 1968 and '69, national schoolboy championships in 1968, '69 and '70, and an NABC title in 1971.

* * *

The 1971-72 season was one of mixed fortunes for the young Chatteris hopeful. It started brightly enough with three victories from four contests, the defeat being a disputed decision while boxing for Eastern Counties at Bremen, West Germany. Dave then inexplicably suffered three points defeats within the space of 12 days.

The first was on the Chatteris club show at Cromwell School when he received a boxing lesson from the vastly experienced 30 year old, Tommy Wallace from Ely. Fighting with tremendous aggression and determination Dave tried everything he knew to try and pin down the cagey southpaw, but could rarely set him up for a big punch. Tommy had never been stopped in his long career in which he reached the 1969 ABA semi-finals as London featherweight champion.

Green attempted to overwhelm Wallace by the sheer weight of his attacks, but was picked off by stiff counter punches. Tommy became more dominant as the bout wore on, but despite the boxing lesson, it was great experience for Dave on the long path which lay ahead. The fight showed Jim Moore that despite his boy's potential, he was not quite ready for this type of opponent.

Outside boxing, Dave's great passion was rabbit shooting which was very much part of country life. From the age of 15 he regularly walked the fields and margins of his father's farm armed with a 410 shotgun seeking rabbits, and also pheasant and partridge when in season. One night, however, he had an accident and sustained a serious injury which could easily have been fatal.

The incident occurred during the evening of 11 November 1971, two days after he had been outpointed by former schoolboy champion, S. Polak, at Watford. With two mates, Ken Carter and Greg Feast, the son of his employer, Dave was in a small shooting-brake on his father's land about three miles from Chatteris. He was sitting on the rear window-ledge, his feet on the seat, arms resting on the roof, and clutching a shotgun in his hands.

It was about 8.30pm when they reached the end of a wooded drove in search of rabbits. As Dave eased himself back inside the vehicle, he took the hammer off the loaded weapon as he had done on countless occasions before. This time, however, the gun went off as he laid it in his lap. The blast ripped a hole in his right side and knocked him through the open window of the vehicle. "Quick, I've shot myself," he screamed as he lay on the ground with blood pouring from the gaping wound.

"Stop mucking about and get back in here," shouted one of his mates thinking Dave was playing one of his practical jokes for which he was renown.

Suddenly, in the torch-light, they saw blood gushing

through his fingers and knew it was serious. Panic stricken, Ken and Greg quickly lowered the back seat of the van, laid Dave out flat and headed for the nearest hospital at Ely about nine miles away. As they approached the city centre they narrowly avoided another disaster when a wheel came off the vehicle as it hurtled around a corner. As it screeched to an abrupt halt, one of the lads ran to a phone box and called an ambulance.

Meanwhile, a crowd gathered beside the van, and unaware of what had occurred some people gasped with horror when they saw how badly Dave was bleeding. His clothes were saturated with blood, and they couldn't understand how such a serious injury could have been sustained by a wheel snapping off.

An ambulance arrived within a few minutes and rushed Green to hospital where he underwent an emergency operation. A total of 65 gunshot pellets were removed from the right side of his body together with bits of shirt button. A further 15 were left in because complications could have arisen by attempting to remove them. More than 15 internal and external stitches were required to close the wound, and Dave was left with a nine inch permanent scar as a reminder of his near miss with death. "They said it got me in the only safe place on my body," he recalled. "Anywhere else and I would not have survived."

At first it was feared that his promising boxing career was over, but after two weeks in hospital, he recovered well and was back at work in January. As soon as he was able he resumed training, and despite the nasty injury, worked hard, got himself fit and was raring to get back into action.

There was plenty of opportunity because early 1972 was another extremely busy time for the Chatteris club in which they took on another trainer, Peter 'Happy' Laws. Apart from their own show at Cromwell School, there were bookings for members at Watford, Norwich and Somersham within a week. Green, Cole and Bernie Wing were also due to box at Leicester Grand Hall, but the show was cancelled at short notice.

Despite his enforced inactivity for almost three months, Dave didn't return to the ring with an easy touch. On a special charity dinner-show at the Melody Rooms, Norwich, on 28 January, his opponent was Stable Lads lightweight champion, Tommy Wallace, who had beaten him at Chatteris in October. Since that defeat, Green had longed to face Tommy again because despite recognising his class, was convinced he could beat him. Jim Moore strongly advised him against the fight, but Dave insisted they agree to it.

Before guest of honour, Henry Cooper, the pair staged a real war in what was the final bout of the evening, and unquestionably the best. Wallace again took the decision, but Dave was not too concerned with the result, realising that it was only through good fortune that he was boxing at all. As he lay in his hospital bed less than three months earlier, he had been convinced he would never box again.

The Wallace fight restored all Dave's confidence, and within the space of three weeks he scored four victories including three inside the distance in dramatic fashion. Against veteran, J. Wiley, at Watford, he ignored Jim Moore's instructions to box and be patient. Fed up with his opponents persistent holding, he went flat out to end the fight in the second round. A series of vicious body punches knocked Wiley to a standstill and the fight was stopped after one minute of the round.

The following evening at Watton, Norfolk, Green faced reigning Metropolitan Police welterweight champion, Chris Mikellides, who later that year would win a European Police championship. After taking some heavy punches to the head in the opening round, he floored the policeman twice in the second. Dave attacked from the start of the third, and a right followed by a tremendous left hook floored Mikellides for the count. It was fully a minute before he recovered.

Against Freddie Williams at Northampton two weeks later, the contest was surprisingly reduced to one of two-minute rounds. By the end of each session, the power of Green's punches was beginning to tell, and had the fight been over the normal three-minute rounds he would have won by stoppage. Instead, he had to settle for a points victory.

Through sheer hard work and determination, Dave had recovered his form of the previous season. Still not 19, he then faced the vastly experienced Derek Hollyoak (Repton) in the lightweight semi-final of the North East London divisional championships at York Hall, Bethnal Green, on 9 March. Hollyoak, the reigning London ABA featherweight champion, had won national schoolboy championships in 1968 and '69, boxed for England at Under 19 level, and against East Germany and Denmark as a full international.

Although Green was beaten on a majority decision, he gave the Repton man all the trouble he could handle. He received a great ovation at the end of the fight, and made a lot of friends in the East End that night. He also met up with several old opponents, two of whom had better fortune. Joey Chapman won the bantamweight championship and Tommy Wallace the feather, while Hollyoak took the lightweight championship, beating Gary Dunks in the final. All were, however, beaten in the London finals three weeks later, although another Green opponent, Dave Smith, won the flyweight title.

In typical fashion, Dave quickly put the latest set-back down to experience. The following week he scored a narrow victory over Paul Fitzgerald (Eltham) on a Rotary Club dinner-show at the plush Copdock Hotel, Ipswich. Although Fitzgerald reversed the decision at Great Yarmouth a few weeks later, Green continued to win more bouts than he lost.

Irrespective of the results, he had developed into an exciting all-action young fighter who thrilled audiences wherever he fought. His non-stop aggression was backed up by good boxing ability, a strong chin and superb fitness. At Peterborough in April, boxing for Eastern Counties against a West German select team, he thrashed 18 year old L. Wagner (Bremen) in the opening round.

Green's impressive display caught the eye of England international team manager, David James. After the fight he invited him to attend training sessions at Crystal Palace with the England Under 21 squad. Afterwards, Dave told the *Cambridgeshire Times*: "I had a great time and it did me a lot of good. I sparred with two international boxers, and afterwards we watched a cine film of the sparring. This showed up all my faults, and I am now awaiting developments from the session." Later in the year, he joined the squad on a training weekend at Sofia Gardens, Cardiff.

On 11 May, at the Rex Ballroom, Cambridge, Green confirmed his excellent form when he captained Eastern Counties in a 4-4 draw against another West Germany select team on a sell-out show organised by Chatteris ABC in conjunction with Cambridge & District Sporting Club. Boxing at light-welterweight, Dave was too powerful for opponent, M. Heyden (Wesel), who was stopped with one minute remaining of the final round. The victory earned him the award for being best Eastern Counties boxer of the evening which was presented by his idol Alan Rudkin who was guest of honour.

Green wound up the 1971-72 season losing on points to South East London divisional lightweight champion, Dave Allen (St Mary's, Chatham), on Ipswich ABC's big outdoor show at Christchurch Park. Again it was a case of being beaten by a top class opponent – Allen being ranked six in the national amateur lightweight ratings.

3

NO EASY PICKINGS

As Dave's boxing career developed, Jim Moore ensured that whenever possible, he faced good class opposition. "The only way he can learn is by facing the best," Jim told a local reporter. "We know his capabilities and intend to bring him along steadily because everyone at the club has very high hopes for him."

The new season started in fine style. Representing Eastern Counties against London ABA at Norwich on 28 September 1972, Green took a close decision over talented Mickey Spencer (Fitzroy Lodge). It was the shock of the match, won 5-3 by London, but showed the natural ability Dave possessed.

Spencer, the fourth ranked featherweight in Britain, having won the London title in March, was described by *Boxing News* as the brightest prospect of the championships in which he beat Tommy Wallace (Ely) in the semi-final. In June he represented England at the European U21 championships at Bucharest, and had been expected to be too skilful for Green. They were supposed to have boxed a return at Northampton three weeks later, but Mickey pulled out. Instead, Dave faced Mickey Ryce of Abingdon and took a unanimous decision.

In the meantime he proved that the victory over Spencer was no fluke. At Beccles seven days later he clearly outpointed Dave Allen, thus reversing a decision which went against him three months earlier.

Although Jim Moore was delighted with his man's success, it was beginning to create some difficulty. Jim wanted to use Dave in a show-piece top-of-the-bill contest at Chatteris on 27 October in which boxers from Kettering, Northampton, Belgrave, Norwich, Beccles, Colchester, Ipswich, Boston, St Neots and HMS Ganges had been invited to take part. The original plan was to match him with reigning ABA featherweight champion, Kirkland Laing, but when the Clifton club temporarily withdrew from all competitions, the contest fell through.

Green was the Chatteris club's best prospect for years, and there were few boxers of his class and weight in the Eastern Counties. Local papers reported all of his fights and rarely a week passed without there being some mention of his progress. Moore went to great lengths to try and find him another opponent, but without success because nobody wanted to fight him on his home ground.

Although he was outpointed by two-time NABC champion and future England international, Des Gwilliam at Kettering, Dave showed real class in outpointing current England representative, Peter Turrell (Beccles), at Cambridge on 9 November. Nine days earlier, Turrell had represented his country against the USSR at the Royal Albert Hall, and had also been selected to face Czechoslovakia at Prague in December. He had been beaten only twice in the last two years, one of which was in May 1972 when he won a silver medal at a gruelling multi-nations tournament in Holland over seven days.

It was a truly magnificent performance by Green whose non-stop aggression clinched a majority decision in a very close contest. Jim Moore considered it to be his best victory to date. He was particularly impressive in the second round when he shook the England international with three consecutive right hooks.

The victory elevated Dave into the *Boxing News* light-welterweight ratings at number 10 making him the first amateur boxer from Chatteris to be ranked. Turrell, rated at three when Green beat him, dropped to number six. Of equal interest was the fact that in the lightweight division, previous opponents, Derek Hollyoak, Des Gwilliam, Mickey Spencer and Tommy Wallace were rated at four, five, eight and nine respectively, an indication of the quality of opponents Dave was facing.

Green's impressive form again caught the attention of the England selectors, and he was on the short-list to box at lightweight in the international at Prague. Jim Moore, however, asked that he wasn't selected because he was finding it increasingly difficult to make the weight, and in the future intended boxing at 10st.

It was a period of mixed fortune for Green because within a week of beating Turrell, he was then on the wrong end of an extremely questionable decision against RAF champion, Tony Meakins. "David won every round," Jim Moore told the *Cambridgeshire Times*. "It was one of those bad decisions."

He later wrote to Bert Barnes, secretary of the mid-Anglia Division of the ABA expressing concern about the standard of judging in the Beds, Herts and Bucks division. Even Meakins admitted after the contest that he thought Dave had done enough to get the decision. The following week, a bold headline appeared on the sports page of the *Cambridgeshire Times*: "DIABOLICAL DECISION ROBS GREEN."

Once again, however, Dave showed his character, and put the disappointment out of his mind. On a charity dinner-show at Bournemouth Pier Pavillion before an audience of 500, he scored another notable victory, taking a majority decision over Irish star, Paul Carson, whom he outboxed in two of the three rounds.

A panel of observers, including John Conteh and Peter Waterman, voted him the most stylish boxer of the evening. His prize was a beautiful silver replica of a boxing ring which had been purchased from a top London jeweller and presented by *Boxing World*. Dave had taken part in one of the early contests, and with Bournemouth being a 380 mile round trip from Chatteris, he and Jim Moore had already left for home by the time the presentation was due to be made. "It was a fine display by David, and he certainly deserved the special award," remarked Moore on being told.

Other officials of the Chatteris club were thrilled when they heard the news, and at a meeting, agreed to organise a special event at the local Working Mens Club on 16 December. Highlight of the evening was the presentation of the trophy to Dave by Councillor Palmer Hayes, Chairman of Chatteris Urban District Council. A photograph entitled "Reward for Style" appeared in the *Cambridgeshire Times* the following week.

Meanwhile, Green and Moore travelled to West Germany with an Eastern Counties team for a match against Wesel to celebrate the club's 50th anniversary. It was a huge event, and a crowd of more than 3,000 watched the tournament, including 30 members of Cambridge & District Sporting Club who sponsored the English team.

Dave, who was captain of Eastern Counties, was their only winner in a heavy defeat, knocking out Reinhard Ruloss in one minute 46 seconds of the first round. He attacked from the opening bell, hammered his way through his opponent's defence, trapped him in a corner and then floored him for the count. It was one of the most sensational victories of his amateur career, and won him a prize of a transistor radio as best boxer of the evening, and also the Watney-Mann cup for being the best English fighter of the visit.

The *Cambridgeshire Times* continued to give good coverage of his fights, and on 15 December praised his performance in Germany under the headline: "SENSATIONAL WIN FOR DAVID GREEN." Four weeks later, a large article described his continued progress and what he meant to the Fens.

In an interview with the sports editor, Jim Moore described the difficulty of finding Dave opponents, claiming that even boys who had beaten him in the past didn't want to know. An example of Jim's frustrations occurred in mid-January when he and Dave made a 120 mile round-trip to Dunstable only to find that his opponent, Alex Gower (Repton), had withdrawn at the last minute. A match was made with C. Courier from Gloucester, but he withdrew on the day after his trainer had studied Green's record.

"He is one of the best prospects the Eastern Counties have ever had let alone Chatteris," Moore told the reporter. "He must be one of the best in the country."

Describing Dave as a box-fighter, Jim said: "He is aggressive inside the ring, and couples that aggressiveness with good footwork and boxing ability. He can adapt himself to his opponent. When he boxed Peter Turrell, he knew all about him, and so he out-boxed him."

Apart from the solid boxer-trainer relationship which had developed between Green and Moore, they had also become good friends. They travelled thousands of miles together to boxing shows and shared some amusing moments. During the trip to Wesel, they shared a twin-bedded room at a local hotel, but on the first night Dave didn't sleep very well. "I don't reckon much to these continental quilts," he moaned next morning. "I didn't keep very warm last night."

Jim couldn't understand it because despite the freezing temperature outside, he had been warm and snug. He therefore decided to watch Dave as he prepared to get into bed the next night. To his amazement, he undid the tapes at one end of the duvet, then climbed inside as though it were a sleeping bag. He laughed out loud when Jim told him he was supposed to get underneath it. "No wonder I didn't keep very warm last night," he chuckled.

Dave was a mischievous lad gifted with a good sense of humour. He was cheeky and loved playing practical jokes, and there were many occasions when he made Jim laugh. One of the first times was one evening when Jim and his wife were driving Dave to a boxing show in the Midlands. As they approached Rutland they came across a group of night cyclists. One elderly man was riding a tricycle, and as they passed him, Green, who was about 14 and sitting in the back seat, wound down the window and called out: "Notice your dad hasn't taken your noddy wheels off then!"

About a mile further on they were held up at roadworks. As they waited Dave became fidgety and kept looking out of the window. Eventually, he saw the group of cyclists approaching, and slid down in the seat hoping they would pass by. Suddenly, there was a tap on the window, and the man on the tricycle called out: "How d'ya do!"

* * *

The long awaited return between Green and Peter Turrell took place at Cromwell Community College, Chatteris, on 2 February 1973. They had been due to meet at Beccles four weeks earlier, but Peter was suffering from flu and had to withdraw at short notice. Strong and confident, Dave confirmed his *Boxing News* rating by again proving to be the better man. His solid left hand work gave him the edge particularly in a convincing opening round.

Turrell, however, countered well and always hit back when hurt, but made the mistake of trying to mix it with an opponent who was physically stronger. Using his vast experience, Peter piled on the pressure during the final round, but Dave remained composed, and boxing strictly to orders held his own to take a close, but well-earned decision. All three judges made him the winner.

The crowd-pleasing main event saved the show from being a complete flop. There were only four other contests and an exhibition, two of which involved boxers from the same club. It was an extremely disappointing evening for the Chatteris club, and in particular secretary/matchmaker, Jim Moore, who was let down by the non-arrival of boxers from three RAF stations. The show was in fact an example of what was the best and worst in amateur boxing. Apart from the excitement during the Green-Turrell fight which had attracted a large crowd, and a gruelling novice bout which started the evening, the absenteeism was an ongoing problem which plagued the amateur sport.

Moore worked single-handed for Chatteris. Apart from arranging contests in his capacity as matchmaker, he would also put up the ring for club shows and take it down again afterwards. He took Green to most of his fights, and nine days later accompanied him to Randers, Denmark, where Dave was the only member of an eight man Eastern Counties team to score a victory in a match against a local team. He was awarded a unanimous decision over H.O. Christensen, who would later become Danish amateur middleweight champion, but the team lost 7-1.

The victory in Denmark was Green's fourth in succession and provided perfect preparation for the forthcoming Eastern Counties championships at Ipswich. They were the first in East Anglia under the ABA's revised national qualifying scheme. In previous seasons his only route towards an ABA title was through the North East London divisional championships.

In the light-welterweight final against Jim Kelly of Peterborough, Dave oozed confidence as he jabbed, stalked and finally stopped his crafty and durable opponent. Although Kelly matched his determination for most of the contest, Green raised the pace sharply towards the end of each round. In the third, his power and strength finally told as tremendous body shots knocked all the fight out of Kelly, and the contest was stopped with just 45 seconds remaining.

It was an highly impressive performance, and *Boxing News* described Dave as:

> ...the brilliant young Chatteris boxer who reminds one of his illustrious home town idol, Eric Boon.

By virtue of becoming Eastern Counties champion, Dave progressed to the ABA quarter-finals under the new scheme. Yet again, however, he found himself really up against it. Boxing for Eastern Counties against Midland Counties at Beccles on 17 March, his opponent was classy Billy Finnegan from the Golden Gloves Club, Birmingham, who was rated number two in Great Britain. A winner of 50 out of 60 amateur contests, he won an NABC title back in 1964, and had eliminated former ABA featherweight champion, Kirkland Laing, two weeks earlier at Longbridge.

Although the overall standard of quarter-final contests was described as being below par compared with the Area championships at Ipswich and Longbridge, the Green-Finnegan bout was an exception. Close and gruelling, it was the fight of the night.

After sizing each other up, Finnegan soon showed his resourcefulness by hammering two-fisted combinations to the body at close quarters. Although at one stage, Green looked on the verge of a dramatic victory during a splendid second round when he scored with some heavy body punches, Billy's experience enabled him to weather the storm. Skilfully picking up points while keeping the aggressive Chatteris fighter at bay with accurate straight lefts, he showed real class.

Green, however, would not be denied and opened a gash on Finnegan's left eyebrow in the fiercely contested final round as each desperately sought victory. At the end both were bleeding freely, but it was the Midlands champion who took the unanimous decision. He progressed to the ABA final at Wembley only to lose on a cut eye to Neville Cole who won his third title. Within nine months, however, Finnegan was established as a full England international.

Despite Dave's failure to progress in the ABA championships, Jim Moore was convinced that he had the ability to beat Finnegan. Whilst refusing to make excuses for the defeat, he felt that the difficulty in getting good sparring partners was hindering his progress.

Although Green was beaten by Kirkland Laing two weeks after the Finnegan fight, he ended the season on a high by hammering out victories on consecutive nights at Overstone and Thurmaston.

The day after meeting Laing, Dave was one of many past and present Chatteris boxers to attend a buffet dance at the

Dave 'Boy' Green (left), with his manager and life-long friend Andy Smith.

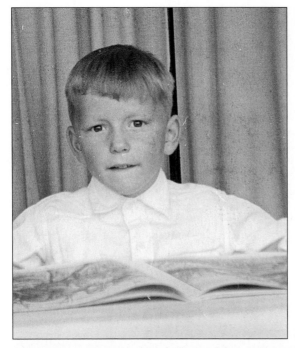

Dave aged six years – his first school photograph.

King Edward Primary School football team 1963–64, captained by Dave (front row – centre).

Chatteris Amateur Boxing Club champions 1969–70; from the left, Brian Goodenough, Bernie Wing, Malcolm McGarvey, Jim Moore (trainer), Dave 'Boy' Green and Dave Cole.

Dave 'Boy' Green aged 15 years.

Dave training at Chatteris Boxing Club with Jim Moore.

Dave (right), competing in a long-distance race at Cromwell School sports day against rival David Smalley.

Dave (right), with school cross-country rivals David Smalley (left) and Peter Carter.

Green (right), outpoints England international, Peter Turrell, at Chatteris on 2 February 1973.

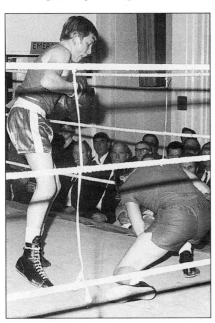

Green (left), floors John Scott at Somersham on 7 February 1970.

Green (left), attacks M. Heyden (Germany) whom he stopped at Cambridge on 11 May 1972.

Councillor Palmer Hayes presents Dave with a trophy for being 'stylist of the evening', following a contest at Bournemouth in November 1972.

Dave, brother Michael and their parents on a day trip to Great Yarmouth.

Helped by Andy Smith, Green pounds the heavy bag at his professional training quarters at St. Ives.

Eric Boon congratulates Green on beating Derek Simpson at Cambridge on 12 February 1975.

Dave meets world heavyweight champion, Muhammed Ali, at Quaglino's, London, in March 1976.

local Working Mens Club organised to raise funds for the boxing club. Being the rising star, he was very much the centre of attention as he chatted with former boxers Tony Parmenter, Ambrose Hurd, Brian Smart and Bill Kirby, and also Matty Payne, a trainer at the club who had retired only a couple of years earlier having won 130 of 168 contests. He was given particular encouragement by 58 year old, Vic Buddle, a top light-heavyweight in the Eastern Counties region 35 years earlier.

A farewell presentation was made to Dick Leader who had resigned after eight years as club secretary, matchmaker and press officer. He was manager of the Chatteris branch of Trustee Savings Bank, but was moving back to St Neots.

* * *

By the start of the 1973-74 amateur season, Dave had been working at the carrot farm for over two years. The strenuous work not only kept him extremely fit, but continued to develop him physically, particularly in his shoulders. Consequently, he could no longer comfortably make the light-welterweight limit of 10st.

Deciding to move up to welterweight, he made determined preparations for the new season, and didn't box until mid-October at Thurmaston. His opponent was England international, Harry Watson, who had outpointed him at the same venue the previous November.

Watson, a Worksop postman, had since reached the ABA welterweight final, but was disqualified against Terry Waller for persistent use of the head. Green, however, knew that if he was to achieve his ambition of winning an ABA title and England vest, he had to fight men of Harry's calibre.

Watson was a youngster who could match Dave for power, and in another close fight he again got the decision. Many ringsiders, however, considered the Chatteris man unlucky. He was desperate for a third meeting, but a proposed contest later in the year fell through when Harry sustained a broken nose.

The second defeat by Watson only served to make Dave more determined than ever. Five days later at Hemel Hempstead, he really turned on the style to outpoint Gerry McManus in a special contest. Yet when his opponent was late arriving he was convinced that he had again turned up at a Markyate club show only to discover he had no opponent. On the same bill, Jimmy Batten took his unbeaten amateur record to 71.

The victory over McManus proved to be the start of a sensational run of success for the aggressive Green. After five victories in as many weeks, he ruthlessly stopped Kirkland Laing after two minutes 50 seconds of the opening round at Thurmaston.

Five days earlier, representing an Eastern Counties and London select team against Jutland at Beccles, he had stopped Hans Madsen in the opening round. A series of vicious shots to the ribs put the Dane on the canvas three times before the referee stepped in.

Dave was in devastating form, and the move up to welterweight had given him increased power. Albert Hillman (Orpington) was stopped in two rounds at Northampton, and making a rare appearance in London, Green stopped Kent champion, Martin Hooker, in the opening round on a Repton club show at York Hall. Hooker was sent to the floor on three occasions from vicious body attacks after which the referee intervened.

Although Dave won four consecutive fights inside two rounds prior to Christmas 1973, his punching power eventually had an adverse effect. It became extremely difficult to get fights for him, and the contest with Hooker in February 1974 was his first for eight weeks.

At a Cambridge Sporting Club dinner-show at the Guildhall in January, Dave was obliged to box an exhibition with Ipswich teenager, Dean Hurd, because nobody would fight him. They had challenged ABA champion, Terry Waller, who had pulled out of an earlier fight with Green at Northampton, but been rejected.

46

Explaining his difficulty to the press, Jim Moore said: "They wanted us to fight Waller in London later this month, so I suggested tonight as well, but they said it was too risky."

The fact was, Dave's punching power had scared opponents off. Contact was made with clubs at Birmingham, Hull, Bristol, Bournemouth and Coventry, but nobody was prepared to travel to the Fens. Jim tried to get him on a show at Hemel Hempstead, but again no opponent could be found. Those pursuing ABA championships didn't want to know either because they preferred to wait until title bouts before facing him.

The fight against Martin Hooker at York Hall only took place following a dispute between Jim Moore and the organisers of the show. Some weeks earlier he received a telephone call asking for Dave to travel to London to face a particular opponent whom he realised was a raw novice. Jim reminded the club secretary that as Green was an open class champion, the contest had to be over three-minute rounds. He was assured it was acceptable. In the weeks leading up to the contest, Jim received regular calls and believed that Dave's crowd-pleasing style was essential to the success of the show. When they arrived at the venue, Moore was approached by the opponent's trainer who said: "Thanks Jim for taking this fight over two-minute rounds."

Moore stressed that he had agreed to three-minute rounds which was the only reason they travelled. A lengthy debate then took place over the duration of the rounds, but without agreement. The other party insisted that he couldn't allow his boy to face Green over three-minute rounds.

Having travelled all the way from Chatteris, Moore confronted the promoter who tried to fob it off by putting a £10 note into his pocket. When he checked the contest board, he found the bout was listed for two-minute rounds. The promoter insisted that's what was agreed over the telephone, and why he had given him the £10 in appreciation.

"What do you think of us," snapped Moore, "because we come out of the countryside, we're a load of monkeys?" Jim stood his ground and was eventually asked if Dave would fight Hooker, to which he agreed. "David, go out and stop this lad as quick as you can," said Moore quietly once they were in the dressing-room. "Then let's get away from here and back home." Green duly obliged.

Early in 1974, Dave was ranked number six in the welterweight division immediately behind Harry Watson. He was progressing well, and a number of critics shared his belief that he could be a real threat in the forthcoming ABA championships.

The first step towards his dream was achieved in impressive style when he won the Eastern Counties title at Beccles on 2 March by stopping 19-year-old Ray Duffy of Ipswich in the opening round. It was Green's first fight in the competition because having drawn a bye in the first round, his semi-final opponent, H. Williams, withdrew claiming he was not strong enough to face Dave.

Determination etched grimly across his face, Green pressed forward from the opening bell. Jabbing to the head and hooking powerfully to the body, he forced Duffy to the ropes. Whilst the Ipswich man managed to avoid most of the head punches, those to the body were crippling. He was put under tremendous pressure, and Dave finally got to him in a neutral corner. A barrage of vicious body punches doubled Ray up and prompted the referee to call a halt after one minute 56 seconds. It was a particularly good performance by Green who had suffered from flu the previous week and lost more than six pounds in weight.

Dave kept sharp in securing a repeat points victory over Mickey Ryce of Abingdon, conqueror of England representative Alex Gower. Ryce suffered three rounds of physical torture, and only his skill and courage kept him there until the final bell. It was a mature performance from the Chatteris man who was boxing better than at any time in his career.

Next stop was the ABA quarter-finals where he faced old opponent, Kirkland Laing (Clifton), at Aston Works, Longbridge on 23 March. Representing the Home and Eastern Counties against Midland and Southern Counties, Dave continued his good form taking a unanimous decision with scores of 60-57, 59-58, and 59-58.

Laing had heard the story about Dave getting shot, and when they met for the weigh in, he lifted his shirt, pointed to the scar, and said: "That's where I'm going to hit you tonight." Green had other ideas, and the talented former ABA featherweight champion was allowed to show only glimpses of his silky skills as Dave bundled forward aggressively to make his power tell. Desperate for survival, Kirkland received a public warning in the final round for persistent holding.

Victory put Green into the English semi-finals at City Hall, Hull, the furthest he had progressed in the prestigious championships. His power and aggression made him one of the most exciting fighters in the competition, and followers of the sport were really starting to take notice. Many believed that he was emerging as the main threat to reigning ABA welterweight champion, Terry Waller, who had his sights set on a fifth national title.

At Hull, Dave faced North West Counties champion, Alf Barnes, (Raven Club, Warrington), and fought in his usual aggressive style from the opening bell. He slammed away to the body, threw hooks and uppercuts to the head, but Alf refused to go down. Although he looked in serious trouble during round two, he survived and came back to extend Green. Constant pressure throughout the final round, however, ensured that Dave took a unanimous decision with scores of 59-57, 59-57 and 60-54 to guarantee himself a fight against Waller in the championship semi-finals the following week.

Since the start of the season, fans and critics had recognised a dramatic increase in the power and accuracy of Dave's punching, yet very few knew how it had come about. Although he worked extremely hard at strength and fitness training, he was by this stage the only senior member at the Chatteris club. Consequently, he became continually frustrated at the fact that he had nobody to spar with.

Jim Moore knew Green was a special breed of fighter who badly needed regular sparring. "Why don't you go and see Andy Smith?" he suggested one day at the beginning of November 1973. "He's got loads of boys over at his gym."

Smith was a highly respected professional manager who for about six years had run a thriving gym at Huntingdon. Among the fighters in his camp was European heavyweight champion, Joe Bugner.

Dave was thrilled at the suggestion, and the following Sunday morning Jim drove him to the gym. Smith was very receptive, and on discovering Green's status, invited him to return the following Sunday and train with his boxers.

The move was a wonderful experience for Dave. Not only did it give him an insight into the serious business of professional boxing which is far removed from the amateur game, but also provided him with some much needed sparring. Jamaican born, Des Morrison, an established professional from Bedford, was training to fight Joe Tetteh for the British light-welterweight championship at Shoreditch on 27 November. Being about the same weight, Green was invited to spar with him. It was the highlight of his visit.

Andy Smith was impressed by Green's attitude and determination, and invited him to train at the gym each Tuesday and Thursday for the next three weeks, as well as Sunday mornings. Dave was delighted because the training was far more intense and varied than he had been used to. Although he kept extremely fit by running each day, sparring was the greatest asset.

Apart from Des Morrison, he also benefited from workouts with Mickey Laud, a local welterweight 13 years his senior and veteran of over 60 professional contests since 1962.

Despite training with professionals, Green's mind was still firmly set on winning an ABA championship. Having not thought beyond that goal, he was therefore somewhat surprised when Andy Smith took him aside one day and asked if he had considered turning professional.

Andy was an astute judge of fighters, and recognised that Dave's aggressive style would be well suited to the paid ranks.

"You are 21 in June," he remarked, "so you can't afford to wait much longer." Mutual respect had already developed between the two, and after some discussion it was agreed that win or lose in the ABA championships, Dave would become a professional under Smith's management.

The ABA semi-finals took place at Belle View, Manchester, on 17 April 1974, just seven days after Green's victory over Alf Barnes. His fight with Terry Waller was one of the main attractions, and a bus load of fans travelled from the Fens to support him. Even in his junior days, car loads of local people went to most of his fights, and numbers increased as he developed into a top class senior.

Although Waller was a slight favourite, the power-punching displays of Green had been the talking point of the season. It was an intriguing match, and many people thought he would hit too hard for the reigning champion.

The contest was an absolute thriller which more than lived up to expectations. Thunderous applause greeted both boxers at the end, and 'nobbins' were thrown into the ring. Although Waller took a unanimous decision, he had never been made to work harder. Green was spectacular in defeat, and his display gave Chatteris its greatest night of sporting excitement since the glory days of Eric Boon.

Speaking on BBC television, commentator, Harry Carpenter, described the fight as: "One of the outstanding amateur contests of not only this year, but any other year."

Knowing his only chance of success was to get in close, Green pushed forward from the first bell. Waller, however, had the longer reach, and his accurate left jab gave him the edge in the opening round. He was a classic boxer of vast experience who had seen it all before at every level. An England international since 1967, he had won a junior ABA title back in 1962, and four senior championships at three weights, the first being in 1967.

The second round was a sheer test of strength. Whilst Terry was still effective with his jab, Green waded forward relentlessly looking to blast his way to victory. After taking a

51

series of left and right hooks to head and body, Waller hung on grimly and was cautioned for the second time.

The capacity crowd were on their feet from virtually the start of the hard, bruising and absorbing final session. People at home sat on the edge of their seats, eyes glued to television screens. "Waller has not had as tough a contest as this in years, ...a superb performance by Green,...the Chatteris boy has come to fight and is testing the champion to the hilt and sometimes a bit beyond it," Carpenter excitedly told the nation.

Despite Dave's power and aggression, Waller hit him with every punch in the book, albeit with no obvious effect. Showing incredible resilience, Green continued to power forward and there must have been moments when Terry wondered what he had to do to thwart him.

The reigning champion looked extremely tired midway through the round, but Dave was also feeling the effects of the non-stop battle. Yet with amazing courage and will-power both found extra reserves of energy to throw testing punches from all angles until the final bell. It was gripping stuff which had the crowd screaming with excitement throughout. At the end there was so much noise that neither boxer nor the referee heard the bell.

Dave's display had been one of raw aggression and determination. He learned a great deal from Waller who went on to take his fifth ABA championship by outpointing Erroll McKenzie in the final at Wembley two weeks later. In doing so he equalled Dick McTaggart's post-war title winning record.

Predictably, there were soon rumours that Dave was to turn professional, but this was denied by Jim Moore. Despite the agreement with Andy Smith, Jim told the press that Dave's fine performance must put him in line for an England vest. The plan was for him to have a rest, then travel with a Cambridgeshire Sporting Club team to box in Germany.

"He will make that trip because he wants to get an England vest," said Moore. "David has no immediate plans to turn professional. We have not discussed it, but if it happens it will certainly be at a later date."

Despite his comments, Moore allowed Dave to step in as a late substitute on a Northampton Amateur Boxing Club show just five days after losing to Waller. Boxing at only half pace, he comfortably outpointed Tony Meakins (RAF) who had beaten him at Abingdon in November 1972.

After the fight he decided it was the ideal time to quit the amateurs. His employer was opposed to the idea, and offered to make him manager of the whole Southery carrot-farm operation if he resisted the temptation to turn professional. Dave knew it was a big step to take and before making a final decision, sought his fathers advice. "Have a go son," Ken Green told him, "because it will be too late in two years time, and then you will regret it."

His father told him what he wanted to hear, but coming from a close family, he needed that support. "It was the perfect situation," he remarked when recalling his decision to become professional, "because it meant I left the amateurs on a winning note."

Although Dave failed to win a national ABA championship, his amateur career was one to be proud of. He won 51 of 70 senior contests, 22 inside the distance. Only Billy Taylor and Mario Stango managed to stop him. From the moment he stepped into the ring as an ambitious 13 year old schoolboy, he faced good quality opposition. This is highlighted by the fact that just five weeks after his first contest in March 1967, future opponents, Terry Waller and Mickey Spencer, won ABA championships at light and bantamweight respectively. Mickey was only 17 at the time.

Throughout his amateur days Dave was described as being ebullient, jovial and friendly. His array of cups and other trophies have been proudly retained and displayed as memories of those enjoyable, albeit, unpaid days.

53

4

TURNS PROFESSIONAL

Although he fell just short of top championship class, Dave Green was a highly respected amateur. From a total of 105 junior and senior contests, he won 74 of which 33 were inside the distance. He was stopped only twice, and never knocked out. His thrilling contest with Terry Waller was shown on national television, and attracted the interest of a number of professional managers and promoters who knew he would become a good ticket seller.

Green's aggressive style was well suited to the professional game, but despite the interest, he looked no further than Andy Smith. Dave had great respect for him almost from the day they first met. More importantly, he felt Andy was a man he could completely trust. They quickly agreed professional terms, and following application to the British Boxing Board of Control at the beginning of August 1974, Green was granted a professional licence the following month.

By this time, Smith had moved his training camp to St Ives where he took possession of a former Victorian primary school which he renovated and turned into a well-equipped gymnasium. Hanging outside the front entrance was a blue notice prominently bearing the words ANDY'S BOXING ACADEMY.

Situated at Pig Lane, the gym contained everything required by a professional fighter. Facilities included two heavy bags, a speed-ball, benches and well-equipped wall-bars for pull-ups. Mirrors were fixed to all the walls to aid shadow-boxing, and the ring erected in a corner of the large ground floor room. At the back were changing rooms and a shower. A good manager and provider, Andy Smith personally cleaned the premises every night after training.

The atmosphere at the gym was always relaxed, yet professional. It was a great attraction, particularly on Sunday mornings which were open house. Locals were allowed to watch the fighters training, and budding youngsters encouraged to spar under Andy Smith's supervision just as Green had about 12 months earlier. People soaked up the atmosphere, and at the end Andy would walk round with a hat inviting spectators to make donations to the local amateur boxing club, which he formed back in 1948.

Apart from Green, Morrison, Gale and Laud, other professionals in the camp included heavyweights Joe Bugner, Dave Roden, and Bjorn Rudi from Norway who Andy Smith had recently signed.

The Hungarian-born Bugner, who lived at St Ives, was the real star, and attracted tremendous attention. Having turned professional in 1967, he progressed to take the British, European and Commonwealth titles from Henry Cooper in 1971. Although he lost them to Jack Bodell six months later, Joe regained the European title in 1972, and by the time Dave joined the camp, had successfully defended it on three occasions. He had lost just five of more than 50 contests, two of which were on points to Muhammed Ali and Joe Frazier.

Very soon after joining the camp, Dave recognised the respect all the boxers had for Andy. Everyone, including Bugner, called him "Mr Smith" all of the time. He was an extremely professional man who cared for his fighters and ensured they did the right things. "I realised he must be a bit special," recalled Green, "and it didn't take me long to know why."

He immediately fell into line, addressing his new manager as "Mr Smith", and continued to do so throughout his life. "He earned my respect," said Dave. "If he wanted me at a place at any given time, I always complied."

Once it became known that Dave's amateur days were over, articles appeared in local newspapers comparing him with another Chatteris favourite, Eric Boon. Known as 'Golden Boy' and 'Boy Boon', the former lightweight champion was a legendary puncher. Having a similar style, Green was already seen as the new ring tiger of the Fens, and soon adopted the name of Dave 'Boy' Green.

When a group of local reporters visited the St Ives gym, Dave told them: "A lot of people say I fight like Boon. I have heard them during my fights shouting out: 'Come on Boy Boon'. My father saw Boon fight at Chatteris, and says he was a real banger."

Andy Smith agreed that there were striking similarities between the two. "The great thing with Eric Boon was that he could be boxed off the park and still come back to knock his man out in the last round. That is the type of fighter David is too," he told his audience.

"He is an exciting little fighter," continued Smith. "To me, that is great, provided he tightens up a bit so he does not get hit so much himself when he goes to work."

"He is a Laud type," said Andy referring to a well known local fighting family. "When the other boy is worn out, he will still be there fighting. That was the great thing about the Laud brothers from this area. They all had the same country stamina."

Andy Smith demanded total dedication from his fighters, and the decision to turn professional completely transformed Dave's life. Unlike his amateur days when he trained twice a week, he found himself at the St Ives gym every evening as well as retaining his job at the farm.

A strenuous programme was mapped out to ensure that he was adequately prepared when he made his professional debut. Loving sport and fitness training, Green adapted well because he knew that success required maximum effort.

Training went according to plan, and by October Smith was

satisfied that Dave was ready for his professional debut. He was matched with Barton McAllister, a journeyman fighter from South London, and the fight scheduled to take place at the Anglo American Sporting Club in London on 16 October.

Although both boxers attended the weigh in ceremony at 1pm, McAllister failed to show up for the fight in the evening. Despite efforts by the promoters, no substitute could be found at such short notice. It was a great disappointment, not only for Green, but also a group of 10 supporters who had hired a minibus to take them from Chatteris to the capital.

The situation was extremely frustrating because a professional debut is generally the most daunting occasion in a fighter's career. Dave had trained hard and psyched himself up for the contest, but all to no avail. It meant he would have to endure the torment all over again. His only consolation was that he received his £50 purse. He never found out why McAllister failed to show up, but was quick to comment: "Obviously he didn't fancy it."

In the meantime, Dave had a more pressing engagement – his wedding 10 days later. He and fianceé, Kay Curson, who lived with her mother at Sutton, had met at a disco back in 1971. She was 16 and he was two years older. After some initial chat, Kay asked Dave what he did. She burst out laughing when he said he was a boxer. As he weighed only eight stone at the time she couldn't believe he was big enough. The only boxer she had ever heard of was Muhammed Ali.

There was, however, instant mutual attraction. They started dating, quickly fell in love, and became engaged in 1973. Although she knew nothing about boxing, Kay did go to some of Dave's amateur fights.

They were married at Kay's local church at Sutton on 26 October 1974. "We chose that day because that's when the clocks went back," said Dave with a cheeky grin. "It gave us an extra hour in bed." The real reason why they chose that date was because it was Kay's uncle Freddie's birthday. He was her mother's brother, and had been her best friend since her father died two years earlier. She wanted him to give her away, but he was too shy and nervous to do so. Instead, another uncle performed the task. Dave's best man was John Garner who had been his closest friend at school.

About 80 people attended the couple's reception at Chatteris Community College hall. Dave and Kay paid for the food, and his father and Kay's mother, Betty, shared the cost of the bar which was open all evening.

After a five day honeymoon in London, the couple started married life living with Kay's mother, with whom Dave built a close relationship. Neither had much in the way of savings, and could not afford a place of their own. Although they looked to rent somewhere there was nothing they liked within their price range. Kay worked as a hairdresser in order to support herself, while Dave's only income was his £15 weekly wage from the farm.

Kay was once quoted by a local newspaper as saying they were so poor when they got married, that all they owned were two second-hand minis, and a double bed which was given to them as a wedding present. "It wasn't the ideal way to start married life," said Dave, "but it didn't really matter because we had each other."

Their poor financial situation made Dave even more determined to succeed as a fighter. On returning from honeymoon, he went straight back to the gym and resumed his exhausting routine. He was luckier than many young boxers setting out on the hard professional road because he was able to get quality sparring from the start. Apart from Des Morrison and Mickey Laud with whom he sparred as an amateur, he also had the benefit of regular work-outs with Jeff Gale, a promising welterweight who had lost just one of nine contests.

* * *

Dave's professional debut finally took place on a big promotion at Nottingham Ice Stadium on 10 December 1974.

Top of the bill was a contest between local man Dave Needham and Paddy Maguire for the vacant British bantamweight championship. The undercard featured Maurice Hope, Tony Poole from Kettering, and Green's stable-mate, Jeff Gale, who faced former British welterweight champion, Bobby Arthur.

Local newspapers gave him good pre-fight coverage and sent reporters to Nottingham to cover the event. Dave personally sold 20 tickets to loyal fans, whilst others travelled to the arena and paid on the night.

Again it was a nerve-racking experience for the young debutant. After arriving at the venue, he was told that his was the second fight of the evening. Preparations were made, including careful taping of the hands, gloving-up and warming-up exercises. As the minutes ticked by, the adrenaline was really pumping. All Dave wanted to do was get into the ring. Suddenly, the dressing-room door swung open. "Sorry son, you've been put back to last," growled the whip engaged by the promoter to escort fighters to the ring.

"I was gutted," said Dave, "but there was nothing we could do. I was having my first fight so I had to do as I was told."

With the main event going the full 15 rounds, the wait seemed like an eternity, but Green was fortunate to have Andy Smith with him. He had seen it all before because such last minute changes are all part of the professional scene. He kept the youngster calm and relaxed until they started the warm-up procedure all over again.

When he finally got into the ring, Dave made the perfect start to the paid ranks, knocking out Yotham Kunda in two rounds. Although the opening session was scrappy, Kunda was rocked by a heavy left-right combination, and by the bell was bleeding heavily from the nose.

In the second, Dave opened him up with good body shots towards the end of the round, then crashed a short right to the chin. Kunda crashed face downwards on the floor and did not stir as referee, John Coyle, completed the count after two minutes 56 seconds. It was several minutes before he recovered.

The most significant thing about Green's victory was his punching power. Kunda, a Zambian boxing out of Swansea, had not previously been stopped, and two months earlier took undefeated light-middleweight, Jimmy Batten, the distance.

Dave hadn't gone into the contest with the intention of looking spectacular. In fact, Andy Smith had told him to take things easy. "But the opening came and I took it," recalled Green. "It was a great start."

The result left Smith with a headache. "It's going to be difficult to get fights for David in the next few months after this," he remarked. "There are not many six-round fighters around. But I am not saying it is a problem I shall not enjoy."

After a short break for Christmas, Green started training for a fight at the Royal Albert Hall on 21 January. John H. Stracey was scheduled to meet Hedgemon Lewis of America in an eliminator for the world welterweight title, but the show was cancelled when John was suddenly rushed to hospital with just a few days to go. Dave's fight, however, was switched to a dinner show at the Anglo American Sporting Club, Park Lane, in honour of Sir Stanley Rous, CBE.

Although he boxed a day earlier than originally planned, Dave still secured another explosive victory inside two rounds. Hefty wallops around the rib cage put opponent, Dave Coombs of Northwich, on the floor twice for counts of nine. More body shots, followed by a right to the chin put him down again, and he was counted out in the act of rising after one minute 56 seconds of the round.

It was a quick night for the diners because the main event of the three-fight bill also ended quickly. Alan Minter, a professional since 1972, knocked out Henry Cooper from Scotland in the opening round.

Andy Smith firmly believed in keeping his fighters busy, and planned to have Dave boxing at least once a month. Having recently been granted a promoters licence, he staged a dinner show at Cambridge Guildhall on 12 February in conjunction with a local sporting club.

In what was the first professional boxing show in the university city for more than a decade, Green was elevated to the main event scheduled for eight two-minute rounds. A popular amateur, he already had plenty of local support, and drew a full-house of over 300. In the audience were Joe Bugner, Eric Boon, Newmarket jockeys, Greville Starkey, Brian Jago and Frankie Durr, along with film star, Trevor Howard, who was attending as a member of a London sporting club party.

Dave's opponent was 27-year-old Derek Simpson from Kilmarnock, a veteran of 50 contests of which he had won 24 and drawn four. A professional since 1969, he had won his last two inside the distance, and was therefore seen as stern opposition for the Chatteris youngster.

Knowing Simpson would not fold quickly, Andy Smith urged his charge to take his time. Anxious to learn, Dave changed his style dramatically during this fight. Instead of the barn-storming aggression of his amateur days, he was more controlled, and displayed good long-range punching on the move. Solid body shots gave him early superiority, but he impressed observers with the skill of his left jab.

An extended delay occurred after round three because all the lights in the hall suddenly failed. When they eventually resumed boxing, Simpson used all his experience and made Dave battle hard.

In round seven, the Chatteris man stepped up the pace, catching the Scot with stiff jolting punches from both hands, and a ramrod left jab landed flush on the left eye. Simpson pawed at it anxiously before retreating to his corner in obvious discomfort, and signalled his retirement. "I thought the eye had burst," he remarked later, "I knew I was behind on points."

Eric Boon went to Green's dressing-room immediately after the fight and congratulated him on a fine performance. "Marvellous, – the boy has great potential," he told a local reporter. "I think a British title is a certainty, and the world title is not beyond the bounds of possibility. He's improving so fast it is ridiculous. He is aggressive and knows what he is doing."

"I haven't had such a good night for a long time," said Trevor Howard who also visited Dave's dressing-room to congratulate him. "Damn good show," he remarked as he shook hands.

Recognising that Dave was a bit special, Andy Smith knew the importance of making him more identifiable. He remarked that there must be thousands of Dave Greens in the country and suggested that he therefore adopt the name of Dave 'Boy' Green. The word 'Boy' was part of local dialogue meaning 'mate', and had also been used by Eric Boon in the early stages of his career.

Billed as Dave 'Boy' Green, the Chatteris prospect made his first appearance on a major London promotion four weeks later when he faced Barton McAllister at Wembley. Top of the bill was the world light-heavyweight title contest between John Conteh and Lonnie Bennett.

It was regarded as another important learning fight for Green because McAllister, a 29-year-old Jamaican had been a professional since 1971. He had won 16 and drawn two of his 48 contests. A regular performer, he had already boxed on four occasions during 1975, winning twice. Just eight days before facing Green, he lost on points over eight rounds to former Irish amateur international, Jim Montague, and in January was outpointed by Dave's old amateur foe, Mickey Ryce.

Resorting to his more familiar aggressive style of fighting, Dave quickly had the Jamaican covering up and looking extremely uncomfortable from vicious hooks to the body. When the referee called a halt midway through round two, he was well on top, although the official ending was due to a gash over Barton's left eye.

Four victories, all inside the distance within the space of three months was a tremendous start to Green's professional career. Yet it so very nearly went wrong in his next fight against George Salmon at Cambridge Guildhall on 8 April.

Boxing out of Stoke, George was another Jamaican journey-man fighter similar to Barton McAllister. He had won 10 and drawn two of his 24 pro fights since 1973, but had the distinction of having never been stopped despite facing good class opponents including Tony Poole (twice) and Steve Angel. Andy Smith warned Dave that it would be tough, but he could never have foreseen how close his man came to defeat.

By the third round Green was well in control when he was suddenly caught by a terrific left uppercut to the point of the chin. Although he didn't go down, he was rocked to his heels and in serious trouble. "For a few moments, everything went black," he remarked when recalling the fight. "I had never been hit like that before."

Despite his predicament, he hung on bravely and was helped by Salmon's wild attempts to finish it. As George waded in hopelessly off-balance, Dave rammed a solid left to the chin which floored him for a count of four.

"Did you switch those lights off again?" Green asked Andy Smith when he returned to the corner. The manager just smiled, sponged him down and prepared him for the next round. "Keep your hands up and take your time," he said calmly as the bell sounded for round four. Whilst obeying the manager's instructions, Green forced the pace for the rest of the fight to take a comfortable decision. Referee, Harry Gibbs' score of 80-77 indicated that Green had won six and drawn two of the eight rounds.

"George Salmon gave me one of my hardest fights at that stage of my career," said Dave. "In boxing, you learn to respect people, and that is very important in life."

Green certainly respected his next opponent, Tommy Joyce from Doncaster, and regarded it as a privilege when matched with him the following month. He remembered Tommy as a top class amateur, and expecting a difficult fight, trained exceptionally hard.

A Scottish international from 1968 to 1970, Joyce won a bronze medal in the 1970 Commonwealth Games at Edinburgh, and was beaten by Terry Waller in the ABA semi-finals the same year. Six years older than Green, he turned professional in 1971 and was unbeaten in his first 15 contests. He had since become something of a journeyman, and by the time they met at the Anglo American Sporting Club on 12 May 1975, had lost 12 and drawn two of 33 contests.

All of his 19 victories had been on points, but despite his undoubted skill Tommy could not keep the aggressive Chatteris fighter at bay. By round two he was grazed above the left eye, and rocked by a vicious left hook to the head early in the third.

After a period of sustained pressure against the ropes, Joyce went to the floor for a count of eight. Blood streaming from his nose, he rose gamely, but was given no respite. Despite giving away four pounds in weight, Green hammered him around the ring, unleashing savage blows from both hands. Two thudding rights to the ribs sent Tommy to the floor grimacing in pain. Although he started to climb to his feet, referee Benny Caplan counted him out at two minutes 35 seconds of the third round.

The victory really brought Dave to notice, and three weeks later he had what would be the first of 20 fights at the Royal Albert Hall. It was a wonderful venue to watch boxing, and Mike Barrett's annual 'Eve of the Derby' promotion was a feast for the fans. Top of the bill saw Chris Finnegan defending his British light-heavyweight title against Johnny Frankham, while the under-card included John H. Stracey, Vernon Sollas, Albert Hillman, Danny McAlinden, and a contest between Joey Singleton and Alan Salter, both of whom would become opponents of Green in the months ahead.

Dave, who had celebrated his 22nd birthday the previous day, faced a genuine hard man, Angus McMillan from Glasgow, seven years his elder and vastly more experienced. He had been stopped only once in 31 professional contests, (seven defeats), and faced a number of top men including Jim Watt, Joey Singleton and Johnny Cheshire.

Although Green won clearly on points, he was made to work hard. The Scot's skilful boxing kept him in contention during the early rounds, and he staggered Dave with a hard right as the bell ended the third. In the later stages of the contest, over eight two-minute rounds, McMillan took a lot of punishment as the extremely strong and fit youngster piled on the pressure. Referee Mike Jacobs' score of 80-77 indicated that Green had not lost a round, drawing two.

Andy Smith always said that Dave would learn nothing from knocking over no-hope opponents. He explained to reporters why he had insisted that the fight with McMillan be over two-minute rounds. "Over eight threes I knew Dave would knock him out," he remarked. "I want him to learn. He's got to be able to go the distance because a string of quick wins won't teach him anything."

The philosophy was good, but the problem Andy faced was getting the right opponents. Tommy Joyce and Barton McAllister were experienced men who had been expected to stay with Green, but he destroyed them both in quick time.

Smith was, nevertheless, delighted with Dave's progress, and in one interview said: "As an amateur he used to walk in and take everything. I've had to instil some boxing into him – and if you look at what he's done in his first season as a pro, you've got to admit he's made tremendous progress. In 12 months time he could well be ready for the British title."

The solid relationship which had developed between the two was built on respect, trust and Andy's ability to handle people. Dave had good reason to be grateful for the way his manager handled one particular situation which could otherwise have affected his attitude and discipline towards training.

One Saturday night during his first few months as a professional, he and Kay were invited to a party at St Ives where the drinks flowed freely. Dave got very drunk, collapsed, and had to be taken home. When he awoke the next morning he felt terrible. "I can't go training this morning," he groaned to Kay.

"Well, you had better telephone Mr Smith and tell him," she replied.

Dave walked to a 'phone box and called the gym. "Mr Smith, I had a bit of a good night last night," he said sheepishly. "I won't be able to make the gym this morning."

"David," he replied. "I've been in boxing all my life and I've been drinking most of my life, but I have never missed a training session through drink. So you get up here as soon as you can."

"I'm on my way," said Green.

At an appropriate moment Smith took the youngster aside. "If you want to be a boxer, let's do it professionally," he said quietly. "If you want to be a drinker, go on your way and start drinking."

Dave was made to understand the seriousness of professional boxing, and from that day was completely disciplined. The situation also strengthened the respect he had for his manager because of the way he dealt with it.

✦ 5 ✦

STEP UP IN CLASS

Despite having had only seven contests, Green was ranked at number nine in the welterweight division of *Boxing News* July rankings. His stable-mate, Jeff Gale, was at five. Two months later, the trade paper published short profiles of the top ten welterweights in Britain. Dave was described as:

> Damaging puncher with either hand. Aggressive and crowd-pleasing style, good body-puncher and left-hooker, should get plenty of exposure this season. Green looks the ideal type for the pro game, and by this time next year could be in a challenging position for the title.

An illustrated two-page feature about him appeared in the same edition under the headline "New Chatteris Thunderbolt?"

After a four month break, Green returned to the ring at the Royal Albert Hall against Al Stewart of Burscough over eight three-minute rounds in a contest made at 10st 7. It was another full house with an incredible atmosphere because the main event was a return between Johnny Frankham and Chris Finnegan. The attractive under-card featured Danny McAlinden, John L. Gardner, Tom Imrie and Bobby Arthur, all appearing in eight rounders.

Stewart's only defeat from eight contests was in December 1974 when an eye injury forced him to retire after five rounds against Derek Simpson. He had been inactive since that fight, but had previously boxed a draw with George Salmon, and in his only Albert Hall appearance knocked out Allan Jones of Merthyr in the opening round.

Once again, Dave made light of an opponent expected to extend him. He found Stewart easy to hit, although towards the end of the opening round a degree of needle developed when Al went to the canvas after appearing to be tripped. On rising he shoulder-charged Green to the floor whereupon both were sternly lectured by referee, Doug Jenkins.

When Stewart landed a heavy shot to the head early in round two, Green hit back immediately. Attacking relentlessly, he hammered Al into a corner and floored him with a left hook to the body. Although he rose at the count of one, he was soon under tremendous pressure.

A buckling left hook doubled Stewart up, another left sent his gumshield spinning across the ring, and a following right sent him back to the floor. Without bothering to count, referee Jenkins waved it off.

"Wonderful," said Andy Smith. "I did not expect Dave to do the job so convincingly so early."

Even after just eight professional contests, Smith had no doubts what the future held for his young prospect. "I think without a doubt David will be British and European champion, and go for a world title," he told Pat Ringham in an exclusive interview for the *Cambridgeshire Times*. "I am not just sitting here in St Ives with stars in my eyes, I am involved with the connoisseurs of boxing, and they all agree that this boy has the hallmark of a great boxer." Smith admitted that Dave's aggressive big-hit style meant opponents had to be paid a larger percentage of the purse just to get them into the ring with him.

Even after a handful of fights, seasoned boxing journalists were impressed by the uninhibited old-fashioned way Green punched to the body with both hands. He was just the same in the gym where he let them go, much to the discomfort of his sparring partners.

"It may not be spectacular to watch," remarked Eric Boon who took a genuine but unobtrusive interest in Dave's progress, "but when you belt them downstairs, the accumulative effects can be both tiring and painful. By the middle rounds of a fight their mouths are beginning to hang open."

Looking ahead, Andy Smith wanted Chatteris to become synonymous with the name of David Green just as St Ives had with Joe Bugner who dominated boxing in that area and created tremendous interest in the locality. He believed Green had arrived on the scene at just the right moment.

On the wall of his office adjacent to the gym, Smith had a perpetual reminder of the past and future – two six foot high portraits of Boon and Green. "They stare at me all the time," he remarked. "One was one of the greats of the past and the other, well I'm sure he's going to be one of the greats of the future."

Dave benefited greatly from sparring with Des Morrison and Jeff Gale, leading contenders for the British light-welter and welterweight championships respectively. His performance over Al Stewart had been very impressive, and sufficient for Albert Hall matchmaker, Mickey Duff, to book him to meet Alan Salter of Peckham on the next show at the venue on 25 November. Before that, however, Green topped Andy Smith's promotion at Cambridge Guildhall on 10 November against Brian Jones from Croeserw, South Wales, over eight rounds.

Jones, a southpaw, was managed by former British junior welterweight champion, Des Rea. After a lay-off for six months, he had come back to win his last two contests and take his overall record to 12 wins and a draw from 17 contests. That good form, however, counted for nothing once he got into the ring with Green who scored a spectacular knock-out after just 55 seconds of round two.

Powerful combinations of hooks to head and body put Jones under terrible pressure, and it was another case of the Chatteris man being too strong and aggressive for an opponent expected to test him. The end came when a left hook smashed the Welshman into the ropes. As he lurched drunkenly forward, a vicious right caught him flush on the chin. They were magnificent, yet frightening blows which sent Jones crashing to the canvas. He never looked like beating the count, and the crowd fell silent because they realised he was badly hurt.

Brian lay motionless for all of six minutes as his seconds and a doctor worked to revive him. Even after being helped to his stool, it was some time before he was able to leave the ring. In the meantime, Andy Smith ushered Green back to the dressing-room because he was extremely concerned about his opponent's condition.

"With this sort of punching power, this boy has world championship potential," Smith told a reporter who spoke to them afterwards. Dave, however, was unable to enjoy his moment of triumph because he felt physically sick. He was not helped when he saw Jones being carried to an ambulance on a stretcher some while later.

Examination at Addenbrookes Hospital, Cambridge, revealed that the Welshman was suffering from severe concussion. Although he was detained overnight for observation, there were no lasting effects, and he was discharged the following day.

* * *

Despite his rapid progress, Green was being sensibly brought along by Andy Smith. "I didn't want him to turn pro until he had matured," Smith remarked at one of his many press conferences. "Once he came with me it was all about taking one step at a time and not getting too excited."

The same applied to purse money. "At this stage of the game, money is not important," Smith told Dave. "Boxing comes in three stages. The first is to make sure you keep winning. For a British title you must take on who is out there, but then you must make sure the money is right."

Even in the very early stages of his career, Dave had the

benefit of Andy, not just as a manager, but also a financial adviser and friend. An extremely astute man with money, he insisted that the young fighter kept his job at the farm, and advised him to put all his ring earnings into a bank account.

Knowing that Dave and Kay didn't have their own house, he suggested they saved up and made it a priority. In less than 12 months, the money from Dave's fights was sufficient for a deposit. Prompted by the manager, he and Kay went house-hunting, and in November 1975 bought a three bedroom semi at 48 Birch Avenue, Chatteris, costing about £8,000.

From the day they were married, Dave and Kay had an agreement that they wouldn't buy anything unless they could afford it. They avoided hire purchase schemes, preferring to save up for things they needed. Consequently, when they moved into their new house, they had very little in the way of furniture – just a double bed, three piece suite, black and white television and a number of secondhand items. As they had no washing machine, Kay went to the launderette every Sunday morning while Dave was at the gym.

By this time, she had changed her job and was working in a laboratory at Cadbury Schweppes in Cambridge. Her weekly wage of £11 was double what she had earned as a hairdresser. Even so they still struggled to make ends meet, but knew that getting their own property was of paramount importance.

"Right from the start, Mr Smith said I should be looking ahead to buy our own place," said Dave. "In many ways he was like a second father to me."

Smith also got on very well with Dave's parents who, despite knowing very little about boxing, supported their son's career wholeheartedly. They trusted Andy, and whatever advice he gave Dave was good enough for them. "If every boxer had parents like yours, I'd have no problems," he told Dave.

Every decision Smith made was in the best interests of his boxers. He was very much his own man, and whilst he had a good working relationship with the top promoters, Harry

Levene, Jarvis Astaire, Mickey Duff and Mike Barrett, he always made sure he got the right money for his fighters. All he demanded in return was dedication and loyalty.

Green was totally dedicated. He was up at 5am every morning to do his running, usually at least four miles. He liked to run alone so there was nobody to distract him or hold him back. He was already convinced that if he put in the work he could make it to the top. That drove him on, often doing an extra mile in order to reach peak fitness.

At 6.30am he left home for the farm, worked non-stop all day, then returned home, changed his clothes and set off for the gym. He trained every evening from 5.30pm until 7pm after which he returned home, had his tea and was in bed by 9pm. It was a daily routine, week in, week out.

Although he was earning good money as a boxer, Dave missed out on the social scene as a young man. "I had to be dedicated," he recalled, "but my wife was marvellous. There aren't many women who would put up with such a life."

Andy Smith always believed in rigorous training sessions, and from the day he turned professional Green had the benefit of working with good men. "I feel if you are lucky enough to have hard preparation, the contests come easy," Smith often remarked. "We always try to make sparring harder than the fights. There are no punches pulled."

As Dave prepared for his fight with Alan Salter at the Royal Albert Hall, Smith instilled into him that the 25 year old Peckham man was his best opponent to date. In his last contest he unsuccessfully challenged Joey Singleton for the British light-welterweight title, losing in nine rounds due to a cut eye. He had previously fought magnificently against Joey in a non-title bout only to lose a highly controversial decision by half a point which caused an uproar.

Although his record of 13 wins and a draw from 30 contests was not particularly impressive, Salter was a known puncher with a reputation for gameness. He was an extremely popular small hall fighter who thrilled the crowds with his hit-or-be-hit style. Some critics felt he would be too experienced for Dave, although most agreed that a good old-fashioned punch-up seemed assured.

Green's exciting style was already making the London audiences sit up and take notice. His popularity was increasing rapidly, and for this fight he personally sold £1,200 worth of tickets. The Albert Hall was packed to capacity, and his fans from the Fens made themselves heard as he climbed into the ring.

"Take your time to feel him out in the first round, and see what he is like," said Andy Smith in the corner as they awaited the opening bell. He knew a lot was riding on the fight, and didn't want Dave to take unnecessary chances. Completely ignoring the manager's final words, the fired-up Green strode straight to the centre of the ring, circled Salter and quickly

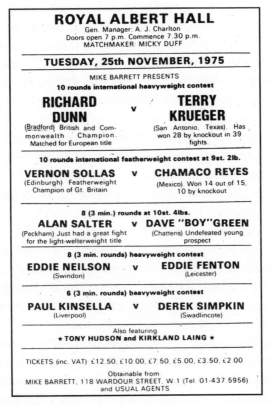

Poster advertising contest between Green and Alan Salter

73

rammed home powerful jabs. Heavy hooks followed, and Alan's face was looking flushed within seconds. A thudding left made Salter's legs sag, and he took a barrage of shots before a right to the jaw sent him to the floor.

Up at six, Salter was immediately under heavy pressure, and could do nothing to keep the powerful Chatteris man away. A left and right combination put him down again, and he took the count of eight on one knee. On rising, he attempted to fight back, but coldly and precisely Green picked his shots. A vicious left hook to the jaw made Salter crumble to the floor with blood dripping from his nose. Although he gamely rose at seven, he looked bemused, and referee, Mike Jacobs, threw protective arms around him and led him to the corner. It had taken Dave just 85 seconds to score his 10th straight victory, and certainly his most important. Salter announced his retirement from the ring immediately after the fight.

Meanwhile, Green apologised to his manager for disobeying orders. "Sorry Mr Smith," he said as he walked back to his corner. "I didn't mean it to go that quick." Andy just laughed.

"A wonderful, wonderful performance," enthused Smith before assembled reporters back in the dressing-room. "He stole the show in just one and a half minutes. The crowd were stunned at the ferocity of his punching. It was out of this world. Salter is one of the toughest men in the business, and he couldn't stand up to it."

Dave sat in silence as his manager held conference, shielding him from the press just as he did with Joe Bugner in his early days. "What pleased me so much," continued Andy, "was that he worked on Salter clinically and methodically like a surgeon."

Before the fight, Smith had been criticised in some quarters for allowing Green to face Salter. Dave's success, however, put him in something of a predicament because he also managed Des Morrison and Jeff Gale. In an interview with *Boxing News*, he said: "It's a unique situation because Dave Green can operate at either weight division. Rather than have him fight Morrison or Gale, we'll divert him on to the European scene, and take progressive steps towards winning the European title."

Describing Green as "a fighter in the Carmen Basilio mould", Smith still wanted him to box every four weeks or so for the next eight or nine months, but was already experiencing difficulty getting British boxers to face him.

Boxing News described Green as the most exciting newcomer of 1975, and predicted he would fight for a major title at light-welter or welterweight during 1976. He was already ranked as third contender for Joey Singleton's light-welterweight title behind Morrison and Billy Waith.

Unlike many young prospects, Green was not given an easy ride to the top by being matched with a series of inadequate opponents. Andy Smith ensured that whenever possible, he faced men of differing styles and levels of experience at both welter and light-welterweight.

Dave's next opponent was George McGurk of Jarrow whom he faced at the Royal Albert Hall on 20 January 1976. Whilst only being a lightweight, he was ranked number two in Britain, and was expected to provide a real test. He was an experienced fighter who had been stopped only twice in 42 contests spanning six years. Both were as a result of injury. A damaged arm forced him to retire against Jean-Baptiste Piedvache in France 12 months earlier, whilst a badly cut cheek caused the referee to pull him out against Jimmy Revie in October 1975.

McGurk's most notable victory was to halt unbeaten Vernon Sollas at Earls Court in 1973. Sollas was ahead when George tagged him with a left hook in round six. He was managed by former British Empire and European featherweight champion, Al Phillips, who told the press: "George really fancies his chances. He says he will match punches with Green, and really believes he can knock him over. He feels he has a punch to do the job."

Support for Green continued to grow, and he sold over

£2,000 worth of tickets himself. His employer purchased a batch of 22 for the farmhands, provided two minibuses, and gave each man a half day off to support their workmate.

More than 200 local fans, including at least 100 from Chatteris, made the journey to the Royal Albert Hall. It was the most support Dave had received since turning professional. "We've always had keen support for boxing in this area," he told the *Chatteris Advertiser.* "Maybe I'll get a fan club soon."

George McGurk had never been knocked out, but before travelling to London, Green said he aimed to ruin that record. Andy Smith also bubbled with enthusiasm about his man's chances. "Dave looks so good at the moment that I will be surprised if it goes five rounds," he remarked.

Despite McGurk's credentials and confidence before the fight, Green was awesome as he unleashed a ferocious barrage of body shots. George had no answer to his power, and was on the floor twice in the opening round. After taking a count of four in the first minute, a vicious right to the body put him down for eight. A plaintive gesture towards his groin was ignored by referee, Mark Hart.

Although he wasn't afraid to have a go, McGurk was clearly living on borrowed time. More strength draining shots downstairs soon had him gasping and holding on, and his only respite was when Green received a warning for a kidney punch.

The inevitable finish came towards the end of round two when a left hook to the body made George gasp. He slid to the floor and was counted out on his knees. There was some booing from spectators who thought he could have got up, but in reality there was no point – the body punches were crippling him.

Gracious in defeat, McGurk said: "My only hope was that he might get fed up with hitting me after three or four rounds. He's just phenomenal – a savage, wild man. He's certainly got the killer instinct."

Andy Smith was thrilled, and described Dave the best entertainer, crowd-wise, in the whole of Great Britain. "People want to see someone they are frightened to take their eyes off in case he scores a knockout. Green is like that," he enthused. "What particularly pleased me was the contrast from his amateur days. Then, he just stood there and punched."

Whilst Dave's performance thrilled the vast majority of fans, particularly those from Chatteris and March, it meant there was no chance of him fighting on Smith's next promotion at Cambridge. "There's just no one to fight," he shrugged. "It's disappointing for the locals, but I reckon the best I can do is have him go three or four rounds with Jeff Gale in an exhibition. That would probably be better than a real fight in any case."

The day after the fight with McGurk, Smith issued a challenge to British light-welterweight champion, Joey Singleton. "If Singleton's manager wants to put his money where his mouth is, we will make it a winner-take-all fight," he told the *Cambridge Evening News*. "And if he is not willing to do that, he can have a side-bet of anything between £200 and £2,000 on the fight."

The background to Smith's outburst was that a few days earlier, Singleton's manager, Charlie Atkinson, revealed that a proposed fight with Jim Watt for the British lightweight championship, had fallen through. Not a single purse offer had been made before the deadline of 31 December. Anxious for action, Joey was prepared to fight any light or light-welterweight in Britain.

"If Dave Green wants his chance at 10 stone, we'll fight him tomorrow for a reasonable pay-day," Atkinson told *Boxing News*. "Honestly, Green is made to order for clever boxers like Singleton."

At the time Smith chose to ignore the remarks, but after Dave's performances against Salter and McGurk, realised Green was knocking on the championship door. He said he was annoyed with "the big headed attitude" of the Singleton camp, but added: "I don't need to start campaigning for a title fight for David – the public will demand it."

Within a week of Smith's remarks, Green was matched with

Billy Waith of Cardiff over 12 rounds. The British Boxing Board of Control approved the promoter's application for the contest to be a final eliminator for Singleton's title.

Smith viewed the contest as an important step in Dave's progression. "We could have got a direct shot at Joey Singleton," he told *Boxing News* editor, Graham Houston, "but we can't afford to miss out opponents on the way up."

The fight was scheduled to take place at the Royal Albert Hall on 17 February 1976 as the chief support to Chris Finnegan's light-heavyweight title defence against Roy John. When Chris was suddenly forced to quit boxing with a torn retina, the show was cancelled, and the Green-Waith contest re-scheduled to 2nd March.

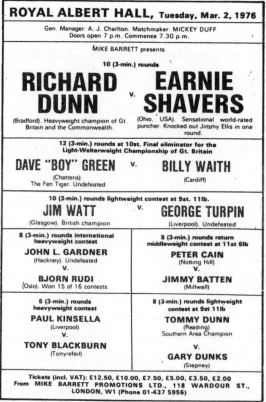

Poster advertising light-welterweight championship eliminator between Green and Billy Waith

For the McGurk fight, Dave had scaled 10 stone, and his performance convinced Andy Smith that he could retain his power at light-welterweight. "I particularly wanted the match with Waith because he has a great deal of boxing ability for Dave to oppose," said Smith at a press conference to announce the contest. "I took the fight as an education for Green, and a great preparation for a fight with Singleton. I have great respect for Waith."

Responding to Charlie Atkinson's earlier remarks, Smith said: "People like Charlie should be pleased there are fighters like Green on the scene so that their fighters can earn a living from them. Singleton would get a bigger pay-day against Green than for any other British fight."

* * *

Billy Waith was a seasoned professional who had never been stopped in 39 contests, and only floored twice. With 27 victories and three draws to his credit he was, pound for pound, probably the cleverest defensive boxer in Britain.

His career started promisingly, a draw being the only blot during his first 15 contests. Subsequent defeats were usually at the hands of good fighters. In October 1972, Billy was out-pointed by Howard Hayes in an eliminator for the British featherweight title. In June the following year he lost on points to world-rated Arnold Taylor at Johannesburg, and 12 months later lost a decision to Jim Watt in a final eliminator for the British lightweight title.

Good quality fighters, Des Morrison, Pat McCormack and Watt outpointed him during 1975, an indication that he represented Green's stiffest test to date. The fight was a great opportunity for Billy to get himself established. A professional since 1970, he had rarely enjoyed the spotlight, and it was the first time he had featured on a major promotion in London. He saw it as a chance not to be missed, and had no doubt about the outcome.

"Green is taking a big step too soon," he remarked in a pre-fight interview. "He's got the right name – 'Boy' – maybe he'll be a man one day, but I just can't see how he can beat me." On reflection, it was an amusing remark because on his debut, the Welshman was billed as Billy 'Boy' Waith.

Billy argued that Green had never fought anybody of class, and knocking out everyone meant little. "He comes in swinging with both hands and they stand there letting him hit them," he continued. "That's madness. I've been in this game too long to do the same. I wonder what he'll be like when I land a few on his chin?"

The Welshman said he would be doing Dave a favour by beating him. "A defeat will set him back 12 months, and that won't be bad," he insisted. "He can learn the game. He could be a good fighter one day."

There were, of course, plenty of people who disagreed with Waith, none more so than Eric Boon who saw Green as the best prospect he had ever seen. He often took the trouble to go the St Ives gym and watch him train, and remarked: "What I like so much about him is his will to win."

Andy Smith agreed with Boon. "Pound for pound, David is the best prospect I have seen too," he remarked, but acknowledged that Waith's experience would be a severe test. Green's carefully planned career had so far gone without a hitch, but by pitching him in with a man as mature and experienced as Waith, Smith admitted he was taking a calculated risk.

The scene was set, and opinions divided about Green's ability to power his way to victory, or whether Waith's experience and ring skills would be decisive. Bill Matthews, boxing correspondent for the Press Association, reckoned it could be 'Fight of the Year':

> Something special it should be. Green, the Tiger of the Fens, is raw-boned, mean, dedicated and a murderous puncher. Waith is a chirpy extrovert, experienced and armed with an iron chin and fluent skills.

The fight lived up to all expectations, and Green rose to the occasion magnificently. Fighting with a ferocity rarely seen in a British ring, he dug deep to hammer brave Billy Waith to defeat after two minutes 35 seconds of round 11.

At the weigh in earlier in the day both men scaled 9st 13, but even as they stood side-by-side, Green looked much the stronger.

The early rounds went very much as expected, with the Chatteris man ploughing forward unloading heavy swinging punches, while the skilful Welshman blocked, smothered and tried to sway out of range.

Billy generally looked confident in the face of aggression, taunting and teasing his less experienced opponent. When Dave caught him with a huge left cross in round two, he simply held his right glove to the side of his head and invited him to do it again.

In the third, Green pressured the Welshman into a corner, crouched cat-like searching for an opening. Failing to find one, he withdrew in despair whereupon Billy tapped him playfully on the head.

Sheer pressure, however, ensured that Dave won the opening four rounds. He whacked away at every part of the target in front of him, and although the skilful Waith took many punches on the arms and gloves, plenty more got through.

Billy didn't really get into the fight until the fifth round. A chopping right sent his gum shield flying across the ring, but composing himself well he started to put his shots together and pick up much needed points. He became more purposeful, and scored with well-placed jabs to Green's head. A chopping right stopped Dave in his tracks just before the bell.

After weathering Green's early aggression in the sixth, Billy hit back stubbornly. A vicious left-right combination made Dave back away, and with the Welshman keeping up the pressure until the bell, some ringsiders sensed he could be poised to cause an upset.

Green resumed control in round seven as he probed and prodded with his stiff accurate left jab before letting loose the familiar hooks to Waith's body. Although a nasty looking cut appeared over Billy's left eye, the blood trickled down the side of his face and did not impair his vision.

Powerful swings to the body from Green in round eight drove Waith backwards, but he re-grouped and danced on his toes to show that he was not in trouble. The crowd roared as he rallied strongly and took the fight to Green who grimaced and gave ground. Solid punches to head and body made Dave cover up in what was developing into one of the best fights of the year.

It was absorbing stuff, and as Green entered new territory in the ninth, there were plenty of bets being taken on the Welshman. It looked anybody's fight as Billy stood his ground and countered Green's aggression. As the round progressed, however, the Chatteris man's incredible strength and fitness became decisive. He threw a lot of punches, and although many missed the target or were blocked, Waith still absorbed some energy-sapping wallops. His gum shield was again dislodged as a swinging right crashed against the side of his face to send perspiration spraying over ringside reporters.

By the 10th, both men were showing signs of battle. Green had a swelling under his right eye and was bleeding from the nose, whilst the cut over Waith's left eye still seeped blood. Although the general consensus of opinion was that Dave was a couple of rounds ahead, it was in this session that he showed the stuff champions are made of.

Following an exchange of blows in the centre of the ring, the Chatteris man was driven to the ropes and momentarily looked in trouble. Gritting his teeth, he pulled himself together, and amid deafening cheers from the packed house, hit back and really began to nail the Welshman. Billy was hammered across the ring into the ropes, and at the bell was under terrible pressure. He visibly wilted after trading punches in what was one of the best rounds of fighting seen at the Albert Hall during recent years.

Green's enthusiasm and determination to finish the job

earned him a warning from referee Sid Nathan, for dangerous use of the head. He was also cautioned when a couple of swinging rights strayed into the kidney region, although Billy's evasive turning tactics contributed to the misdemeanour.

Although Dave looked exhausted as he slumped to his stool at the end of the gruelling round, he was far from finished. Feverous work by his cornermen who drenched him with water, sponged and massaged his neck, head, arms and legs during the 60 second interval, brought him back to life. At the bell he was on his feet ready to resume combat.

Focused and grimly determined, he moved forward purposefully. He was totally ruthless as he lashed out at Waith who now moved on heavy legs. His arms hung limp at his sides as he tried to bob and weave, but the strength had been completely hammered out of him.

Green had no intention of letting his man off the hook. Despite never having fought longer than eight two-minute rounds, he dredged up the strength to launch a non-stop barrage of vicious punches to the Welshman's head. There was no let-up, and as Billy sagged against the ropes looking certain to drop, referee Nathan jumped in and called it off.

It had been an incredible fight and the scenes at the end were special. Fans all around the ringside stood and cheered, grown men danced with delight, while veteran pressmen smiled as they scribbled frantically on their notepads.

Green leapt into the air and hugged Andy Smith before striding across the ring to commiserate with his beaten opponent. Billy had given everything and was glorious in defeat. He was never on the floor, and deserved the wonderful ovation he received as he left the ring.

With wife Kay watching him for the first time as a professional, Dave chose the right night for the finest hour in his short but exciting career. Joe Bugner and John Conteh were among the many boxing personalities present. BBC television cameras were also there.

The fight was a huge challenge to Dave, yet he met it superbly, proving that he was much more than just a walk-in banger. At the end he was punching as hard as during the opening session.

Showing ruthless desire for victory, he found untapped reserves of stamina and will-power at a crucial stage. He also displayed great maturity and ring-generalship by standing back and jabbing when Waith proved too elusive to catch with big shots. The decisive factor, however, was Green's staying power. When the going got really tough, he dug deep, hit back to regain control, and pounded the resistance out of a brave and experienced opponent.

Dave left the ring to rapturous applause, not only from his 1,000 or so travelling fans, but also the Londoners who had taken him into their hearts. There was a real spring in his step as he walked arm-in-arm with Andy Smith along a corridor towards the dressing-room. "You enjoyed that didn't you son?" remarked the manager. "I did, I loved every minute of it," replied the jubilant fighter.

They were followed by a dozen or more reporters anxious for comments about the fight, and Dave's future. "It couldn't have gone better if I'd written the script," a delighted Andy Smith told them once they had all settled down. "Who, but someone remarkable, could find the strength to stop a man after 11 rounds of almost non-stop punching."

"Singleton is the logical fight for us now," he continued. "We could have by-passed Waith, but David needed this fight to further his ring education. It was a wonderful experience for him."

Never a boastful man, Green quietly told his audience that although he took some good shots, he always knew what he was doing. He had always remained confident he would catch up with Billy before the end of the scheduled 12 rounds.

"This is my best performance," he remarked. "I could have gone another four or five rounds. I've certainly not got any worries about being strong at the weight."

Dave was full of praise for Waith. "He's the cleverest man I've ever fought," he admitted. "I only caught him half a dozen decent body blows. I had to go at his head in the end." He then amazed newsmen by saying he would be back at work the next morning. He couldn't let his workmates down because 20 of them and his boss had travelled from the Fens to watch him fight.

As Green was being interviewed, a man rushed into the dressing-room clutching a programme. "God," he yelled with tears in his eyes, "I've known young Dave for years. I just want him to put his name on this and I'll die happy." The Fen Tiger duly obliged.

In an adjoining dressing-room, Billy Waith was quick to praise his conqueror. "He is super fit," he told reporters. "He really hurt me in the 10th round, and that's what got me. He'll be too much for Singleton."

A few minutes later, Billy sportingly went to Green's dressing-room and congratulated him. "I thought that if I could stick with you for eight or ten rounds taking the shots, you would tire and I could get to you," he remarked with a smile. Green replied by telling the Welshman that he brought about his own downfall. "When you opened up, you left yourself wide open," he remarked. It was moving stuff between two good professionals.

The press were full of praise for the mature performance by Green. Former fighters also recognised that he was emerging as an exciting prospect. Writing in *Boxing News* a couple of weeks later, Henry Cooper said:

> It's nice to see a natural puncher like Dave Green coming to the fore... He still has a lot to learn, but what I like about him is that he looks a born fighter and a born puncher.

With Green now firmly established as the official contender for Joey Singleton's title, it was just a matter of time before the fight was arranged. Meanwhile, Charlie Atkinson told *Boxing News* editor, Graham Houston, that he hadn't bothered to go to the Royal Albert Hall. "Once you've seen one round of Dave Green, you've seen them all," he remarked. "Neither he nor Waith are in Joey's class."

Some weeks later, Charlie qualified his remarks, telling

Houston that he meant no offense to Dave. "We expect a tough fight with Dave Green, but Joey's looking tremendous, and punching hard in the gym," he remarked. "We're not selling Green short, but I don't think he has the ability to change tactics. Joey will set a fast pace, and I promise you something, if Green runs out of steam, he'll be in an awful lot of trouble."

* * *

Despite the intensity of his fight with Billy Waith, Dave was in action again 18 days later at the Empire Pool, Wembley, against experienced Italian, Guiseppe Minotti. The eight three-minute rounds contest at 10st 2 was a support to John H. Stracey's world welterweight title defence against Hedgemon Lewis of America.

As part of his preparation for the Minotti fight, Green was invited to spar with Lewis at the fashionable Quaglinos in London's west end. It was a wonderful opportunity for him because the American was genuine world class. A professional since 1966, he first boxed for a world title back in 1971, losing on points to Jose Napoles.

Andy Smith jumped at the opportunity the moment it was offered, but reserved the right to withdraw Green the moment proceedings ceased to be to his advantage.

Dave sparred four rounds with Lewis each day for a week without taking a fee. The experience was reward enough. "This way I can pull him out at anytime I feel I need to, but I am happy he is in there with this fellow," said Smith. "Dave is more an American type of fighter, and can learn a lot from this."

For the majority of the time, Dave was Lewis' only sparring partner. The sessions were hard and frequently flared into explosive action between the world rated contender with only six defeats from 61 contests, and the young hopeful who didn't know how to hold back. "He is good – a great mover," said Green. "I am learning how to move under pressure myself. He makes me think all the time."

Although Dave was there to learn, he still showed enough ability and enthusiasm to impress one of boxing's greatest ever trainers, Eddie Futch, manager of Lewis, and a veteran of countless world championship fights.

"This Green is a terrific prospect for a boy who has had only 12 fights," he remarked. "He can punch, he is a surprisingly good boxer and mover for that type of fighter, and has a pretty good jab into the bargain. All those factors combined, strength, power, youth and skill add up to one thing – a championship contender. He could go all the way."

"He's certainly no ordinary sparring partner – he is a good strong young fighter." added Futch.

Later that week, Eddie was less pleased when Andy Smith suddenly pulled Dave out without warning. Smith, however, was quick to give his side of the story. "Four rounds in each session was enough for Lewis," he told the press, "although Dave was ready to give him eight rounds if they wanted it. Lewis was trying to look good, but if they had been fighting for real, Green would have knocked him out any time after the eighth round. I really believe he is going to be a world champion."

Earlier in the week, Lewis' training had been disgracefully interrupted by a Muhammed Ali – Richard Dunn publicity stunt. It incensed him, although Harry Levene did later telephone to apologise. Green, meanwhile, seized the opportunity to meet the world heavyweight champion and posed for photographs with him.

At Wembley, on 20 March, Green stopped Minotti, his first overseas opponent, in four rounds immediately following the Stracey fight. Although the Italian proved durable, and countered well enough to draw blood from Dave's nose in round three, he took a real hammering in the fourth. Big shots thudded to head and body as Green turned on the power in a workmanlike performance. A vicious right swing sent Minotti staggering into a corner and in no position to defend himself, prompting referee, Mike Jacobs, to intervene.

Anxious to keep Dave busy whilst awaiting a title shot

against Singleton, Andy Smith reached agreement with Mike Barrett for two contests at the Royal Albert Hall within the space of 21 days during April. Green's opponent for the first was former Spanish champion, Jesus Rodriguez Dela Rosa, but by the morning of the fight he had failed to arrive in London. Following a series of frantic telephone calls, matchmaker, Mickey Duff, secured the services of Jim Montague from Belfast as a late substitute.

Montague's manager, Johnny Griffin, had previously turned down a fight with Green. Jim was furious because, being a southpaw, he believed he had the style to cause an upset. He told Griffin that if they were ever offered Green again, the match was to be taken.

Jim flew into London on the afternoon of the fight, and at 10st 9 was almost half a stone heavier than Dave (10-1¼). Despite the weight advantage, he was a tough opponent, having been stopped only once in his career, on a cut eye. Green hit him with everything, but the Irishman remained standing at the end of eight rounds.

Referee, Roland Dakin's score of 80-76½ meant that Dave had won all but one round, the other being halved. Andy Smith was delighted with the outcome because he had always maintained that if his man was to become world class, he would need experience which would not come by beating opponents within the first few rounds.

"As far as we are concerned, it worked out wonderfully," Smith told reporters. "It was the type of fight Dave needs at this stage of his career."

Montague, a fully-fledged welterweight, put up a brave performance to become only the third professional to take Green the distance. He had to withstand a terrible battering, especially during the first four rounds as the Chatteris man sought an early victory. Somehow, he soaked it up, and even hit back viciously in the sixth to thunderous applause.

"Jim really surprised me," admitted Green. "I kept up the pressure and hit him with a lot of good punches, but he stuck at it. He was great."

Dave was back at the Albert Hall three weeks later against Herbie McLean from Edinburgh in an eight rounds contest at 10st 2. The Scot had been stopped only twice in a 27 fight career containing 15 victories and three draws. A points defeat to Alan Salter at Walworth 12 months earlier was his only setback in his last seven contests.

Back in 1972, after winning his first seven professional fights, McLean fought Tony Riley in a final eliminator for the British light-welterweight title, but was stopped in 11 rounds. He readily accepted the contest with Green because he saw it as a chance to re-establish himself as a top contender in the division.

For Green, the fight was seen as nothing more than a warm-up because Mike Barrett announced that the eagerly awaited clash with Joey Singleton would top his Derby Eve promotion at the Albert Hall on 1 June. Dave was guaranteed a purse of £2,400, the largest of his career so far.

Taking no chances, Dave sensibly boxed within himself and took his time before cutting down the brave, but limited McLean. Cut over the left eye in the third, Herbie took a stream of hurtful hooks throughout round four. He looked set for a real hiding, but manager, Tommy Gilmore, sensibly retired him at the end of the round.

Dave was unscathed, and despite his desire to get straight back into the gym to prepare for the fight with Singleton, Andy Smith persuaded him to have a 10 day break to freshen up.

✦ 6 ✦

BRITISH CHAMPION

The fight between Dave 'Boy' Green and Joey Singleton was a huge attraction – a classic fighter v boxer encounter, guaranteeing Dave his best pay-day since turning professional. With all tickets sold, promoter Mike Barrett likened it to great domestic encounters of the past such as Boon v Danahar, Charnley v Curvis, and Frankie Taylor v Lennie Williams.

Despite being an admirer of Singleton's craft and skill, Barrett described Dave as being the most colourful and attractive fighter in Britain since Terry Downes. His popularity had escalated dramatically, and it was his exciting brand of fighting which had generated such massive interest. Despite having been a professional for only 18 months, he was already something of a cult figure. For this contest he sold over £8,000 worth of tickets, delivered many of them personally, and even arranged transport for local people.

By this stage, Green was affectionately known as 'The Fen Tiger', mainly because of his style, determination and the area he came from. For centuries, men from the locality had been referred to as 'Fen Tigers' because of the way they worked in adverse conditions. They were renown for being a species of people who never gave up until they achieved their objective. They lived by the seasons, were masters of country lore, and made a living from their local environment. In Dave Green, local people saw him as a fighter who would keep going against all odds to achieve his aim.

Chatteris, with a population of approximately 5,600, was not a wealthy town. A detached house could be purchased for about £15,000, and although cars had replaced horses, many were old ones. Dave's progress towards the championship challenge, however, had an incredible impact on the locality. The town boxing club had revived, and it's headquarters at Bridge Street was busier than ever before. Nine months earlier there were very few members, but suddenly youngsters queued at the door on training nights, all wanting to become budding Dave Greens.

The George Hotel in the High Street, where Freddie Mills once trained for a world title fight, again became a central meeting place for boxing fans. Elderly folk who remembered Mills, Boon and other national heroes, were re-vitalised by Green's success, and he was the talk of the pubs, cafes and on the buses. Fen Tiger T-shirts rolled off the production lines at Tony Powell Sports, on the Honeysome industrial estate from early May, and during the build up to the fight were worn by many people in the town.

When a local newspaper reporter decided to savour the atmosphere in the town as the fight with Singleton drew near, he found people comparing Dave to Eric Boon. "The thing about Boon was he knew how to take a punch," said one old-timer. "Green's the same – he's a good boy."

"Boon used to put 'em to sleep." said another old character playing darts in the public bar of The George. "Green does the same."

At school, children proudly wore their Dave 'Boy' Green T-shirts, and loved to talk about him because he was already their champion.

His success was bringing townsfolk together, and it was estimated that at least 2,000 Chatteris folk would travel to London for the fight. There was hardly a man or woman in the town without a relative making the trip. Dave was having exactly the same effect as Boon almost 40 years earlier. A local bookmaker who watched some of Boon's fights, moaned that he couldn't be at the Albert Hall because there were six race meetings the same day.

Sticking rigorously to a strict training schedule devised by Andy Smith, Dave received great support from his employer who gave him two weeks off work to concentrate on his preparation. His day began at 7.30am with six miles of running including sprint work. After resting at home until 11.30am, he moved to the gym where he went through a calisthenics programme and several rounds on the speedball.

Sparring commenced at 5.30pm, and he worked between

ROYAL ALBERT HALL

TUESDAY, 1st JUNE, 1976

Gen. Manager: A. J. Charlton
Matchmaker: MICKEY DUFF

Doors open 7 p.m. Commence 7.30 p.m.

MIKE BARRETT Presents
15 (3 min.) rounds at 10st for

THE LIGHT-WELTERWEIGHT CHAMPIONSHIP OF GREAT BRITAIN

JOEY SINGLETON	v	DAVID "Boy" GREEN
(Kirkby) Champion		(Chatteris) Challenger The Fen Tiger

The Fight you've all been waiting for!

8 (3 min.) rounds featherweight contest at 9st

MARK BLISS	v	LES PICKETT
(Tottenham) Southern Area champion		(Merthyr) Welsh champion

Plus supporting contests featuring the following stars

MAURICE HOPE	JOHN L. GARDNER	JIMMY BATTEN	STEVE FENTON
(Hackney) Lt-Middleweight Champion of Great Britain	(Hackney) Unbeaten heavyweight prospect	(Millwall) Albert Hall favourite	(Leicester) A crowd-pleaser

TICKETS (incl. VAT): £12.50, £10.00, £7.50, £5.00, £3.50, £2.00

From: Mike Barrett Promotions Ltd., 118 Wardour Street, London W.1. (01-437 5956)

Poster advertising British light-welterweight championship fight between Green and Joey Singleton

92

six and eight hard rounds, often with as many as four sparring partners. Dave took everything very seriously. As soon as the gum shield went in, the smile disappeared from his face, and he was ready for work as if it was the real thing. No punches were pulled, and onlookers often winced as he let go vicious shots, particularly to the body.

Green was fortunate to have good class men such as Des Morrison and Jeff Gale in his camp. Not only could they look after themselves, they also provided a quality of sparring which would have cost Andy Smith a great deal of money.

Morrison acted the role of Joey Singleton by imitating his hit-and-run style. Under the watchful eye of Smith, Dave was urged to cut off the ring and maintain relentless pressure. Des, who lost a disputed decision to Singleton at Manchester in November 1975, strongly fancied Green to win. "It should be a classic contest between a fighter and a fast mover," he told a reporter from the *Cambridge Evening News*, "but Joey can't really hit at all, so I think Dave will stop him."

Although he already possessed incredible strength built up over the past few years stacking crates and humping bags of carrots all day, weight training was also part of Dave's daily routine. He spent long periods punching upwards with 20lb weights gripped tightly in his hands, and for hours also pounded away with a heavy hammer at a local blacksmiths forge. It was yet another comparison with Eric Boon who used to work and train at his father's forge.

From the moment the fight was signed, Green was big news. Throughout the training period, Andy Smith held a series of press conferences, one of which was at a plush St Ives hotel. So many national newspaper reporters wanted to be there that they chartered a coach from Fleet Street.

Smith was in no doubt that his charge would become champion. "I think Joey Singleton is a very good quality British champion," he told them, "but I believe Dave Green is world potential. He has that extra something that portrays world class."

"I just don't think Singleton has the strength to keep him at bay for 15 rounds," he continued. "It will be like King Canute trying to hold back the tide."

Predicting that Green would stop the champion inside 10 rounds, Smith added: "No man of Joey's size would be able to last any longer."

On the question of Dave actually losing his first professional contest, the manager just couldn't see it happening. "We are going to hit him with a new kind of punch... the 'muck-spreader'," he remarked.

Smith was confident about Dave's ability to travel the full 15 rounds if necessary. "As far as fitness is concerned, Green is one of the most superbly fit athletes I have ever seen in my life," he enthused. "He will be tuned to perfection. When he steps into the ring, he will be feeling right both mentally and physically. And I think that when this kid is right, there is not a light-welterweight in Europe who can stay with him."

"The guy is box-office magic," continued the manager with absolute sincerity. "Singleton can thank Green for his big pay-day. With his style, he wouldn't have had a hope of making money against anyone else."

Despite the enthusiasm and support for his fighter, Smith never went over the top or tried to create a false impression. It was not his style, and having been in boxing a long time, he genuinely believed everything he said. Having steered Joe Bugner to world level and made him a rich man, he now wanted to do the same for Dave Green.

Smith talked of Green as being a rare breed – a British fighter in the same mould as Rocky Marciano and Carmen Basilio. "Britain needs someone like Dave Green to excite them," he remarked. "I think he will become one of the biggest names in British boxing. He is all-action, colourful, and the fans love the way he fights. We need him as champion – he'll bring fire and personality back into the game."

Looking beyond the Singleton fight, Smith admitted having long-range plans for Dave. In particular, he fancied a fight with reigning world welterweight champion, John H. Stracey. "It would be a greater attraction than the Boon-Danahar classic," he remarked. "Such a fight may be a long way off, but it's my dream if you like. But I am sure David is strong enough, young enough and good enough to challenge Stracey."

Green was equally confident of success. "Singleton must be good to be British champion," he told the reporters, "but I think I have the punches to slow him down. I won't get impatient, but he has to get in punching range to hit me."

* * *

Despite all the excitement about Dave, Singleton's handlers believed their man had the know-how to halt the challenger's progress. They were confident that Joey would be too fast and too smart. "The bigger the occasion, the better Joey fights," his manager, Charlie Atkinson, told the press. "This boy is like ice. Green's people can shout all they want, but it won't worry Joey."

Singleton came from Kirkby, an area of Liverpool plagued by hooliganism and graffiti. Boarded-up shops bore testimony of the viciousness and anti-social behaviour which ran through the streets of the satellite town made up of numerous blocks of flats and anonymous brown-bricked housing estates.

One of six children from a boxing family, Joey was a superb amateur, winning 200 of 212 junior and senior contests. A National Schoolboy champion in 1966, he won a junior ABA title in 1968, and was ABA lightweight champion in 1971. In September that year he won a gold medal at the pre-Olympic tournament in Munich, although loss of form and a cartilage injury forced him to miss the games the following year. He represented England at international level against Scotland, Wales, East Germany and Zambia.

Singleton turned professional in March 1973 with a points victory over Barton McAllister, and followed it up with a decision over another Green opponent, Angus McMillan. In only his third contest, Joey boxed a 10-rounder, outpointing

Jess Harper to take the vacant Central Area light-welterweight title.

Despite having been a professional for almost two years longer than Green, injury had limited Joey to just 12 contests. Yet he had almost twice as much ring experience, having boxed a total of 111 rounds to Dave's 66. He was very much the boxer of the pair, having won only two contests inside the distance.

Singleton won the British title in November 1974, outpointing Pat McCormack over 15 rounds. Successful defences the following year against Alan Salter (rsf 9) and Green's stable-mate, Des Morrison (points), ensured that he won a Lonsdale belt outright. His stamina was not in doubt, having finished strongly to outpoint McCormack and Morrison. He also displayed great courage and resilience against McCormack who floored him in the opening round.

Joey's sole defeat was against Jim Montague in November 1973, when a badly cut scalp caused the referee to intervene.

"I have a lot of respect for Dave Green," Singleton said in an interview, "but I fought fellows like him when I beat the Russians, Hungarians and Poles as an amateur. Those fellows were tough, strong and punched just as hard. Dave's style is nothing new to me."

A church-going Roman Catholic, Joey admitted that he took Holy Communion before his fights. "I will pray to God to look after me – and Dave," he told a *Cambridge Evening News* reporter. "I don't want Dave to get cut to pieces, but a fight is a fight. If he gets a cut, I won't lay off it."

* * *

The weekend before the fight, Green and wife Kay, joined Andy Smith and his wife at Cromer on the Norfolk coast before travelling to London on the Monday. Dave was toned to perfection, but had become edgy, so Smith decided to take him away to a relaxed environment to concentrate his mind for the biggest fight of his life.

"About five minutes before I go into the ring, I get a bit nervous," admitted Dave, "but once I get in there, it all goes."

"I love to fight, and I like the big occasion," he continued. "It gives me a big lift when the fans start cheering for me as I get in the ring. I think Singleton will be more nervous than me."

Although he still enjoyed working on the farm, boxing very much controlled Dave's life. He was already earning good money, and his rapid rise up the British rankings helped him and Kay furnish their new home at Birch Avenue, and have luxuries neither had ever been able to afford.

Green, who would be 23 the day after the fight, was 11-8 on favourite to take the title. Knowing that success would take him to further riches, he was determined not to slip up.

* * *

Eric Boon was among the army of fanatical Fenland supporters who travelled to London in their hundreds by coach, car and rail to witness the biggest test of their idol's professional career. "It brings it all back," he said before leaving his home at Wicken. "There is a tremendous feeling of excitement in the air. I think David will wear Singleton down and stop him."

Dave's workmates from the farm decided to travel by car instead of their usual coach. Anticipating victory, they planned celebrations which would keep them in the capital long after most other fans had departed for home.

It was a night of incredible drama and atmosphere, and the Royal Albert Hall was packed long before the fight. There were plenty of amusing moments, and even before the boxing commenced, a small group of Green supporters dressed as true country yokels, clambered into the ring and held a banner high above their heads. Led by a character playing a ukulele, others in smocks and carrot costumes performed cossack dancing around the ringside.

The antics were the idea of Dave's greatest fan, Rod

Marriner, and carried out at the invitation of promoter, Mike Barrett. Rod, a market trader and former amateur boxer, was first drawn towards Green in 1966, when he faced Mario Stango in his first schoolboy contest. Despite being raw, he loved Dave's intense will to win, and decided to keep an eye on him.

When Dave fought George Salmon at Cambridge, Marriner sat close to his corner screaming advice throughout. "Be first, use your jab," he shouted, much to the annoyance of Andy Smith. "Would you like to come up here in the corner because you seem to know better than me," snapped the manager sarcastically at one point.

Because of his passion and admiration for Green, Rod eventually got to know Andy Smith largely due to the fact that the manager's son, Robert, a prominent schoolboy boxer, often helped him get into Dave's dressing-room after fights. Being a fanatical fan, Rod had lots of ideas he wanted to develop, but was reluctant to say anything because he saw Smith as being very protective and not wanting intruders.

For the Alan Salter fight, Marriner ordered a small batch of T-shirts from a shop at Cambridge, and had the words DAVE 'BOY' GREEN – THE FEN TIGER printed on the front. He and a few mates wore them at the Albert Hall, and after the fight, Smith asked where they got them.

Rod told Andy he would like to start a fan club, get masses of T-shirts printed, and create a newsletter. Smith rejected the ideas because he didn't want any hangers-on. Privately, however, he liked the T-shirt idea, took it on board and made his own arrangements leading up to the Singleton fight.

Smith gradually warmed to Rod, and even invited him to his house at St Ives to spend time with Dave a few days before the Singleton fight. It was the start of what would become a lifelong friendship.

Anxious to develop a theme for what was the most important fight of Dave's career, Rod decided that it would be amusing if he and his close mates dressed up as Fen farmers. One of the group, Danny Blundell, a car dealer from Royston, whose son Mark would later become a top motor racing driver, agreed to provide a van.

Another friend of Marriner's, who worked for an advertising business, designed some large posters bearing the words; DAVE 'BOY' GREEN – THE THRESHING MACHINE. These were attached to the sides of the van.

The group dressed up in smocks and farm boots splattered with imitation cow's muck, and a local newspaper, the *Royston Crow*, photographed them in Blundell's garden with the van.

On the day of the fight, Rod telephoned Mike Barrett and told him what they were doing. Mike loved it, and invited them to assemble at a particular entrance at the Royal Albert Hall early that evening.

Dressed in their country gear, and calling themselves the Dave 'Boy' Green Clunch Supporter's Club, they set off for London full of excitement. The name was thought up by Marriner on the spur of the moment for the benefit of the local newspaper. In his opinion, it sounded agricultural because at Melbourn, a small village near Royston, there were some pits which local farmers always referred to as the old clunch pits.

Throughout the afternoon the group toured the streets of the capital much to the amusement of the crowds who cheered them heartily. At the agreed time, they arrived at the rear of the Albert Hall, parked the van, and on Mike Barrett's instruction, were given free entry to a corridor leading to the dressing-rooms. There, they waited until called into the auditorium and made their way to the ring. Their harmless antics provided a great start to the evening, and Londoners in the crowd lapped it up. After they left the ring the canvas was covered with debris and had to be swept before the boxing could commence. Yet it was all part of the fun because many ringsiders thought the imitation cow's muck was real and that the individuals had come straight from a farm.

There were so many people in the crowd wearing Fen Tiger T-shirts that one lad told a newspaper reporter: "If there are burglars in Chatteris tonight, they'll have a bonanza. There's nobody in – not even at the Police Station."

At about 9pm Dave Green made a sensational entry to the arena. Dressed in a new tiger-skin dressing-gown made and donated by Tony Powell Sports, he received a deafening reception. Stern-faced and focused, he thrust his arms into the air to acknowledge his loyal fans.

Singleton followed a few minutes later, and as he passed the rows of Green fans clad in Fen Tiger T-shirts, he was taunted with remarks of "you're in trouble." The prediction was spot on because at the opening bell, Green was off his stool in a flash intent on waging war.

Roars of "David...David...David," rang around the grand arena with a deafening blast as the Chatteris man slammed his first punches on target. Grimly determined, he stalked Joey around the ring. He jabbed solidly, and within a minute Singleton was looking flushed about the face and forehead.

An overhand right to the chin wobbled the champion, and there were frantic shouts of "claim him" from his corner as Green banged away. Although Joey jabbed gamely to stay in contention, Dave won the round with ease and set the pattern of the fight.

The champion started round two with a series of quick left jabs, but was soon shaken by a solid right lead to the head. Green was determined to dictate matters, and cleverly cut off the ring as Joey tried to retreat. With nowhere to go, the champion decided to stand and trade punches with the Chatteris man – a decision he must have deeply regretted. Green was too strong, and bored in attacking the body to open the way for powerful jabs. Singleton was getting caught easily which was an obvious concern to his corner.

Singleton tried to turn the fight around early in the third by ramming five or six sharp left jabs into Green's face. Although his supporters were encouraged, Dave was determined to be the master. He was quickly back on the attack forcing Joey to the ropes where he landed powerful hooks to head and body.

As the champion tried to hit back, Green was ruthless, hammering home another salvo of accurate heavy shots. Showing great boxing ability, he slammed three straight left jabs to the face, and glared at Singleton as the bell ended the round. If his fans wanted action, the young farm worker was not disappointing them, and they roared approval as he strode back to his corner.

Singleton began the fourth with good flurries of left jabs, but again Green waded through them and made him give ground. In a futile attempt to match his challenger for strength Joey again foolishly tried to trade punches. "Don't fight, Joey – box. Jab and run," yelled an anxious Charlie Atkinson from the corner.

Although the champion had some success, Green was much stronger, and his punches carried more power. Singleton was driven to the corners of the ring where he was battered unmercifully. Heavy blows thudded against his head and body from every angle as the challenger sought to end hostilities. His noisy fans sensed a dramatic victory, and there were shouts for him to deliver 'the carrot-cruncher' and 'the muck-spreader'.

After a clash of heads, Joey emerged with a nasty looking cut above his left eye. During another furious exchange his right eyelid was ripped, and bled profusely. Then, as the dramatic action-packed round progressed, Green sustained a cut by the corner of his right eyebrow. He would later claim it was the first time he had ever been cut.

During the interval, referee Harry Gibbs went to each corner, inspected the injuries and told both boxers to be careful with their heads. Some ringsiders even called for him to stop the fight because Singleton was taking a bad beating.

The fifth round saw the champion bravely make his last stand. Attacking with both hands, he forced Green to back off for a while, but just as he appeared to have weathered the storm, Dave hit back. Crunching punches knocked Joey's head from side to side as the challenger resumed control. Apart from being a savage fighter, he also showed he was a class boxer as he cleverly moved around the ring to continue his onslaught. By the end of the round, Singleton looked a spent force.

In all probability, Dave had won the five completed rounds, and referee Gibbs again took a long look at the champion's injuries during the interval. Somewhat surprisingly, he allowed him to continue, but with hindsight it was poor judgement. Blood streamed down his face early in round six, and spattered over ringside reporters when Green hit him.

Looking much the fresher of the two, Dave continued to attack furiously. Although Singleton did his best to survive, he didn't have the strength or power to hold him off. He was driven around the ring and into corners where huge punches cannoned into his sides.

Joey took a sustained beating for most of the round as jabs, hooks, uppercuts and clubbing right swings all found their target. Although the brave Kirkby man took everything without once going to the floor, the end was clearly in sight. A flurry of ramrod left jabs to the face had him at a standstill when the bell came to his rescue.

Charlie Atkinson was a shrewd and compassionate manager. Knowing that Green was too strong, he called Harry Gibbs to the corner and signalled Joey's retirement. Although it was officially announced that cuts had brought about the ending, the title had been torn from Singleton by a determined young challenger who stalked and savaged him from the opening bell. He took a terrible battering, and only his courage and ability to ride many of Dave's ferocious punches, kept him upright.

The Albert Hall erupted when the decision was announced, and many of Dave's excited fans rushed to the ringside. There was a stampede to get inside the ropes, and although a few succeeded, they were quickly removed. As order was restored, Green blew kisses to all four sides of the ring. "David...David...David," chanted his supporters as the Lonsdale belt was strapped around his waist.

It was refreshing the way his fans, some wearing smocks

and wellington boots, with corn-stalks in their hair, greeted his triumph. It was good humoured, and they set a pattern of behaviour to serve as an example to less disciplined sport-goers.

Things were just as hectic in the dressing-room a short while later as scores of Fenland supporters tried to get in to congratulate their man. The press boys were also there in numbers because the next day, Dave would be headline news. Once it was calm, Andy Smith addressed them in his usual inimitable way.

"David proved he's got real boxing ability," he remarked. "Our plan was to outdo the thing the other man does best – to outjab him. Once you dominate the jabbing, you can go to work with the swings and hooks. We meant to show how well David can box, and I expect a lot of you were surprised."

"David cut down the ring on him to the size of a postage stamp, and Joey had nowhere to run," continued Smith who was full of praise for both boxers. "Singleton did everything he could have done. When he knew he couldn't win by jabbing, he stood and fought, but the difference was that Green is a fighter with world-class potential."

"I thought Singleton defended his title well – a true champion," said Smith. "He really took some stick, and if it hadn't been a title fight, I think the referee would have stopped it earlier."

Asked by one reporter if Dave's tiger-skin dressing-gown was real, Andy replied: "Sure, we skinned it at Woburn Abbey first thing this morning. The Duke of Bedford is still looking for it."

Although the new champion never had any doubts about the outcome of the fight, he also had great respect for his opponent. "He was certainly a brave man," he remarked. "I was surprised he took so much, but I don't think he could have gone another two rounds even without his cuts."

Despite being absolutely thrilled at his victory, Dave was quite emotional. "I feel great," he enthused. "I just can't believe it has happened. My supporters were fantastic – I did it for them."

"It's all a dream really," he continued with tears in his eyes.

"I never expected success so soon. As an amateur, I was just a fighter and always got beat by the best boys. Then Mr Smith taught me to box a bit, and it's all come together."

Yet it was the manner of his victory which marked Dave as a young man with a future at world level. Although Singleton displayed incredible bravery, Green was just too strong and persistent. He attacked from the opening bell with thudding punches which hammered all the resistance out of the champion.

Amongst the crowd was Dave's wife Kay, watching him as a professional for only the second time. She was accompanied by his parents, Ken and Mary, brother Michael and several other relatives. His former amateur trainer, Jim Moore, was there, as was Isle of Ely MP, Clement Freud.

Talking to reporters, Ken Green said: "It has been Dave's ambition to be a champion ever since he started boxing. I feel very excited and very proud." With a broad smile across her face, mum Mary had less to say, adding: "I feel more relieved than anything."

Clement Freud was one of the first people to congratulate Dave. Warmly shaking the new champion's hand, he said: "Census shows Chatteris has 7,000 folk. How come there are 7,500 here tonight?"

"Do you know, two new Liberal candidates had their first campaign meeting near Chatteris recently?" he continued. "Waste of time they said – all they talked about was the fight."

Turning to Andy Smith, the MP said jokingly: "I tell you what Andy, it was a hell of a better fight than we had in the Commons last week. It's great for Chatteris."

Eric Boon also visited the dressing-room. Before the fight he received an incredible reception when introduced from the ring. Only that afforded to Green when he was pronounced champion was greater. "You were great," he told Dave, "simply great."

Dave never forgot that moment, and years later remarked: "It meant the world to me when Eric Boon came into my dressing-room after the fight. He was my inspiration."

He also retained vivid memories of the fight, in particular the moment when he eye-balled Singleton in the centre of the ring whilst receiving the referee's final instructions. "I was really fired up," he recalled. "I knew that if he couldn't hurt me, he was in serious trouble."

Green's victory led to incredible scenes in and around the Royal Albert Hall. The man with the ukulele played vigorously in the corridors, while others sang country songs. Passers-by laughed and cheered, and threw money into a hat.

Although Rod Marriner and his mates were described as "crazy people from the Fens", none of the group actually came from that area. Despite some reports to the contrary only he and his mates dressed up that night. They did, however, set a precedent, and hundreds copied them on subsequent trips to the capital to support their idol.

Dave had an incredible personality, and was like a magnet to ordinary folk in the street. Locals, Vince Wayman, his brother Ralph, and a lad named Roger from Manea paid £12.50 for their tickets, and had followed him since his amateur days. "I'm not kidding," Ralph told a local reporter, "Green could have been a professional footballer or a runner. Steve Austin would have lost his job, and no one would ever have heard of Brendan Foster."

The local ladies also took a shine to Dave. In the days following his success over Joey Singleton, it was estimated that he received cards from more than half the females in Chatteris. Kay recalled how one girl made a personal delivery to their front door, then ran down the path for all she was worth. "She must have thought I'd be mad," she said with a smile.

* * *

Becoming champion meant a great deal to Dave, and it also brought tremendous pride and honour to the people of Chatteris. Local councillors were quick to show their appreciation of his achievement by organising a civic reception and victory celebration parade.

Dave and Kay returned home the morning after the fight to a rapturous reception. It was the perfect setting for the new champion to celebrate his 23rd birthday. At 12 noon, he, Kay and Andy Smith boarded a dray loaned by Cottenham potato merchants, Richard Creek Limited, which was drawn by two Suffolk Punch horses. It was much the same as after Eric Boon had beaten Arthur Danahar in their historic pre-war lightweight championship thriller.

Hundreds of fans cheered wildly every time Dave held the Lonsdale belt aloft. Standing at his side, Andy Smith stoked up the atmosphere as he waved the pair of red gloves used to batter Singleton to defeat.

Amid all the excitement, youngsters climbed aboard the dray as it was drawn through the streets from Slade End to Cromwell Community College where Green once attended school. There he was greeted by a tightly packed crowd of about 500, many of whom were children wearing Fen Tiger T-shirts. Almost spontaneously they burst into song with *"Happy Birthday"*.

The British champion was greeted on the hastily erected platform by Miss Hilda Clarke, Chairman of Chatteris Borough Council, who was performing the first official duty of her second term in office. She was accompanied by Parish Clerk, Charles Dobbs, and fellow councillors.

Above the platform hung a banner boldly bearing the words:

THE WORLD CROWN AND WHO KNOWS? – WELCOME TO DAVE THE CHAMPION.

Welcoming Dave home, Councillor Clarke explained that she had known him and his parents all of their lives. She said that his well deserved glory had once again placed Chatteris on the map, and people of the town wished to thank him.

Presenting Dave with an inscribed silver tray, the councillor expressed her admiration for the way he had progressed to become champion. She was confident that he

106

would continue to have the support and interest of everyone in the locality, all of whom would be willing him to become world champion.

Green's former headmasters, Dennis Hall of King Edward and Donald Cooper from Cromwell College both described him as a helpful pupil who excelled at all sports. "We were proud of him as a pupil, and we're proud of him now," they both remarked.

Mr Hall, who had known Dave since he was seven, said that Chatteris should be proud of him. "We are," echoed the crowd loudly.

Dick Leader, former secretary of Chatteris Boxing Club where Green began his career as a schoolboy, travelled to the town especially for the occasion. In a short speech, he said he was thrilled he had reached such heights. "They used to say nice guys don't win anything," he remarked, "but David has proved that wrong."

An elated Andy Smith said: "Green's displays have made him a big attraction, and he is probably Britain's most popular champion after John Stracey. But he has a lot to learn. We must get our priorities right and take things gradually. Time is on his side."

Referring to the Singleton fight, Smith said that Dave often outboxed the accepted master of skills, just to prove he could do it. "I was delighted with the way he fought," admitted Andy. "He could have won just as well by smashing through him all the time. Instead he mixed in the boxing skill and got the same result. He was great." Smith spoke for everyone when he concluded his speech with the words: "It couldn't happen to a nicer bloke."

Dave found the civic reception more of an ordeal than his fight with Singleton. With a plaster over his cut right eye, he looked tense as he sat through the speeches of congratulation. "I am a better boxer than talker I think," he remarked when called upon to respond, "but it is fantastic the support I have received right through my career."

"I would like to thank Mr Smith who has really brought me

on," he added. "I just don't know what to say – there are so many people to thank."

After the ceremony was over, Dave went off in the dray surrounded by hero-worshipping youngsters. Wife Kay clutched a handful of the many cards and telegrams which made it the best birthday of his life. The day belonged to him, and was sufficiently important to attract many representatives from the national press and television, all anxious to record how a small Fenland town welcomed home a local boxing hero.

Despite his incredible success and the attention it had attracted, it didn't change Dave in the slightest. He still had an appetite for work, and at 7.30am the next morning he was back at the farm raring to go. There were plenty of interruptions, however, because he had the Lonsdale Belt in the boot of his car. Throughout the day, mates from far around turned up wanting to take photos of it. Nobody was refused because they were the people Dave grew up with, and he never forgot them.

Not many fighters would have turned up for work the morning after winning a major championship, but that's the way Dave was. Despite not having gone to bed until about 3am, it was just another day to him. Not only did he love the work environment where he was on the go all the time, he was also extremely grateful to his employer for all the help he had given him.

Dave and Kay on their wedding day – 26 October 1974.

Green poses with Hedgemon Lewis with whom he sparred at Quaglinos in March 1976, Eddie Futch (left) and Andy Smith.

Green with Andy Smith and Joe Bugner at the Boxing Writers Club dinner in January 1977 when he received the Young Boxer of the Year award.

Dave's training often included work at a blacksmith's forge at Wicken owned by former amateur boxer, Wally Redditt (left).

Dave poses with his father after an early professional success.

Green scores with a left jab to the face of Billy Waith whom he stopped in 11 rounds at the Royal Albert Hall on 2 March 1976.

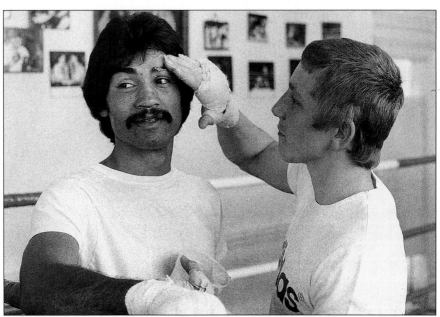

Dave greases the face of Carlos Palomino with whom he sparred at the Thomas A'Beckett gym in June 1976.

Shooting was one of Dave's favourite pastimes.

The famous Fen Tiger T-shirt.

Determination and aggression always showed on Dave's face when training and in a fight.

Dave is joined by his parents after taking the British light-welterweight title from Joey Singleton at the Royal Albert Hall on 1 June 1976.

Dave and Kay celebrate at a reception at Cromwell Community College the following day.

Dave was taken around the streets of Chatteris on a dray drawn by two Suffolk Punch horses the day after his victory over Joey Singleton.

Ken Green proudly wears the Lonsdale belt at his farm.

Dave gives a skipping demonstration to children at a local school.

Green (left), attacks Joey Singleton in their
championship fight at the Royal Albert Hall on 1 June
1976.

Dave and Kay relax at Lands End in August
1979.

Dave back at work a few days after beating
Jean-Baptiste Piedvache for the European
title on 7 December 1976.

✦ *7* ✦

COUNTDOWN TO EUROPE

Becoming British champion made Green the leading contender for the European title held by 33 year old Cemal Kamaci of Turkey. Andy Smith was convinced that his man would have too much power and enthusiasm for the ageing champion, but had to rely on the promoters to stage it. "We'd love the fight to be in Britain, but would be prepared to travel if we had to," he remarked at a press conference. "The thing about Green is that he is a puncher, and you haven't got to worry too much about points decisions."

Within 18 months, Dave had undoubtedly become, pound for pound, one of the most exciting British fighters for many years. There was already premature talk in the press about the mouth-watering prospect of an all-British showdown with world welterweight champion, John H. Stracey. Such hopes, however, were quickly dashed in a statement by Board of Control General Secretary, Ray Clarke. "Such a suggestion is an insult to Stracey and most unfair to Green," he told Colin Hart of *The Sun*.

Whilst such a contest would have been the biggest money-spinner in Britain outside the heavyweight division, Clarke was talking good sense. Dave was a novice compared with Stracey, a professional since 1969. He had been beaten on just three occasions in 49 fights, courtesy of one controversial points

109

decision, a disqualification and a cut eye. In comparison, Green had engaged in only 16 contests, and was half a stone lighter.

Whilst conceding that Dave needed more experience before meeting Stracey, Andy Smith believed that public opinion could force the fight within a year.

Green's immediate reward for becoming British champion, was a fight at Wembley on 22 June on the undercard of Stracey's world title defence against Carlos Palomino of Mexico. He was matched with Giampiero Mereu of Italy over 10 rounds at 10st 2 in the chief supporting contest. When Mereu withdrew through injury five days before the fight, Ernesto Bergamesco, a 26-year-old slaughterman from Naples, was brought in as a late substitute.

Andy Smith was not keen on the replacement because Green had been preparing to fight a southpaw. Once the fight got underway, however, it was clear that the Italian was likely to go the same way as most of Dave's previous opponents. His intentions were clear during the referee's final instructions, and Bergamesco looked slightly taken aback when his smile to the British champion was confronted by a menacing glare. Green went straight into action, and within seconds of the opening bell was pumping stiff left jabs into Bergamesco's face. By the end of the round, the Italian was already showing signs of wilting.

Flashes of needle crept in during the second when Bergamesco, under heavy pressure, suddenly butted Dave and then offered to shake hands. Not known for niceties inside the ropes, Green brushed aside the extended glove and slammed a hard right to the head. Towards the end of the round the Italian appeared to be looking for a way out by turning his back and indicating to referee, Roland Dakin, that he had injured his left hand.

Heavy driving rights had Bergamesco in trouble during the third, and one massive right almost ended the fight in this round when the Italian was cut over the left eye. He had to be motioned out for the fourth, and was again on the receiving end of a torrent of solid left jabs.

Green steamed out for round five, and a vicious left hook had Bergamesco reeling on the ropes. The British champion poured it on until referee Dakin jumped in with just 21 seconds gone.

Later in the evening, John Stracey lost his world welterweight title when he was hammered to defeat in 12 rounds by Carlos Palomino. The result put an end to any speculation that he would defend his title against Green.

On a more practical level, Mike Barrett and Mickey Duff travelled to Monte Carlo later that week for the Carlos Monzon – Rodrigo Valdez world middleweight title fight. Whilst there they had talks with Willy Zeller, manager of European champion, Cemal Kamaci, who was based in Germany. On his return to Britain, Barrett revealed that the Turk wanted the equivalent of £23,000 to defend his title against Green in London. "It was too much to pay." he remarked, "but if it goes to purse offers, I'm sure the fight will come to this country."

Dave's continued progress earned him number 14 spot in *Boxing News'* world light-welterweight ratings for July 1976, and the following month he was nominated by the European Boxing Union as official contender for Kamaci's title. Mickey Duff told the press that every effort would be made to stage the fight at Wembley or the Royal Albert Hall.

In the meantime, Green took a well-earned holiday in Majorca. After seven fights in six months, Andy Smith was anxious that his man relaxed and freshened up before embarking on a programme of fights which would hopefully lead to the European championship.

* * *

Despite his hectic boxing schedule, Dave never forgot his roots or the people who supported him. Together with Eric Boon, he opened the summer fete at King Edward School, Chatteris, which attracted a crowd of over 1,000. At the conclusion of speeches, they and their wives were presented with buttonholes and bouquets of flowers by a group of pupils. The Lonsdale belt was displayed to excited onlookers, and Dave donated two autographed Fen Tiger T-shirts and a pair of boxing boots to be auctioned for school funds.

During the holidays, Green and Andy Smith put on a film show for children at Colville School, Cherry Hinton, organised by Cambridge City Councillor, John Phillips. Films were shown of Dave and Joe Bugner in action.

The gestures were so typical of Dave, a generous and caring young man who fully appreciated his own good fortune. Since turning professional, he had been inundated with invitations to attend functions, and he rarely declined. In February 1975, after just three paid contests, he was guest of honour at a schoolboy and junior boxing tournament staged by March Amateur Boxing Club. In December the same year, he presented trophies at a show organised by Wisbech Boys Boxing Club, and on 8 April 1976 he was guest of honour at Ely and District ABC dinner-show.

On returning to the gym after his summer break, Dave was given a good variety of sparring partners to work with. They included former ABA middleweight champion, Malcolm Heath, 1976 light-welterweight finalist, Ricky Beaumont, both from the Hull Fish Traders Club, and also old amateur opponent, Harry Watson, who had turned professional under Andy Smith. Heath weighed 12st and stood six feet tall, whilst Beaumont was stocky at 5ft 7.

Despite the intensity of their work, Dave and his sparring partners always got on well. In the gym dressing-room one evening after an explosive session, Ricky asked about the scar on his body. Green told him about the shotgun accident and explained that 15 lead pellets were still in there. "No they aren't," said Beaumont, "they've moved into your fists."

Back in the ring, Green was in devastating form, stopping both Jean-Pierre Younsi of France and Ugo Di Pietro of Italy in the opening round within the space of four weeks. His brand of naked ferocity and merciless punching convinced critics that only world class fighters would be able to stand up to him.

Following his nomination as official contender for the

European title, interest in Green was incredible. He was making such a name for himself that ahead of the fight with Younsi at the Royal Albert Hall on 14 September, local companies took out a page of good luck adverts in the *Cambridgeshire Times*. They included hairdressers, butchers shops, vegetable growers and removal companies.

Scheduled for 10 rounds, it was the chief supporting contest to the return between Alan Minter and Kevin Finnegan for the British middleweight title. Although Younsi was leading contender for the French title, he was completely overwhelmed by Green who attacked relentlessly from the opening bell.

The Frenchman was stunned by Dave's first punch, a heavy right in the opening 15 seconds. From that moment it was just a matter of how long he could survive as jabs, vicious left hooks, crosses and swings to head and body pinned him in a corner. Green was sensational, and poured it on until referee, Mark Hart, called a halt with 10 seconds of the round remaining.

"I was pleased Dave didn't let him off the hook, but I was glad it was stopped when it was," said Andy Smith in the dressing-room. "Younsi was out on his feet, and a couple more punches might have done him serious harm."

Smith said they had been working on different punches – straight ones as well as hooks and swings. "They're coming from all angles now, and it's impossible for the opponent to anticipate them," he remarked enthusiastically.

It was a similar story against Di Pietro at Wembley four weeks later when Green's sheer power reduced the Italian to a cowering wreck after only two minutes 10 seconds. Even during the preliminaries he avoided eye contact with Green whose grim fixed stare was a sign of things to come.

At the opening bell, Dave was off his stool like a rocket, smashing punches from all angles. Ribs reddened from a vicious body attack, Di Pietro tried to move out of range and use the ring, but the British champion stayed right on top of him. Lefts and rights snapped the Italian's head back as he

113

was hammered around the ring, and an accumulation of heavy punches eventually sent him to his knees.

Twice holder of the Italian lightweight title, and a professional since 1970, Di Pietro was never given the chance to extend Green. When he rose with the count at seven, the British champion was on him in a flash, pouring in heavy punches to head and body. A mighty right swing to the side of the head sent him to the floor again, and as he cowered in the corner he looked appealingly at his seconds for help.

The Italian gamely climbed to his feet at nine, but Green leapt forward and hammered him unmercifully without reply. His attack was so intense that he almost floored referee, Sid Nathan, who took a glancing blow to the chest as he jumped in to call a halt. Despite the fight having lasted less than a round, Di Pietro's pale skin was a mass of red weals at the end. Although it was his 28th birthday, Dave Green was the only one celebrating.

Scheduled for eight rounds, the fight had been a support to the British, European and Commonwealth heavyweight championship contest between the champion, Richard Dunn, and Green's stable-mate, Joe Bugner, who had retired from the ring a year earlier. Joe also won in the opening round, and it was estimated that he and Dave sold over £10,000 worth of tickets between them.

In a pre-fight interview, Joe had complained about a shortage of sparring partners. When a newspaper reporter asked why he didn't call upon the services of Green, he replied: "Because I don't want to get my ribs caved in."

Bugner had tremendous respect and admiration for Dave, and after his fight with Di Pietro said: "You never know where Green will aim next. There's hooks, swings, garden hoses, muck-spreaders, hatchets, mallets and carrots all thrown in together."

"Don't change for anybody Dave," he said turning to Green. "Do your thing all the time."

Despite his incredible progress in the ring, Green kept his

feet firmly on the ground. Many youngsters in his position would have let success go to their heads, but he preferred to stick with the routine and lifestyle he knew. Consequently, he was back at the carrot farm the morning after each fight doing the same chores as his workmates.

Relaxing after a fight was never Dave's style. "All my life I have worked with the lads," he remarked. "I like working with them. I mean, I am a country boy brought up on farming."

He admitted that humping bags of carrots about all day was demanding work. "But we get paid for it," he continued. "Around these parts, we like to earn our money."

Dave was fortunate to have an accommodating employer who always allowed him up to two weeks off work to prepare for important fights. His hours were also considerably modified to fit in with his demanding training routine for all other contests.

* * *

Despite continued negotiations with Cemal Kamaci, there was speculation that he would retire from boxing rather than face Green. Meanwhile, Dave was anxious to get back into action because victories like those over Younsi and Di Pietro left him with energy to burn. "I wouldn't mind another fight next Tuesday," he remarked after destroying the Italian. "I am still raring to go."

Taking full advantage of the situation, Mike Barrett and Mickey Duff promptly featured Green in the main event of their promotion at the Royal Albert Hall just 14 days after beating Di Pietro. His opponent, Ramiro 'Clay' Bolanos, a 26-year-old from Ecuador, represented a move to the fringe of world class. A veteran of 62 contests, of which he had lost 10 and drawn two, he was outpointed by world ranked light-welterweight, Randy Shields, at Los Angeles in his last fight.

A professional since 1967, Bolanos met Kuniaki Shibata for the WBC junior lightweight title in Tokyo during 1974. He survived a second round knockdown to take the champion into the 15th and final round before being stopped.

Bolanos had fought four world champions in his 10 year career. He was outpointed by WBA featherweight champion, Ernesto Marcel, WBC champion Clemente Sanchez, and WBC junior lightweight title holder, Ricardo Arrendondo in non-title bouts, but outpointed Arrendondo in another 10 rounder in November 1975. He was a known crowd-pleaser, and 29 of his 50 victories had come inside the distance.

Although Mike Barrett was convinced that Dave was already world-class, he believed Bolanos was just the opponent he needed to express his true quality. "Green is a real iron man who reminds me so much of Roberto Duran," he told Graham Houston of *Boxing News*. "The fight fraternity have already recognised Dave's ability, but he's now on the verge of the breakthrough to wider public recognition."

Green fully justified the promoters faith as he hammered the experienced Bolanos to defeat in four rounds. Although victory was officially due to a cut right eye, the man from Ecuador was heading for a real thumping. Blood gushed from the injury, and there were no complaints when referee, Roland Dakin, called a halt after one minute 30 seconds of the round.

The South American entered the ring wearing a stunning dressing-gown of gold and black circles on a mauve background. In the opening round he looked confident and well-balanced, and soon showed that he was a quality boxer with a good left hand.

Although Green made a cautious start, probing with his left jab, he was busy enough to prevent Bolanos settling into a rhythm. He only lashed out with two-fisted attacks when the South American covered up.

Showing more aggression in the second, the well-schooled Bolanos wanted to fight in bursts. Although he stung Dave with some sharp punches to the face, he found the British champion ready to move up a gear to match him. Yet it wasn't until the latter part of the round that he was able to land his heavy body shots.

By round three, Dave realised that Bolanos was a different and braver breed of opponent than many others he had fought. He took a series of vicious head punches, but still came back for more. Early in the round, two rights from the British champion landed flush on the nose, and when he switched his attack to the body, the South American looked in trouble for the first time.

Although Green's punches were heavier, it was a tremendous round. An awesome left hook opened a nasty gash over the South American's right eye, but he hit back with great bravery. Blood poured from the injury, and Dave's hair, body and white trunks were splattered with claret as he surged forward pouring stiff jabs and hooks to every area of the target. At the end of the round, referee Dakin went to Bolanos' corner and took a careful look at his injury before allowing him to continue.

Accurate jabs from Green brought the blood flowing again in the opening seconds of the fourth. Although Bolanos tried to throw counter-punches, the British champion was too strong. Sensing the end was near, he backed his man to the ropes where he coldly and professionally made every shot count.

Blood sprayed from the cut every time Dave landed a head punch, and with the South American almost at a standstill, Mr Dakin stepped in and took him to his corner. After a close inspection of the injury, he called it off.

Despite the step-up in class, Dave was not overawed. He showed complete ruthlessness and determination to end proceedings as early as possible. He was delighted with his victory, and when a reporter asked if he wished the fight had gone a bit longer, he replied: "No, I'd seen enough of him."

After the fight, Phil Silver, the manager of Bolanos, said he thought Dave needed more experience to become world class. "He might well become champion, but you can't compare him to Duran at the moment," he remarked. "Certainly he's the best prospect at this stage that I have ever seen, but a really smart fighter might hurt him."

Bolanos, his lips swollen and cheeks puffed up, nodded agreement, but couldn't be sure of the British champion's true potential. "The fight didn't last long enough," he said, "but he sure punches good."

Whilst delighted with his man's performance, Andy Smith was somewhat disappointed about the ending. "The cut deprived Dave of stopping him in a more decisive fashion," he insisted. "He was getting to him with some good shots, and Bolanos was beginning to feel the strain. I don't think it could have gone more than another two rounds."

Smith was also somewhat aggrieved that details of Green's next fight were released before the Albert Hall show. In what Wembley promoter, Harry Levene, described as: 'Great Britain v USA – A Great Value For Money Programme', Dave was one of four reigning British champions due to feature in 10 round contests against American opposition just 14 days later. Matched against world number eight ranked light-welterweight, Jimmy Heair, he shared top billing with Alan Minter, Maurice Hope and Paddy Maguire.

"This was a good opponent and anything could have happened," said Smith referring to Bolanos. "They should have waited until after this fight before making the Wembley announcement."

Despite his comment, the manager had no objection to the choice of opponent. "Heair provides the chance to take a progressive step," he remarked. "He is world class opposition, and represents Dave's hardest test to date."

The importance, however, was to keep Dave busy while the European championship situation was resolved. Smith was sceptical about rumours that Kamaci would retire, and believed it was a ploy to get more money. As the Turk had already declined to box in London, it would clearly be sometime before any agreement was reached.

Meanwhile, Mike Barrett flew to Segovia, Spain, to watch WBC champion, Saensak Muangsurin demolish Spanish title holder, Miguel Velasquez in two rounds. During his trip he had dinner with the Thai's manager, Lupe Sarreal, and discussed a possible championship defence against Green in London. Although it was early days, Barrett hoped to stage the fight on his Derby Eve programme in June the following year.

On his return to London, Mike said he believed Dave had "a hell of a chance against the world champion." In the meantime, however, capturing the European championship remained the main priority.

* * *

Jimmy Heair, from El Paso, but based in Los Angeles, was described as the Texas State light-welterweight champion. He was a vastly experienced man who had fought in the rings of Argentina, Australia, Puerto Rico, Mexico and Thailand.

With the reputation of being a sound boxer with a good chin, he had never been knocked out in over 100 contests starting as a 14 year old 10 years earlier. He had stayed the distance with world class fighters Hector Thompson, Nicolino Locche and Armando Muniz, and had amassed 50 victories and a draw from 62 professional fights. Amongst his successes was a points victory over former WBC lightweight champion, Chango Carmona.

The son of a Baptist minister, Heair was a busy fighter having already fought on 12 occasions during 1976, losing four. In June he had been outpointed by world welterweight contender Muniz over 12 rounds at El Paso. He was the ideal opponent for Green at this stage of his career. The fans recognised the quality and importance of this fight, and the Empire Pool was packed. Green personally sold over £13,000 worth of tickets, and his faithful band of followers from the Fens lit up the great arena. Shouts of "Tally Ho" from one group could be heard above the clapping and cheering, whilst others blew trumpets and horns.

Andy Smith warned Dave that the American was a tough customer who would push him all the way. Wearing long pink shorts, Heair's confidence bordered upon arrogance. During the referee's final instructions he stuck out his tongue in response to the British champion's icy glare. His gesture, however, only fuelled Green's fire because the greater the challenge, the more he relished it.

EMPIRE POOL, WEMBLEY

Tuesday, November 9th, 1976. Doors open 7 p.m. Commence 8 p.m. Matchmaker MICKEY DUF

HARRY LEVENE presents a great Value For Money programme
International boxing featuring Five National Champions

GREAT BRITAIN v U.S.A.

0 (3 min.) Rounds International Middleweight Contest at 11st 9lbs	10 (3 min.) Rounds International Lt.-Welterweight Contest at 10st 2lbs
ALAN **MINTER**	DAVE "BOY" **GREEN**
(Crawley) British Middleweight Champion	(Chatteris) "The Fen Tiger" British Lt.-Welterweight Champ
v	v
TONY **LICATA**	JIMMY **HEAIR**
(New Orleans) U.S.A. Middleweight Champion	Texas State Lt.-Welterweight Champion. In World Ratings
10 (3 min.) Rounds Light-Middleweight Contest at 11st 2lbs	10 (3 min.) Rounds International Bantamweight Contest at 8st 8lb
MAURICE **HOPE**	PADDY **MAGUIRE**
(Hackney) European, British and Commonwealth Champion	(Brixton) British Bantamweight Champion
v	
RAFAEL **RODRIGUEZ**	JOSE LUIS **NAVARETTE**
(Minneapolis). World Rated. K.O'd Keith Averett (1 Rd.)	(El Paso) Great Crowd-pleaser

Supporting contests will include KRIS SMITH — undefeated Heavyweight Prospect

PRICES	INC. V.A.T.	£3.50	£6.50	£8.50	£12.50	Ringside £15.50

To: HARRY LEVENE   87 WARDOUR STREET, W.1 (01-437 2304)

Please reserve . . . . seats at . . . . Empire Pool, Wembley, on Tuesday, 9th November, 1976. Please enclose stamped addressed envelope for reply. Cheque / Postal Order herewith. TOTAL VALUE £ . . . . p

M . . . .

Poster advertising Green's fight with Jimmy Heair

At the opening bell, he shot from his stool, brushed aside the tall American's long straight left, and got in close enough to launch a savage body attack. Left hooks, short rights and an occasional overarm swing all thumped through Heair's guard. It was a blistering start, but the experienced American, despite wobbling briefly, took it all, re-grouped and hit back to have the crowd roaring with excitement.

Although Green appeared surprised, he composed himself and worked well behind stiff left jabs to open Jimmy up for more heavy shots to head and body. The action continued for the full three minutes, and at the bell, Heair still moved forward hands held high and a grin etched across his face as if to let Dave know he was happy to continue. The British champion momentarily stood his ground whereupon Jimmy tapped him on the elbow as if to acknowledge his class.

Green kept up his relentless attack during the next three rounds giving the American a real pounding. A savage right to the head in the second would have floored less determined opponents, but Jimmy stood firm. Several more hurtful shots forced him to clinch, but before the bell he was trapped on the ropes and punished severely to head and body.

As the fight progressed, Dave jabbed to create openings, and followed up with heavy shots to the head, neck, stomach and kidneys. The American, however, was no ordinary opponent, as he leant slightly backwards, forwards or sideways. When shoved against the ropes during round three, he taunted the British champion with the remark: "I can take anything you've got."

"You can't take this boy," snarled the frustrated Green as he slammed punches to head and body, but Jimmy rolled, clinched and proved that he could.

Heair knew his way around the professional ring, and tried everything to make Green lose concentration. He shrugged off one vicious attack by blowing a kiss, and on other occasions poked out his tongue. "Keep hitting son," he muttered during another toe-to-toe skirmish.

The pace slowed in round five as both men appeared to accept each others toughness. Green, however, showed good boxing skill during the middle rounds and kept piling up the points with clusters of stiff accurate jabs. His change of style was partly due to the fact that he injured his right hand during this round when a heavy blow caught Heair high on the head. The American was unaware of the damage because Dave just gritted his teeth and worked through the pain.

The accuracy of Green's punches caused damage about Heair's face. He was bleeding from the nose, and badly bruised around both eyes. Mr Dakin visited his corner before the start of the sixth, but Jimmy insisted on continuing.

Showing tremendous fitness and stamina, the British

champion increased the pressure during the eighth, and kept it up until the final bell. Throughout the last round he danced around the ring jabbing and landing left leads almost at will. Sheer pressure forced Heair to the ropes, but despite a sustained final onslaught, Dave couldn't floor him.

At the bell there was only one winner, and referee Roland Dakin's score of 100-95 indicated that Green had won every round. Yet despite the one-sided score, it was still the hardest fight of his career.

Heair's contribution had been massive, and the crowd gave him generous applause as he left the ring. In the early rounds Green hit him with such ferocity that it seemed unlikely he would last the distance. His performance was even more remarkable considering he was suffering from jet lag brought about by an airline strike which delayed his trip to the United Kingdom until the day before the fight.

His eyes almost closed, Jimmy described Green as: "A saloon bar fighter with a great left jab who didn't throw a bad punch, and might just get to be world champion."

Green, sporting a bruised left eye, sore knuckles, and with his damaged right hand immersed in a bucket of ice, sat calmly in his dressing-room after the fight to face the usual army of reporters. "It was the hardest fight of my life, the one the fans have wanted to see," he told them. "I caught him with some of my best punches, but he still wouldn't go."

Andy Smith was delighted that his man got valuable experience against Heair, a man whom he praised for a thoroughly professional performance. "It would have taken two men to knock him down," he remarked, "but it was the sort of fight I'd been dreaming about. There are better boxers around who would have buckled under that onslaught which proves just how good the guy was."

"Had Dave not damaged his hand, I would have ordered him to try and force the referee to stop it around the seventh or eighth rounds," continued the manager. "As it was, I told him to box. It pleased me to show in public some of the skills he has shown in the gym these last few months."

The press boys loved interviewing Andy Smith because whilst he gave them what they wanted, he never got carried away by success. He was an eloquent speaker who defined tactics and achievement to the finest detail, and always gave credit where it was due.

Expressing great pride for Green, he said: "Dave showed how to vary his tactics as he proceeded to hit Heair with a succession of left jabs and hooks."

"Things are coming along very nicely," he added. "We all knew he could fight – now he's shown he can box a bit too."

* * *

Whilst Green was kept active, the saga involving European champion, Cemal Kamaci, continued. Long before the Heair fight, Mike Barrett made a bid to stage the contest at the Royal Albert Hall on 7 December. Meanwhile, Kamaci's manager, who held a promoter's licence in Austria, submitted a counter-bid to the EBU, thereby delaying matters even further. Yet when a national newspaper reported that Barrett's offer had been accepted, the waiting finally seemed to be over.

When the news broke, a relieved Andy Smith said: "It's a sprat to catch a mackerel situation if you like. Kamaci will come here for his best pay-day to date, and we will avoid going to his place in Istanbul where Green might get disqualified for punching."

Smith was not so happy a few days later when Barrett stated that he had provisionally pencilled Green in to fight for the world title on 31 May the following year. "I will decide who David Green fights next," he remarked. "Nobody controls me as far as my fighters are concerned, and I will look at things after the Kamaci fight."

Despite Dave's continued success and advancement up the world rankings, Smith kept a cool head. It was a predictable reaction because he knew that one fight could change everything they had worked so hard for.

Unbeknown to the British contingent, yet another twist in

the European saga was just around the corner. In mid-November came the news that Kamaci had finally decided to retire from the ring. The EBU promptly ordered Green to meet Jean-Baptiste Piedvache of France for the vacant title.

With the Albert Hall already booked for 7 December, Mike Barrett moved quickly to secure the fight. He and matchmaker, Mickey Duff, flew to Paris for talks with Piedvache's people who at first wanted the contest staged in the French capital. After tense discussions, however, the Frenchman agreed to a contract that would guarantee him £10,000 after tax.

"There was only one way to get the fight to London, and that was to buy it," admitted Andy Smith. "We promised we would do everything possible to get it staged over here, and that's what we did."

Green had been guaranteed £9,400 to face Kamaci, but after hours of negotiation between Smith, Barrett and Duff, reports indicated that he would receive more to meet Piedvache. Even so, Andy Smith still had some concerns. "I would have preferred Dave to have met Kamaci," he told *Boxing News* editor, Graham Houston. "Kamaci is 33 years old, and recent photos show him to be heavily scarred. I'm only interested in Dave winning the title – the easier the job, the happier I am."

Smith was convinced that despite the huge amount of money he had been offered, Kamaci felt it better to retire as undefeated champion with plenty of ego. "Piedvache is a different proposition," he insisted. "Although I don't think there's a light-welterweight in Europe to beat Green, it will be a harder fight than if he had met the champion."

Meanwhile, Green, whose recent victories had pushed him into *Boxing News'* world rankings at number eight, was told that an X-ray of his injured right hand revealed no fracture. "He will need some physiotherapy, but all should be well in about 10 days," Smith told interested reporters. "Dave Green will be ready to fight on 7 December."

✦ 8 ✦

WORLD CHAMPIONSHIP CONTENDER

Posters advertising Green's European championship venture described him as: 'The Fen Tiger – Britain's most explosive and exciting fighter.' Mike Barrett was in no doubt about the British champion's credentials, and when announcing the fight in London said: "There has never been a boxer outside the heavyweight class to match him as a box-office draw."

The promoter believed the replacement fight was far better than the original because Piedvache, billed as 'The Pride of Paris', was younger and fresher than the veteran Kamaci.

The bulk of Green's training took place at St Ives where his sparring included three round sessions with tall Colin Powers from Paddington with whom Dave concentrated on jabbing. For heavy attacks he worked with Crawley welterweight, Johnny Pincham, whilst lightweight stable-mate, Ricky Beaumont, provided speed.

During the intense sessions, Dave wore Joe Bugner's 16 ounce training gloves instead of his own 12 ounce pair. The reason was two-fold; to put more weight on his arms whilst working, and to protect the sparring partners when he unleashed his vicious attacks.

Bugner had become a great admirer of Dave, and often watched him train, offering an occasional word of advice. "He has always had that ferocity, ever since he was a lad," he told a local newspaper reporter. "The only thing was he couldn't control it. Now he is one of only two boxers in the world who excites me – the other is Muhammed Ali when he is turning the heat on."

For the final week of training, Dave moved to The Horseshoe, Tottenham Court Road, where a gymnasium had been rigged up in one of the rooms. Apart from Green, other fighters on the bill, including Piedvache, Alan Minter and Sugar Ray Seales, all worked out in public between 12 noon and 3pm, Monday to Friday. Although the facilities bore no resemblance to the quarters at St Ives, it was done at the request of the promoter to facilitate press and public for the show.

Andy Smith used the situation to his advantage, and took time out to watch Piedvache doing his work-outs. He and Dave also closely studied a video of the Frenchman in action in an earlier contest.

Whilst in London, Dave and his manager stayed at the Holiday Inn, Swiss Cottage, and Green did his running each morning on Hampstead Heath. Despite being committed to public work-outs, Smith insisted that he only went through the motions whilst he was in the ring. Afterwards he and Colin Powers had serious sparring sessions at the Wellington gym, Highgate.

The gym was at the rear of a pub jointly run by former British champions, Ralph Charles and Vic Andreetti. Being the work-place of fighters trained by George Francis, including John Conteh and Bunny Sterling, it was a hive of activity, and there were plenty of good men with whom Dave could work.

Green arrived for the main press conference dressed in a farm smock and straw hat festooned with wisps of hay and clutching a pitch fork. It was Mike Barrett's idea, but the stunt hit a snag when Piedvache was handed a sword, asked to strip and pose for photographs.

"Non," he said flatly.

He was then asked to at least remove his jacket and waistcoat to justify a cavalier against roundhead image the promoters wanted to sell to the public to boost ticket sales.

"Non," he said again without a flicker of emotion.

Piedvache said that all he would remove was his jacket. He refused to undress for publicity until the evening of the fight.

"I am a boxer not a clown," he said tersely. "Boxing is too important to me. I love it too much – it is too beautiful a sport to be deformed like this."

Cold, composed, yet very dignified, the 28-year-old Frenchman from the Paris suburb of St Maur, was convinced he would end Green's unbeaten run. "The two styles make it a good contrast, but how I win depends on the mood I am in," he said softly. "If I am in a bad temper, I will knock him out."

Married with a six month old daughter, Piedvache had been a professional for six years. His only defeat from 40 contests was on points to then reigning French champion, Jean Saadli, in May 1975. Since then he had won seven in a row, and warmed up for his meeting with Green by taking a clear 10 rounds decision over Italian journeyman, Efisio Pinna, at Perigueux on 19 November.

Piedvache won the French junior lightweight championship in 1974, but outgrew the division. He was a tough man whose jaw had been shattered in 1973 in a fight against Andre Jamet. Yet he was never off his feet, and hung on to win in nine rounds.

His victims included Mike Mayon, 'Zip' Castillo and Lorenzo Trujillo, all American based fighters noted for their durability. His best win was probably against former WBC junior lightweight champion Ricardo Arrendondo of Mexico, whom he outpointed in Paris 10 months before facing Green. His sole British opponent was George McGurk whom he stopped in three rounds in January 1975 due to an arm injury.

Veteran French boxing manager, Jean Bretonnel, believed Piedvache's style made it a fascinating contest. "He is a fast clever fighter, and very brave," he told reporters. "Sometimes he gets into trouble by slugging it out. He's not really a strong fighter physically, but he can be dangerous with his right hand because it is thrown at such speed."

Most British sports writers predicted that Green would win inside the distance, but one of the most accurate assessments came from *Boxing News* editor, Graham Houston:

> I doubt if Piedvache has met anyone who puts so much pressure on an opponent so early in a fight, or faced such a hurtful puncher. I look for Green to overpower the visitor before the 10th round.

Meanwhile, Eric Boon, who had recently recovered from a heart attack, was seen by a number of press boys and asked for his opinion. Confident that Dave would take the title, he said: "I don't think this Frenchman can do anything against Green. Frenchmen are notoriously bad punchers. Green will lick anybody who cannot punch, because of his aggression and stamina."

Dave had rapidly become a throw-back to the days of Billy Walker when venues were completely sold out. For this fight, he personally sold over £13,000 worth of tickets, and it was estimated that 4,000 fans would make the journey from the Fens to support him.

His success as a professional had Chatteris gripped in fight fever. When the local amateur boxing club held their first tournament for three years, they were forced to turn people away. Although there was room for 250, between 50 and 60 were left outside.

"This is all due to Dave Green," said club coach and matchmaker, Jim Moore. "Since he started climbing the pro ladder, interest in boxing in this town is incredible."

Although he had moved on, Dave never forgot the start Jim and the club gave him. Despite being at the peak of his training for Piedvache, he still found time to attend the show, present trophies and give encouragement to many of the young boxers.

His training complete, the British champion watched his favourite football team, Cambridge United, on the Saturday afternoon before travelling back to London. The final couple of days before the fight were spent relaxing at an hotel, and taking brisk walks to keep loose.

Monitoring his weight during the final 24 hours was of the utmost importance to Dave and Andy Smith. At 7am on the morning of the fight he weighed exactly 10 stone. His only intake between then and the weigh-in was a drink of honey and glucose water. The weight remained static, and at the official ceremony at 1pm he was right on the championship limit of 10 stone. Piedvache scaled 9st 13¼.

"He's not like many boys who dry out to the extent of sauna bathing," said Smith. "If this fight had been in warm weather, he'd have made the weight easily. It's always that bit harder when it turns cold."

Poster advertising European light-welterweight championship fight between Green and Jean-Baptiste Piedvache

* * *

Bookmakers, William Hill, who reported tremendous betting on the fight, made Green 2-1 on favourite, with Piedvache at 13-8. The most popular bet, particularly with punters from the Fens, was for Dave to win in round six for which the odds were 16-1. Betting on the contest was all part of the excitement, and odds of 40-1 were offered against him winning in the opening round.

By fight-time, the atmosphere inside the Royal Albert Hall was electric as the packed crowd waited with excited expectation. Piedvache was led to the ring by former European middleweight champion, Jean-Claude Bouttier, who carried the French flag. He was given a warm reception by 200 travelling fans, although there were plenty of jeers from the thousands from the Fens.

Green followed shortly afterwards and received a rapturous reception as he ducked through the ropes wearing his now familiar hooded tiger-skin dressing-gown. In the ring, a Union Jack stood beside him as the audience rose for the national anthems.

The fight was a thriller because from the opening bell Piedvache stood up to Green and caught him with clusters of accurate left jabs. The British champion, however, was unconcerned. He hit back with solid lefts of his own, and a huge right to the head brought the crowd to the boil. Looking to take control early, Dave boxed beautifully throughout the first round, but the Frenchman took it all in his stride. At the bell he looked pointedly at Green as if to let him know he was not going to be intimidated.

Piedvache produced a flurry of fast jabs to the head at the start of round two, but the more solid punching came from the British champion. "Greeny, Greeny, Greeny," yelled his army of supporters as he increased the pressure. Flesh around the Frenchman's left eye began to swell and darken from the power of Dave's punches, and at the end of the round he nodded respectfully at the Chatteris man.

Both men fought hard and were quick to punish each other's mistakes. Solid head punches forced Piedvache to retreat in the third. A right hook made him hold, and left hooks to head and body ensured that Green had won the opening three rounds.

The fourth was closer as the Frenchman stuck close to Dave and scored with his share of solid accurate punches. By round five, however, his left eye was completely closed, and a huge right uppercut from Green forced him to grab and hold.

Piedvache took a real beating in this round, and at one stage the end looked near. Green's power and raw aggression pinned him on the ropes in a neutral corner. It was tense stuff, and blows were exchanged after the bell as the Frenchman desperately tried to rally.

It was an absorbing fight with the advantage swaying one way and then the other. The tables turned again in round six as the game Frenchman outpunched Green and forced him to retreat. Left jabs pounded into Dave's face, but just before the bell he stunned Piedvache with a crushing right to the jaw. The crowd roared as he tried to follow up with left hooks, but the bell came to the Frenchman's rescue.

Although Piedvache clearly won the sixth, Green bounced back in round seven. A fierce left hook crashed against the Frenchman's head. A good right hook was quickly followed by an uppercut. Piedvache, however, was brave and gave as good as he got, drawing blood from the British champion's nose in one exchange.

Despite the handicap of his injured left eye, the Frenchman attacked strongly in round eight. He caught Green almost at will at one stage, and even staggered him on one occasion with a right cross. Left jabs again brought blood dripping from Dave's nose, but he stood his ground and rammed home plenty of his own accurate left jabs.

His left eye a grotesque sight, Piedvache made his major effort. His cornermen screamed with excitement when a left right combination to the jaw appeared to wobble the British champion. On the other side of the ring Andy Smith looked apprehensive as more punches again brought blood streaming from Green's nose.

It was at this stage of the fight that Dave showed his maturity. With victory the only thing on his mind, courage, determination and improved ringcraft pulled him through a difficult situation against an excellent opponent. From being under intense pressure, he hit back quickly with thumping left jabs. As Piedvache backed away, damaging hooks to head and body put the British champion back in control.

The Frenchman had given everything, and during the interval signalled his retirement. His left eye was completely closed, and an ugly shelf of flesh hung from the lid.

Hysteria broke out all around the arena, and crowds flocked to the ringside when they realised Dave had won. The new champion leapt from his stool, a huge grin on his face. Andy Smith scrambled into the ring and hugged his young protegé, and was there minutes later to console him when all the emotion poured out. "When I knew I had won, I was so emotional," Dave admitted later. "I just couldn't hold it back."

It was Green's 22nd straight victory, and 18th inside the distance. Only John Conteh and two Ulster bantamweights, John Kelly and Freddie Gilroy, became British champions of Europe with fewer fights behind them.

Dave fully deserved the tremendous applause he received in becoming one of the greatest sportsmen the Fens had ever known. Close to the ringside, that other great Chatteris hero, Eric Boon, watched on in quiet admiration. Green had not only emulated him by winning the British title, but gone one better by capturing his second major championship in just over six months.

"I put all my efforts into winning," Dave told reporters in the dressing-room. "I can punch a bit, but that's what people pay to see."

Although he won the opening three rounds with comparative ease, Green was then made to work all the way to secure victory. Piedvache was a fine boxer, and at times it became too close for comfort as he took the fight to his aggressive young opponent.

It was a gruelling fight, but Dave boxed intelligently, pacing and containing himself as though expecting to go the full 15 rounds. His strength and stamina were incredible, and ringsiders noticed that Piedvache was tiring badly. When the end came, Green was comfortably ahead on the cards of all three officials. Under the EBU scoring system, German referee, Kurt Halbach, scored 89-85, while ringside judges Arsene Klop (Luxembourg) and Kurd Jensen (Denmark) made it 89-87 and 89-85 respectively, indicating that the British champion lost only one round on each card.

* * *

Although Dave had quickly become a national sporting hero, the people of Chatteris loved him because he was one of their own. They were not the hangers-on type so familiar within boxing, but genuine country folk from a close-knit community. They knew him as a quiet, modest young man who treated everyone with courtesy and respect.

The evening after the Piedvache fight, a special welcome home party with a magnificent buffet was laid on for Dave at The Palace, Chatteris. A band played *"Congratulations"*, and more than 200 Fenland folk jumped to their feet to welcome him as he walked in wearing a pair of sunglasses to conceal the bruises around his eyes.

His supporters club had grown rapidly during recent months, and the committee again did him proud. Later in the evening he was able to watch the fight on a colour television loaned for the occasion by local businessman, Ted Tiley.

Joe Bugner also received a warm welcome, and was greeted by Dave's personal bugler, John Phillips, a Cambridgeshire City Councillor who ran a taxi service. He first saw Green box at Cambridge Guildhall in February 1975, and since then had been at all of his fights. He always carried his bugle and played it whenever Dave made his way to the ring, and also between rounds.

Alec Dawson, Chairman of the Supporters Committee,

presented Dave with an inscribed clock, and read out some congratulatory telegrams, one of which came from the staff and officials of Fenland District Council.

Congratulating Dave on behalf of Chatteris Parish Council, Ray German said they hoped he would soon return home with the world crown.

With customary sincerity, Andy Smith made an impassioned speech in which he assured the gathering that Dave would eventually fight for the world championship:

> "Two years ago, David Green decided he wanted to go professional, and everyone said to me he would never make it because he takes too many punches."

> "He has since won the British and now the European crown, but there are still people who say he will never make it. It's just the same with Joe Bugner."

> "I have a relationship with my boys at training. I have a love in my heart for them."

> "I will promise you one thing – whether David becomes world champion or not depends entirely on him. My job is to get him that opportunity. But I promise you that he will fight for the world championship."

Earlier that day, Parliament was called upon to recognise Green's European championship success. Isle of Ely MP, Clement Freud, put forward a motion, seconded by Paul Hawkins, the member for the constituency in which Dave worked.

The motion put before the House of Commons read:

> "That the House congratulates Dave 'Boy' Green on his magnificent victory in the European light-welterweight championship; recognises that it is the first time an Englishman has ever won this title, and salutes Mr Green's skill, courage and outstanding sportsmanship."

The victory over Piedvache opened up all sorts of possibilities for Dave. From Andy Smith's point of view the most intriguing was a fight with former WBC welterweight champion, John H. Stracey.

134

"This fight keeps lingering in my mind," Smith told Graham Houston of *Boxing News*. "Stracey is not a big welter, and Green could carry a few more pounds. There would not be too much difference in weight."

Since turning professional two years earlier, Dave had never weighed below 9st 13 and had been as high as 10st 5³/₄. The difference was he had not faced a welterweight of Stracey's class.

The manager, however, saw it as a good fight for both men, and reasoned that if Dave lost, he could still move forward to a WBC title fight at light-welter and make defences of his European crown. "Green against Stracey would be a £100,000 fight," enthused Andy. "It would sell out Wembley."

Dave's performance against Piedvache brought glowing reports in the press. Henry Cooper had become a real fan of his, and writing in *Boxing News* commented:

> Dave looked tremendous in the opening rounds against the clever Piedvache. His jabbing was superb, and he seemed to be hitting hard with his right...
>
> Green's performance was superb, and he has the best record of any champion in 1976. I'm sure his manager intends him to have a long holiday. The crowds will flock to see him when he's ready to fight again.

Meanwhile, there was a debate over the gloves used in the fight between Green and the Frenchman. Andy Smith claimed they were eight ounce and not the usual six ounce gloves used at light-welterweight.

"You've only got to look at the photos to see what big gloves they are," he remarked. "The tag on the gloves read: 'size one, eight ounces'."

Smith insisted that Dave would have done a better job on the Frenchman had he been wearing the correct gloves. "The extra padding is obviously more of a disadvantage to a puncher than to a boxer," he insisted. "Green's punching was reduced in effectiveness by one third."

Board of Control Secretary, Ray Clarke, assured *Boxing*

News that the gloves used were not eight ounce. "I weighed them myself on the morning of the fight," he remarked. "They were welterweight gloves. I always try on new gloves, and you get the feel of gloves over the years."

In reality, the size of the gloves was irrelevant because Dave won the title, and in doing so recorded his 12th victory of 1976. Only two opponents had lasted the distance. It was an incredible year, and his achievements were recognised by *Boxing News* who voted him as their 'Fighter of the Year'. He also featured in two of the publication's top four fights of the year – against Piedvache and Billy Waith.

Despite his level of achievement, Green was back at work at the carrot farm just four days after the fight with Piedvache. Although he had been allowed plenty of time off to train, he was eager to get back there once it was over.

He also remembered fans who were unable to attend the fight, and one of the first things he did on returning to Chatteris, was to take his European championship belt to show the residents of Lion Court, an old peoples home. "When I won the British title, they asked if I would take it to show them," Dave told the *Chatteris Advertiser*. "At the time they said they hoped I would win the European title, and I said if I did I would take the belt to show them."

* * *

After two weeks holiday with Kay in Tenerife during early January, Dave returned home refreshed and desperate for action. He went straight back to the gym because he was due to fight at the Royal Albert Hall on 22 February 1977.

Although Green's London fights were promoted by either Harry Levene or Mike Barrett, rival promoter, Jack Solomons, had for some months issued challenges on behalf of All-Ireland lightweight champion, Charlie Nash. In September 1976, he had stopped Joey Singleton in a final eliminator for the British lightweight title, and was undefeated in nine contests. Solomons, who promoted at the World Sporting Club in London, was a bitter rival of Levene and Barrett, and wanted Nash to face Green for the light-welterweight title, but complained that his challenges were repeatedly ignored.

"Solomons knows in his heart of hearts that the fight can never come off, and that is why he is shouting about it so much," remarked Andy Smith. "It is like me challenging you to a fight in the pub because I know a dozen of your mates will not let you fight."

In the meantime, Dave was a principal guest at the 26th annual dinner of the Boxing Writers Club at Quaglino's Restaurant, Mayfair on 26 January. Members had voted him 'Best Young Boxer of the Year', a prestigious award which had been made annually since 1951. Previous winners included John Conteh, John H. Stracey, and Dave's stable-mate, Joe Bugner in 1969. Dave was an established favourite with the boxing writers having been voted runner-up to Vernon Sollas the previous year.

At the Albert Hall, Green faced Mario Guilloti of Argentina over 10 rounds at 10st 7. He was originally booked to fight Ray Hammond of New York, but he was replaced by Juan Cantres, a New York based Puerto Rican, who also pulled out at short notice. The 30 year old Guilloti was, however, a much tougher proposition.

A professional since 1969, he was a bronze medallist in the 1968 Olympics where he eliminated Armando Muniz and Canada's Donato Paduano before losing in the semi-finals. He had lost on seven occasions, five of which were to Miguel Angel Campanino who was to fight for the WBA welterweight title next time out.

Although the fight was made at 10st 7, Andy Smith insisted that Green could still make light-welter. "You take fights as they come along if they suit the purpose," he remarked pointing out that Dave had fought full welters before.

"It's going to be a very good contest for David," insisted Smith, "the type of fight to do him a lot of good, and I will be very happy with a win."

Some cynical fans dismissed Guilloti as just another

substitute, but students of international boxing knew he was unlikely to be demolished quickly. Based in Italy, the South American had a reputation for skill and durability, and the British camp knew he was a tough opponent. More importantly, he stood between a projected £60,000 showdown with John H. Stracey. Negotiations had already been put in place to stage the fight at Wembley on 29 March.

Although Dave comfortably outpointed Guilloti, many fans were disappointed because he was unable to produce the fireworks of previous contests. Referee Sid Nathan's score of 99-97 indicated the new European champion had won six and drawn two of the 10 rounds, yet many people in the audience seemed unable to recognise the South American's skill.

By round five there were bursts of slow handclapping, something Green had never experienced before. During the eighth, sections of the crowd sarcastically cheered Guilloti's elusive moves. Generally, the dissatisfaction came from fans sitting at the back of the arena who could not appreciate the subtleties of the South American's boxing.

Guilloti showed that a fighter can avoid punches without racing around the ring. Short, swarthy and broad-shouldered, he was not the type of opponent to look good against. He frequently made Green miss by a turn of the head, raised his gloves and turned his shoulders to catch the British champion's shots with amazing anticipation. He was a real professional, and it wasn't until the fourth round that Dave really shook him. Even then he recovered quickly to continue his defensive ploys.

As the fight progressed, the British champion became increasingly frustrated at not having an easy target to hit. Yet he never gave up, and kept plugging away with left jabs to generally control the fight. Even so, he didn't have matters entirely his own way.

Working in spurts, Guilloti scored with ease during round five, and drew blood from Green's nose. In the ninth he was close to causing a major upset when a solid combination to the head hurt the Chatteris man and forced him to fight for survival for an uncomfortable 15 seconds.

"I was gone for a moment," admitted Green afterwards. "It was a good punch, and that was only the second time that has happened to me."

Green recovered well, stepped up the pace in the final round and prodded to victory with his left jab. At the final bell, Guilloti smilingly accepted defeat, but booing from sections of the crowd was harsh on the European champion.

"The fans had been led to believe from what they read in the morning papers, that this was a three round job," said Andy Smith. "Naturally they were disappointed. If they had been told this was a tough and experienced fighter who doesn't get stopped, they would have reacted differently. I don't blame the fans."

Explaining that Guilloti could probably go the distance with the best men in the world, Smith said: "I told Dave to keep going the way he was because the win was the most important thing. I was glad when it was all over."

By this time it was well known that Green's next opponent would almost certainly be Stracey. "I was worried because things can go wrong when you've got a big fight coming up," added Smith. He reminded reporters that Joe Bugner was held to a draw by Bill Drover of Canada a month before he faced Henry Cooper, and how Stracey sustained a badly cut eye against Keith Averett at Wembley while marking time before facing Jose Napoles. "All this was in my mind," he remarked.

Green admitted that he found Guilloti extremely hard to hit. "He knew the game," he said. "He kept sticking his thumb out as he jabbed, but he only caught me with that one good shot in the ninth."

Despite the boos at the end, matchmaker Mickey Duff and Wembley promoter, Harry Levene, were delighted with Dave's performance. "He was up against a spoiler and I thought he did very well," said Levene.

Duff gave an accurate assessment of the contest when he told reporters: "I thought it was the most controlled showing of Dave's career. It was the first time he has been made to really think."

Levene and Duff had good reason to be pleased with Green because they had world champion Carlos Palomino contracted to fight in London. When the Mexican challenged John H. Stracey for the WBC welterweight title the previous year, his manager, Jackie McCoy, was obliged to come to an agreement giving Duff and Levene the option on Palomino's first two defences in the event of him winning the title. This was done to protect Stracey's interest.

Palomino made a successful first defence of the title in Los Angeles on 22 January 1977, stopping Armando Muniz in the 15th and final round of a tremendous contest. Duff, who had an interest in the promotion, said that the champion looked a "twenty per cent better fighter" than when he beat Stracey. Before returning to London, he reached agreement with Palomino that his next defence would be against Stracey, or another opponent, at the discretion of the promoter, namely Levene.

Two days after Dave Green beat Guilloti, the long awaited fight between him and Stracey was announced. Although approval was still required from the WBC, it would go ahead at Wembley on 29 March over 12 rounds, and be a final eliminator for Palomino's title.

✦ 9 ✦

FENS – EAST END THRILLER

Green against Stracey was a natural showdown – a fight the fans had been relishing for more than a year. Dave, who had risen to number four in the WBC light-welterweight rankings, had become very much a main event fighter in a short space of time. He was being tipped as a future world champion, whilst John who had been to the very highest level, badly needed to re-establish himself.

Although purse details were not revealed, it was suggested by the press that both men would receive in excess of £30,000. "Some tough terms have been agreed," said Harry Levene during the press conference at London's Sportsman Club, Tottenham Court Road, to announce the fight, "but everything is going up these days. This fight is more expensive than a certain world championship I promoted in the last 18 months. That's inflation for you, but it is going to be a tremendous fight between two tremendous British fighters."

The tough terms referred to by Levene had arisen because Andy Smith insisted that Green received as much as Stracey. John had already accepted terms with the promoter before watching Dave beat Guilloti. Once Smith realised this, he used all his bargaining skills because in his words, "Green was the trump card."

141

"The ball is in my court now," he told the press before negotiations began, "and Stracey can shadow-box at Wembley unless I have the chance to get David as much as him, or even more."

Smith told Dave that they had a choice of a flat rate or a percentage of the gate. Knowing the fight would be a sell-out, the astute Scot advised his man to go for the percentage, and trusting his manager's judgement, Dave agreed.

"It was a huge fight," he said when recalling the situation. "Stracey had a massive following in London, was a former world champion, and the fight was a final eliminator. I believe I made five or six grand more than John because he took the flat rate."

Green was always appreciative of the support given to him by his manager in respect of all matters. "I would never have got where I am if it hadn't been for Mr Smith," he told local reporters when they visited the St Ives gym a few days before the fight. "He has taught me to box and control myself in my punching, and brought me on a bomb. You cannot do half a job. What you need is natural ability, dedication, and the right coach."

Both men were confident of victory when they came face to face at the press conference. "I am glad of the opportunity of meeting Stracey, and I am very confident of beating him," said Dave. "I think I can do a better job than Palomino."

In response, Stracey said: "We are both straightforward fighters so it's certain to be a war. I think I'll stop Dave."

Bookmakers, William Hill, agreed with John, and immediately installed him as a 2-1 on favourite. Green was quoted at 6-4 against.

Despite the fight being a certain box-office winner, it was nevertheless dubbed "The Snarler" v "The Smiler" as a ticket-selling gimmick. "I don't care if Green is a snarler," remarked Stracey. "Snarling never hurt anyone. Don't worry, I'll stop him. I took this fight because I didn't want to finish with Palomino. When I go out, I want to go out fighting."

Once the fight was agreed, Andy Smith immediately

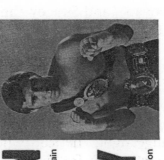

EMPIRE POOL, WEMBLEY

TUESDAY, 29th MARCH, 1977

Doors open 6.30 p.m.   Commence 7.30 p.m.

Matchmaker: MICKEY DUFF

Harry Levene PRESENTS

THE FIGHT OF THE YEAR !!

REMEMBER BOON v DANAHAR ?   CHATTERIS v BETHNAL GREEN ?   HERE IS THE REPEAT !

12 (3 min.) ROUNDS AT 10st. 7lbs. FINAL ELIMINATING CONTEST FOR THE

WELTERWEIGHT CHAMPIONSHIP of the WORLD

THE WINNER WILL MEET CARLOS PALOMINO FOR THE WORLD TITLE IN LONDON ON 14th JUNE, 1977

DAVID 'BOY' GREEN

(Chatteris). "The Fen Tiger".   Light-welterweight Champion of Great Britain and Europe.

v

JOHN H. STRACEY

(Bethnal Green). "The Cockney Bulldog".   Former Welterweight Champion of the World.

★ PLUS FULL STAR SUPPORTING PROGRAMME ★

| Tickets: | £5.50 | £8.50 | £12.50 | £17.50 | Ringside £25.00 |

Printed by Albert Robins & Co. Ltd., 11-19 Vyner Street, E.2 (01-981 0910)

Poster advertising contest between Green and John H. Stracey

143

ordered £20,000 worth of tickets, but within a few days, realised it wasn't enough because the demand was incredible. "Chatteris will be deserted that night," he remarked.

There was massive press coverage, countless articles about both men appearing in the sports pages of local and national newspapers. Comparisons were quickly made with the epic British lightweight championship fight back in February 1939 between Eric Boon of Chatteris and Arthur Danahar from Bethnal Green. Boon won by a knockout in the 14th round of what was rated as one of the greatest fights ever seen in a British ring.

Harry Levene believed that Green against Stracey had the makings of a similar fight, but was of greater importance. It was a world title final eliminator between two world-class fighters.

Ahead of the fight, Green and Stracey were joint guests of honour at a special boxing dinner at the Anglo American Sporting Club in London. After a welcoming speech by club secretary, Kenneth Wolstenholme DFC, and a toast by BBC television commentator, Harry Carpenter, both responded and expressed their confidence of victory.

During the build-up to the fight, some reporters focused on the role played by Dave's wife Kay, who by this time had seen only four of his professional contests. She was, however, an important part of his team, watching his diet and understanding his moods.

"You've got to be keyed up in this game," Dave explained, "and I get a bit nasty sometimes." Paying tribute to Kay, he said: "When you are watching what you eat and drink, it does come as a bit of a bind. I've got a good understanding wife, and she copes with it. It's much easier to have a wife who understands that if you get on, you're both going to benefit."

The first stages of Dave's intensive training programme were done at St Ives, but in early March Andy Smith took him to America to polish up. Joe Bugner was due to fight Ron Lyle at Las Vegas on the 20th of that month, and the manager believed the trip would be good for him. Not only would it give him a taste of the big fight atmosphere in the States, it would also shelter him from the pressure of ticket hunters who would make Chatteris a deserted town on fight night.

The experience matured Dave and gave him even more confidence about his ability. He worked in the same gym as Bugner, and got some tremendous sparring sessions with three good class American middleweights. Andy Smith gave his two boxers equal attention, working with Joe in the morning and Dave during the afternoon. When the Chatteris man returned to Britain he was tuned to perfection, like a grand prix motor car revving up on the starting grid.

"It was absolutely wonderful for David," Andy Smith told the *Chatteris Advertiser* on their return home. "The experience has shown him how good he is. I am delighted with how things worked out. I wanted him to realise that he is not only British and European champion, but also capable of holding his own with the best in the world."

Green's attitude before a fight was always the same – kill or be killed. This one was no exception. He became moody and irritable, and couldn't wait to get to grips with the man who stood between him and a fight for the world championship.

Despite Dave's confidence, many of his fans had concerns because he had never been put under the sort of pressure Stracey would impose. Yet nobody could ever doubt his determination, dedication, aggression or instinct for the fight game. Writing in the *Daily Mirror*, Frank McGee said:

> The theory of those who support Green is that he will overwhelm Stracey with action, sicken him with body punches – as Palomino did – and be, bluntly, too good for him.

The writer, however, predicted that John's pride would take him to victory inside the distance.

Graham Houston, editor of *Boxing News*, also favoured the Londoner, albeit with some reservations:

> I think the fight will end about round eight, with one or the other having to be saved by the referee. My prediction is a win

for Stracey. Green is a willing and able fighter, but I think there are too many doubts about Dave at this high level to pick him to win. Yet when two proud fighters step between the ropes, anything can happen. All we can be fairly sure of is that it will be dramatic for as long as it lasts, and may the best man win.

Although Stracey had not fought since losing to Palomino nine months earlier, he was still a massive obstacle for Green to overcome. Throughout his career he had achieved so much more than Dave, having won a national schoolboy championship in 1965, NABC title (1966), and Junior ABA titles in 1966 and '67. In 1969, he was ABA light-welterweight champion and an England international.

He turned professional with Terry Lawless in 1969, and had won 45 and drawn one of 50 contests, with 37 opponents failing to last the distance. He was undefeated British welterweight champion between 1973-1975, undefeated European champion 1974-75, before becoming WBC world champion.

Stracey had performed at the highest level, and achieved what was thought to be impossible when going to Mexico City in December 1975 and taking the world title from the great Jose Napoles. In the daunting surroundings of the Plaza Bullring, 7000 feet above sea-level, he did it the hard way. Knocked down early in the opening round, he showed tremendous courage to hold on, then grind the champion to a sixth round defeat.

A successful defence against Hedgemon Lewis in March 1976 was followed by the shattering defeat by Palomino three months later. Although John was extremely confident of victory against Green, nobody really knew how much damage he had suffered physically or psychologically from the loss to the Mexican. There were so many ifs and buts about this fight that the only certainty seemed to be that another Fens – East End classic was about to be unveiled.

Eric Boon fancied Green. "If David puts the pressure on as he can, I think it could end as early as four rounds," he told the *Cambridge Evening News*. "I think Stracey has lost his

146

heart and guts. That beating from Palomino has taken everything out of him."

In some respects, Boon's assessment was hard on Stracey because the last thing a boxer loses is his pride. John always had plenty of that, as he showed against Napoles after being floored in the opening round. When he fought Hedgemon Lewis, he was again under tremendous pressure during the first session as the American lashed out with spectacular combinations.

Stracey was also shaken early on in his fights with Roger Menetrey, Vernon Mason, Jack Tillman and Ernie 'Indian Red' Lopez, but pulled himself together and hammered his way to victory. Against Marc Gevais of Canada, he was on the floor in the opening round, but hit back viciously to win in the fourth.

Whilst Green and his manager were extremely confident, they were under no illusions about John's courage and ability to absorb punishment. Having won in Las Vegas, Mexico and Paris, his experience and punching power were other factors in his favour. His handlers insisted that the only time he lost on merit was to Palomino.

By fight night, Green was ready. "I feel great, fantastic," he said firmly. "I have no doubts at all. I am going to win. It's a fight I have been waiting a long time for, and now Mr Smith says it's the right time."

"I think I have the equipment to stop him," he continued. "I just cannot see him staying with me. It's a pity it's not for the world title, but there you are. I just want Stracey. I have no worries – he has got to worry about me."

Going into the fight, Dave had the consolation of knowing that whatever the result, he would still remain British and European light-welterweight champion. Success against Stracey, however, would generate huge financial rewards.

At the weigh-in, Dave was surprisingly heavier at 10st 5 and 14oz to John's 10st $4^3/_4$. Whilst Stracey remained favourite in pre-fight betting, the odds eased slightly to 7-4 on, with Green at 11-8 against.

The fight more than lived up to its billing, and was one of the most exciting seen in a British ring for more than a decade. It contained raw drama, hard punching, and unrestrained, uncompromising action from start to finish. It was about an all-action youngster on the way up, pitted against the more experienced boxer who had tasted life at the highest level, and wanted to go there again.

Some unwarranted boos from a section of the crowd, presumably Stracey supporters, greeted Dave as he climbed into the ring wearing his now familiar hooded dressing-gown of imitation tiger-skin. Meanwhile, Stracey, the Union Jack emblazoned on the back of his white robe, had waited on the ring steps, and ducked between the ropes after the Chatteris man.

Green made an explosive start, and took the initiative from the opening bell. He charged from his corner and practically hurled himself at Stracey, forcing him to the ropes where he was hammered by looping punches to the head and ribs.

Under intense pressure, the Londoner backed away, but Dave stayed right on top of him. Although John eventually scored with two good left hooks which momentarily halted Green, his timing was generally that of a man who had been out of the ring for nine months. Desperation left hooks and uppercuts were woefully short of the mark.

Knowing that Stracey was a slow starter, Dave piled on the pressure as he went in search of an early victory. In his eagerness, he forgot the niceties of the game, and was twice warned for low blows. He was also sternly reprimanded by referee, Harry Gibbs, after Stracey justifiably complained about careless use of the head.

Green's strength was incredible, and John looked very shaky as he was driven from one side of the ring to the other. His face twisted in agony as vicious hooks sank deep into his body, and at one stage when his knees buckled, it looked as though he must go to the floor. Before the end of the round his back was reddened by rope burns, and there were signs of puffiness around the left eye.

148

It was a breathtaking opening session which had the capacity crowd screaming with excitement throughout. The action was so intense that neither man heard the bell, and Harry Gibbs had to pull them apart.

Green kept up his incessant attack during round two, although Stracey boxed with more authority and probably shared the round. He was more composed, and steadied Dave with short effective clusters of punches.

Towards the end of the round, Dave received a further warning for careless use of the head. Clearly angered, Stracey lashed out viciously with both hands the moment they were ordered to box on. Green stood his ground, hit back strongly, and again Mr Gibbs had to drag them apart at the bell.

The swelling above Stracey's left eye worsened during the third. Although he showed signs of rallying when landing good jabs early in the round, he could still not keep his aggressive opponent at bay. Green simply walked through the punches in order to get inside and attack the body. Two hard rights in quick succession landed on John's damaged eye, and he was also punished by hooks to head and body as Green kept up the pressure.

The fourth was as furious as anything which had gone before. Attacking with tigerish ferocity, Dave caught Stracey with a long looping right, jolted his head back with a jab, and hooked to the body with both hands. Yet Stracey never lacked courage, and was always looking to hit back. When backed into Green's corner, he braced his legs, gritted his teeth and banged back with good shots from both hands.

It was gripping stuff which had the crowd screaming. Always looking to go forward, Dave was sometimes too wild, and when his head again crashed into John's face, Harry Gibbs went straight into action. He grabbed Green by his hair, marched him to the far side of the ring and administered a severe finger-wagging caution. "Do that again son, and you're out," he growled making it abundantly clear that this was the final warning.

As expected, it was an extremely tough and rugged fight

with a great deal at stake. Not surprising, there was an element of needle. Almost from the start, Stracey's cornermen had loudly protested about Green's head, and more than once, John had pleaded to Harry Gibbs for defence against it. Always his own man, Gibbs issued a warning when he thought necessary, and on other occasions tapped Dave on the head without stopping the action.

Whilst Green was clearly the main offender, there was an occasion when Stracey lowered his head in what appeared to be retaliation as he bored in. Green pulled his head back with some exaggeration, whereupon Mr Gibbs told him to cut out the acting.

The referee called the fighters together at the start of round five and firmly told them to cool down. As he waved them on, Green tore into Stracey, crashing three rights on the damaged left eye, closing it a little more. He threw everything he had in another raging onslaught as he went in search of victory. John took a lot of punishment in this round, and whenever he tried to punch his way clear, found Green only too willing to trade with him.

By the sixth, Stracey's left eye had narrowed to a mere slit, and he was soon backing away as Green continued his relentless attack. Yet as the round progressed there were signs that the Chatteris man was tiring. Stracey was still strong, and despite the hammering he had taken, was able to increase his punch-rate. He connected with more jabs and hooks than at any stage of the fight, and for the first time looked to be in with a chance of victory. The needle was still there, however, and when words were exchanged at close quarters, Mr Gibbs called them together again and told them to behave.

There was a real turnaround in round seven as Green's pace appeared to slow. His punches became wilder, and the flurries did not last so long and were not as effective. Sensing he was fading, Stracey put his own combinations together and got right back into the fight. Two-fisted attacks crashed through Dave's guard, and a solid left hook hurt him. It was a great round for the Londoner in which they were again talking in the clinches. "Is that the hardest you can hit?" snarled Green trying kidology whilst under pressure.

The fight had reached an extremely interesting stage because it looked as though Stracey had taken Dave's best shots and was now taking control. He stood his ground much more, looked confident, and countered well to pull Dave up short whenever he attacked. Throughout rounds eight and nine he beat Green to the punch, scoring with three and four jab combinations to the head.

Stracey landed more solid punches during the first two minutes of the ninth than at any stage of the fight. It was the moment of truth for Green who showed signs of wilting under John's spirited comeback. At one point he appeared to stumble when caught flush on the chin by a two-fisted combination.

Dave's strength and level of fitness, however, were incredible, and absolutely crucial at this point. Propelled by a burning desire for victory, he fought with intense pride and heart to deny the Londoner at a time when he appeared to be taking over. Taking everything that was thrown at him, it was his turn to dig deep and grit his teeth as he sought for untapped reserves of grit and stamina.

As they came out for round 10, it looked anybody's fight, but Green's determination soon changed all that. Given a timely instruction by Andy Smith, he moved into the blind area on Stracey's left, and sickened the Londoner with a series of rib-bending body shots. Two right swings crashed against the damaged left eye closing it completely.

John had very little left, prompting Harry Gibbs to ask if he wished to continue. Bravely acknowledging that he did, he was soon in trouble again. Green pulled him to the ropes, ruthlessly went to work, and caught him with almost every shot he threw.

Unable to see out of his left eye, Stracey was a defenceless, half-blinded target. All the fight had gone out of him and he was no longer punching back when Mr Gibbs mercifully called it off after one minute 40 seconds of the round. He had given the former world champion every chance, and the stoppage came at exactly the right moment. An ugly purple shelf of flesh jutted out as his left eye closed with Green throwing overarm rights in the general direction of it. One shot too many and the eye could have suffered lasting damage.

Green leapt into the air as Gibbs stepped in. He hugged Andy Smith, and immediately asked: "Do I get a crack at the world title now?"

"After winning a fight like that, you certainly deserve it," enthused his delighted manager.

Although Dave was probably hit harder in this fight than ever before, his tactics had been absolutely correct. He boxed intelligently, mixing fighting with jabbing, hit Stracey hard and often from the opening seconds, and never gave him the room to unload his own big shots. He didn't escape unscathed, and swelling around the right eyebrow and bruising on the cheek bore testimony of John's power.

Back in the dressing-room, Green's familiar fighting snarl changed to a beaming smile as he faced the press. "I am over the moon," he said. "The guv'nor says it's Palomino now – and I am ready."

"Stracey is a great fighter to go 10 rounds like that with me," he continued. "It comes from the bottom when you are fighting like that. He has got some guts. You have to give him that."

Asked whether he was worried about the warnings for butting, Dave replied: "Nothing worries me. I am just there to fight."

Stracey's manager, Terry Lawless said that he wanted to pull his man out of the fight three rounds earlier because of his damaged eye, but John wouldn't let him. "I have always had a lot of respect for Dave Green," he remarked, "but he got away with one or two little indiscretions tonight. I am sure John would have licked him with two eyes."

Stracey was more direct. "It was his 'muck-spreader' which did it – his head. He hit me with it about three times in the first round. My eye started coming up and it grew worse and worse."

Harry Gibbs confirmed afterwards that it was anyone's fight at the end. In his autobiography some years later, he said:

> The fight itself was a rugged one and I issued a number of warnings to both men for the way they were careless with their heads. As early as the first round I had occasion to wag a finger at Green and warn him about his head, but in the second I felt John overplayed it when he showed out to me because David's head was nowhere near that time. Of course it was in the vicinity, but that was inevitable in a close quarter battle.

* * *

A few days after the fight, Dave and Kay accompanied Andy Smith and his family on a memorable four week holiday in the United States. They flew from Heathrow to West Palm Beach, Florida, where they spent two weeks relaxing and totally distanced from boxing. They hired a large American car, and with Dave doing most of the driving, travelled to Cape Canaveral before spending three days at Disneyland.

After visiting one of Andy Smith's sons at St Petersburg, they went to Key West and on to Miami Beach where they spent a week. Andy contacted Angelo Dundee and arranged to visit his gym which was nearby. Among the boxers training there was Commonwealth middleweight champion, Monty Betham, a brilliant boxer and fine technician who had defended his title five times since winning it in July 1975.

Dundee, a great friend of Smith, invited Dave to train at the world-famous gym for a week, and during that time he sparred six rounds with Betham on three occasions. He was also extended the privilege of visiting the personal dressing-room of world heavyweight champion, Muhammed Ali. The whole visit was a great experience.

On his return home, Dave accepted an invitation to complete in a heat of the popular Superstars competition being staged at St Ives Recreation Centre on 9 and 10 May.

Presented by Transworld International and televised by the BBC, Superstars was based on an original idea conceived by Olympic and World figure skating champion, Dick Bulton who started it in America during 1972. The first British competition, won by athlete David Hemery, was staged in 1973. The following year, John Conteh was champion. There was no competition in 1975, but Hemery again won the event in 1976.

Green's opponents in the 1977 men's competition were British and European shot-putt champion, Geoff Capes, football stars, Mike Channon and Malcolm McDonald, Welsh Rugby Union internationals, Gerald Davies and JPR Williams, Keith Remfry (judo) and Olympic rowing silver medallist, Tim Crooks, a late replacement for England cricketer, Derek Randall.

Competitors were given four days preparation at St Ives for the special events. Dave was an absolute fitness fanatic, and once he picked up the tempo, he also trained every day for the Palomino fight which had been set for 14 June.

Hundreds of spectators descended on St Ives for the Superstars event, and gave tremendous encouragement to the competitors. Being the local boy, Dave had more support than the others, and received incredible cheers for his sporting, but highly competitive approach. Before the competition began, Andy Smith described him as "a competitor in the Kevin Keegan mould."

Dave didn't let his fans down, and amassed 33 points to finish a credible third in the gruelling event won by Tim Crooks, with Geoff Capes runner-up.

The competition began with the 50 metre swim in the recreation centre pool. Green battled hard and completed the distance in 35 seconds to finish runner-up to Crooks.

In the first round of the table tennis event, he had the misfortune to be drawn against Williams, a former Wimbledon junior champion, who won 21-11.

At weight-lifting, each competitor was set a task of lifting his own body weight and scoring points on anything above. Although Dave put in an incredible performance, lifting 77.5 kilos, 6.3 kilos above his body weight, he was beaten by the bigger men and finished only sixth.

154

The gym tests comprised of two sections – dips on the parallel bars, and squat thrusts. In winning the event, Dave astonished the audience with an incredible 73 thrusts in 60 seconds. He also did 16 dips on the bars.

He also won the pistol shooting with an amazing score of 49, just one point off the maximum.

The soccer stars picked Green to win the football competition, but this went to Capes, who along with Gerald Davies, scored a single goal. Although Dave was the only non-footballing competitor to show any skills, bad luck and a superb save by Ipswich Town goalkeeper, Paul Cooper, denied him. He finished fifth.

He was also fifth in the 100 metre sprint, but recorded a personal best time of 12.9 seconds.

With each competitor obliged to miss out two of the ten events, Dave chose canoeing and cycling. The 600 metre steeplechase was his final test, and although he went for it from the gun, he was run out of it in the home straight. He finished third in one minute 52.3 seconds.

The competition was a fantastic experience for Dave. He felt confident that given more time to train, he could have taken another championship back to Chatteris. Yet he had no regrets, and considered the intense level of competition in eight events over two days, was an added bonus to his preparations for the Palomino fight.

✦ 10 ✦

WORLD TITLE CHALLENGE

Shortly after the Palomino fight was signed, the European Boxing Union nominated Primo Bandini of Italy as official challenger for Dave's European light-welterweight title. Purse offers were invited by 18 May, thereby putting the proposed contest on a collision course with the world title fight set for 14 June.

Not wishing his man to relinquish the European title, Andy Smith asked the EBU to delay the defence until after Dave had met Palomino. At first they showed little compassion and sent Smith a strongly worded letter demanding action. Andy, however, was a great negotiator, and after a series of letters and telephone calls, persuaded the European governing body to withdraw its demand until after the Palomino fight.

The six weeks leading up to his world title challenge were the most important in Dave's life. He knew the task he faced, but his burning ambition and will to win the crown were immense. Every conceivable effort would be made to ensure that he went into the ring in the peak of fitness.

His employer was again very generous in allowing him time off work to prepare for the fight. Still tanned from his holiday in Florida, Dave did his running every morning at St Ives golf course before going to Andy Smith's house for breakfast and a few hours rest. Press functions and tough sessions in the gym filled the remainder of the day.

As he steadily built towards his peak Dave was put through a series of rigorous training sessions. In sparring, no punches were pulled, and most of his partners were heavily protected around the body as he increased his power and pace. In particular, Jimmy Harrington from Sandy, an ABA middleweight semi-finalist, had a huge foam rubber protector strapped to his body to combat Dave's lethal hooks.

Wearing a pair of Joe Bugner's large training gloves, he hammered the heavy bag during one session before a large invited audience of national newspaper reporters. "Come on son, keep it going," yelled Andy Smith as sweat cascaded from his man's head and body. "Hit them straight – great he's gone."

Throughout each session, Smith watched, almost fatherly as Dave went about his work. He was protective but practical, and there was an air of military precision about the routines he set his fighter.

"These gloves are like sacks of potatoes on me," said Green with a smile as he squatted on the floor once the demanding session was over. Yet it wasn't a show put on to entertain the press, but part of a deadly serious daily routine. Every punch the British champion threw contained power and venom as if the target in front of him was a live opponent in a real fight. Carlos Palomino was fixed firmly in his mind.

Each session was confined to sheer physical graft. There were no dossiers or films of Palomino. "I never watch a lot of films," Dave told the press boys. "I never worry about opponents, I let them worry about me."

Green's continued success and attitude to the fight game had a massive effect throughout East Anglia. It had become a wider picture of what occurred at Chatteris during the period leading up to his fight with Piedvache. Membership of amateur boxing clubs as far afield as March, Wisbech and Peterborough, soared rapidly. As one club secretary told the press: "Every kid around here wants to become a Dave Green."

Despite having become a household name, Dave was still an ordinary Fenland lad. Success hadn't changed him one iota, and he made regular trips to amateur boxing clubs and dinner shows throughout the region. His attendance generated an incredible atmosphere, and he loved giving advice and encouragement to novice boxers of all ages. Nothing was too much trouble for him.

In the days leading up to the Palomino fight, the whole of Chatteris talked about Dave. Pictures of him appeared everywhere – in the newspapers, displayed in the windows of shops and cafes, and on the walls of public houses. In local schools, children made banners ready to string across the streets, regardless of the outcome of the fight.

Elderly folk who remembered Eric Boon had become just as excited about Dave, who by fighting for a world title, was achieving something which eluded the old Chatteris hero. The incredible excitement and atmosphere generated in the town had become a regular feature each time a big fight approached, only this time it was greater than ever before.

At the time, the average weekly wage was £75, a gallon of petrol cost 82p and a pint of bitter 23p. Rod Stewart was number one in the record charts with his single 'First Cut is the Deepest', and in boxing Dave 'Boy' Green was the biggest box-office attraction in the country. For this fight alone he sold £35,000 worth of tickets ranging from £5.50 to £30, at the time a record for any British fighter. Local publicans, particularly John Birch of the Rose and Crown at Manea, and members of Green's supporters club, worked flat out on his behalf.

* * *

Carlos Palomino arrived in London on 2 June, Green's 24th birthday. At a press conference later that day, he posed with the British champion as he blew out the candles on a cake presented for the occasion by promoter, Harry Levene. It was the only celebration Dave had. With preparations for the fight at their peak, he stayed no longer than was necessary because all he wanted to do was get back to St Ives and resume training.

Based in Los Angeles, the 27-year-old world champion was managed by Jackie McCoy. Since becoming a professional in 1972, he had lost only once in 25 contests – a 10 rounds points decision to Andy 'Hawk' Price at San Diego in 1974.

The second of 11 children, Carlos was born to a construction worker in Sonora, Mexico. The family moved to California when he was 10 years old. Although he did not take up boxing until the age of 20 whilst serving in the US Army, he progressed well, and outpointed Sugar Ray Seales to win a National AAU title in 1972.

Boxing helped him to pay for his studies, and he graduated in recreational administration at Long Beach State University, California. He loved working with children, and became a recreation leader in Orange County.

Swarthy and moustached, Palomino was a thoroughly professional fighter with an excellent variety of punches. He had displayed courage and durability after being floored in the opening round when making the first defence of his title against Armando Muniz in January. The fact that he was able to floor and stop his seasoned opponent in the 15th and final round of a gruelling contest, proved that he also had tremendous stamina.

On his previous visit to London when he fought John H. Stracey, he became one of the most popular world champions to visit Britain for a long time. Always modest, articulate and intelligent, he was a fighter who often looked very ordinary in the gym. It was this as much as anything which led to him being generally unfancied by the British press prior to meeting Stracey. Everyone who met him described him as a true gentleman. He had a warm personality, and one American sports writer described him as: "quiet enough to be mistaken for a librarian, articulate enough to be mistaken for a teacher, handsome enough to be mistaken for an entertainer and humble enough to be mistaken for a clergyman."

Green and Palomino had sparred four rounds together at the Thomas A'Beckett gym in London 12 months earlier when the Mexican was preparing to meet Stracey. "I never thought I'd be fighting him," said Carlos at the press conference, "but I do remember he was real strong and came to go to work. I'll be ready for 15 tough rounds if it has to be."

Dave said that he just went to spar with Palomino for the experience. "He was good, but I never thought I'd be fighting him so I didn't take much notice," he remarked. "To be honest, I thought Stracey would win." He forgot to mention that he attacked the Mexican for all he was worth, and knocked his head guard off with a big left hook during the second round.

Andy Smith and Dave were at Wembley when Carlos beat Stracey. During the middle rounds Smith commented that the first man to back off or lose heart would lose the fight. "John backed off," he said afterwards.

At the press conference, Smith remarked: "The man who wins this fight will be the one who is willing to lay his life on the canvas. Stracey wasn't – Green is. Is Palomino willing to die?"

It was a dramatic remark by the manager anxious to stress that Green would be prepared to dig deep, give everything he had, and then look for a bit more.

The press were divided about the possible outcome, although most agreed with Levene that it would be a tremendous contest. In *Boxing News*, Graham Houston wrote:

> We are likely to see rallies and counter-rallies, and lots of hard blows given and taken. It could be sensational... I go for Green to take the championship. Whatever happens, I know he will not let anyone down.

Dave and Andy Smith travelled to London the day before the fight and stayed at the Holiday Inn, Swiss Cottage. Looking relaxed and confident, the British champion scaled 10st 6³/₄ at the official weigh in. Palomino, who had been installed as a 2-1 on favourite by the bookies, was right on the limit of 10st 7.

A capacity crowd descended on Wembley that evening, and all roads leading to the famous arena were jammed solid with traffic. It was a never-to-be-forgotten night, starting with Green's entry to the ring which had to be seen to be believed.

As the lights dimmed, fanfares echoed around the massive Empire Pool. Spotlights directed to one corner, picked out the Union Jack being carried slowly and proudly towards the ring ahead of the British champion and his handlers. It was a moving moment as the Chatteris hero was led through a marvellously patriotic crowd full of anticipation. The country dialects of his faithful Fenland followers who were there in their thousands, and cockney voices from the capital, joined together in a welcome that was breathtaking.

As lights illuminated the ring, thunderous cheers greeted the British champion as he ducked through the ropes clad in his famous tiger-skin dressing-gown. As the lights dimmed again, the fanfares chillingly heralded the arrival of Palomino. "David... David... David..." yelled the huge crowd as the spotlights picked out the champion starting his long walk to the ring.

Undaunted by the chants, Carlos looked an extremely composed professional on his way to do another day's work. He was unconcerned that most people in the arena were hoping to see him beaten. It had been just the same when he faced John Stracey.

Once the two boxers and appointed officials were in the ring, everyone stood for stirring renderings of the national anthems of both countries. Two pairs of gleaming red gloves were then removed from their boxes by an official and handed to the chief seconds.

Green was really pumped up and itching to get into action. He fidgeted and glowered across the ring at Palomino as Andy Smith laced and taped his gloves. Even during the national anthems he kept jigging up and down, forwards and backwards. As Master of Ceremonies, Nat Basso, made the formal introductions, he prowled around the ring, and

161

eventually had to be eased back to his corner to await the start.

The Empire Pool had hosted many great contests over several decades. Back in February 1935, Jack Petersen and Walter Neusel engaged in what was described as "the greatest heavyweight fight for years." There were plenty more at different weights, but Green against Palomino surpassed most. When Harry Levene remarked at a press conference 11 days earlier: "It cannot fail to be a great fight," even he could not have imagined how spectacular it would be.

Every round was bitterly contested, and fortunes swayed one way then the other. Dave's massive army of supporters got right behind him from the start, and he gave them a wonderful run for their money. Not wanting to waste a second, he was off his stool and across the ring before the bell for most rounds.

In what quickly developed into a real world championship encounter, the two men landed and took punches quite evenly during the first four rounds. Green tried to crowd the champion from the opening bell, but was beaten at his own game. Palomino threw fast accurate combinations as if to serve notice on the challenger of the task he faced.

Although Carlos was expected to be the better of the two at long range, it was Green who had the more effective jab. Three straight lefts followed by a heavy right cross gave him a share of a tense opening round which started badly for him.

Right from the start, neither man had to go looking for the other. When Green strode forward at the start of round two, the champion met him. A head-on confrontation quickly developed as both were prepared to take a few shots to land their own. Dave's jab continued to be the better single punch, although when Palomino was under pressure he replied with solid straight shots from both hands.

When both took good shots without flinching early in round three, it was an indication that it was likely to be a long hard fight. "Over the top David," yelled Andy Smith perched on the ring steps as the action hotted up. Green instantly

162

responded to the manager's call, and the infamous 'muck-spreader' found it's target.

Despite his dark, swarthy film-star looks, Palomino was made of stern stuff. He took the punch well, remained composed, and hit back viciously to briefly force Dave to the ropes.

The toe-to-toe combat continued throughout the fourth, with advantage swinging one way and then the other. Green's opening attack was so sustained that midway through the round there were signs that he was getting on top. After taking everything thrown at him, however, the champion hit back. Two left hooks appeared to unsteady Dave, but not for long. By the end of the round he was attacking again with all the ferocity he could muster.

The crowd roared with excitement as sweeping left and rights put Palomino under severe pressure, and stiff left jabs had him blinking. This was Green at his best as he exploded punches to head and body. Like the good champion he was, Carlos took the punches well, and at the bell was hitting back with a vengeance.

Fortunes swayed again in round five in which Palomino looked to be taking over. As Dave attacked, he steadied him with stiff counter-punches. Standing erect, the champion boxed superbly, scoring with uppercuts and flashing right crosses. Green's rhythm was broken, and by the end of the round there were signs of puffiness around his left eyebrow, testimony of the accuracy of Palomino's shots.

Green still tried to push forward in the sixth, but found Carlos a class act. Two quick rights to the chin shook the Chatteris man when he fell short with his own jabs. Again it was give and take, and Green responded magnificently with two good shots to the head. He dug deep, waded forward and drove the champion across the ring near the end of the round.

The British boxer stormed out for the seventh to have perhaps the best round of the fight, smashing punch after punch at Palomino. Although the champion hit back, Green kept up the pressure, forcing him to cover up and try to stay close.

The champion appeared disillusioned when Dave took a good right to the head without flinching, only to respond with an even better one. Realising Palomino was hurt, the Fenland supporters roared their man on as he poured in the punches. A dozen or so found the target, and at the bell the champion looked unsteady. "Beautiful," yelled Andy Smith as his man slumped on to his stool to be sponged down.

The eighth was another tremendous round in which fortunes swayed yet again. When Palomino landed hurtful shots to the body with both hands, Green looked to be wilting. Halfway through the round, he looked in serious trouble for the first time in the fight as heavy blows thudded into his midriff. Yet seconds later he literally hurled himself back into attack, and the champion was cut over his left eye.

Not for the first time, Dave displayed tremendous courage, fought his way out of a difficult situation and appeared to have turned it completely around. Suddenly, the title looked to be within his grasp.

Palomino looked extremely uncomfortable, and it was his turn to dig deep. A good body attack eventually made Green give ground. He bent almost double as hooks slammed into his ribs, and as he backed away the champion's cornermen screamed for him to "go to the body."

Dave looked vulnerable downstairs, but as Palomino continued the offensive, he momentarily dropped his guard. A right from Green crashed against his head. By the end of the round there was a lot of blood on the champion's face, and referee Jim Brimmell went to his corner during the interval to inspect the damage. Manager, Jackie McCoy, assured him that he had it under control.

Dave felt confident of victory, and when he returned to his corner told Andy Smith: "Guv'nor, I'll be world champion in another 20 minutes."

Within half a minute of the start of round nine, Palomino sustained a cut on the right eyelid. The sight of more blood spurred Green on, but the champion remained relaxed, and punched with great accuracy. Dave was forced to back up more and more, and his punches seemed to be less effective. Yet he continued to battle bravely, and one left jab followed by a right under the heart, stopped the champion in his tracks as he tried to set up another attack.

It had been anybody's fight for nine rounds during which both men had gone at a furious pace and appeared capable of maintaining it over the scheduled course. The turning point came, however, during the amazing 10th when Green, his left eye closing rapidly, suddenly appeared to be facing an uphill struggle. Yet Wembley erupted when he suddenly produced his best punch of the fight – a massive overarm right which caught Palomino flush on the chin and forced him to the ropes.

The champion was hurt, and his legs buckled when two more big shots crashed home. Suddenly Green looked on the verge of a dramatic victory. For more than a minute Carlos looked in real trouble, but then as Green rushed in looking to capitalise on his success, he showed what a great champion he was. Pulling himself together, he raised the pace and hit back fiercely. A dozen or more punches were on target, and Dave was forced to give ground. After a clash of heads just before the bell, he reeled away with his left eye almost closed.

Green was still in there as they came out for round 11, but was virtually fighting with one eye. The side of his face was also badly swollen. Although blood still leaked from his eye injuries, Palomino looked ominously fresh and wasted no time going about his job. His greater ring maturity and cool head proved decisive, and his incessant jabbing closed Dave's eye completely.

Severely handicapped, Green began to look clumsy, and midway through the round the champion's class asserted itself. He cut loose, and as Dave retreated in the face of renewed pressure, a perfect left hook caught him flush on the chin. He crashed backwards, his head striking the floor with a sickening thud. Out cold, he lay flat on his back as referee Brimmell completed the count at two minutes five seconds of the round. It was the first time he had been floored as a professional.

Andy Smith immediately jumped into the ring and tugged the gumshield from the mouth of his stricken fighter as he lay quivering on the floor. Dave looked badly hurt, and Smith's own words of: "Green's prepared to die on the canvas," must have flashed through many people's minds.

There were anxious moments as the Chatteris fighter received attention from Board of Control Medical Officer, Dr Adrian Whiteson. The crowd were silent as he lay motionless. His own supporters were stunned, and many were crying while others felt sick in the stomach.

Eventually, after what seemed an eternity, Dave regained his senses and was lifted to his stool. Even then it was several minutes before everyone knew he was okay. The Board of Control doctor later revealed that he was suffering from a whiplash injury which left a large egg-sized lump at the back of his head.

There was relief all around the Empire Pool, and when the Fenland fans regained their composure, they accepted that their hero had done them proud. He proved that he had the biggest heart in British boxing, and was prepared to walk through extreme pain and endurance to achieve his goal. Sadly, it was not to be.

Once he had recovered, Green showed wonderful sportsmanship by walking across the ring to congratulate Palomino. Seconds later he applauded vigorously as the champion was presented with the world championship trophy. Anxious to thank the crowd for their support, he then strolled around the ring clapping his hands and shaking his fist defiantly, assuring them he had fully recovered.

Dave deserved the wonderful applause he received because although he was beaten, he produced one of the greatest world title challenges ever by a British boxer. Old-timers at ringside recalled Tommy Farr's courageous bid to beat Joe Louis in 1937, and more recently, Chris Finnegan's brave challenge against Bob Foster. Green, however, surpassed the efforts of those two gallant fighters because right up until the dramatic finish, he was in with a genuine chance of victory.

Fighting with typical ferocity throughout, he landed viciously to the body, and constantly connected with his crude, but effective 'muck-spreader'. Although Palomino's punches were accurate and solid, he never batted an eyelid. From the very first bell, he waded forward throwing punches in the way to which he was accustomed. Despite often being outboxed, he had fabulous moments in the fight, displaying immense courage and strength to launch wave after wave of attacks.

The fight had everything – entertainment and action from beginning to end, a change in fortunes within a short space of time, and the dramatic sudden and conclusive one-punch finish. There was never a moment when Palomino could afford to relax, yet he proved to be a magnificent champion. He had class, stayed cool under pressure, and was technically in a different league to the Briton. He never budged an inch when the going got really tough, and even the army of Fenland supporters could not begrudge him victory.

Dave was devastated at the outcome of the fight, and it was easy to understand his heartbreak and frustration as he hammered on his dressing-room wall with both fists once the reality set in. "I'm sorry Mr Smith," he sobbed. "I wanted to win it for you."

The fight would become headline news the next day, and the dressing-room was soon packed with reporters anxious to note the minutest comment. Armed with tape-recorders and notepads, they rapidly, but orderly, fired questions at the beaten hero and his manager.

"Did they count me out?" asked Green as he sat on a table feeling the effects of the fight.

"I thought I was ahead, but I didn't see the punch coming," he told them. "The next think I knew, I was getting up."

"With my eye closed, I was trying to move around all the time to see better," he continued. "But what a persistent fighter. He just keeps coming. I can see there's another Dave Green about. He was cut and I felt really good, really strong and relaxed. But he just got me before I got him."

Despite his gruelling battle, Dave was still extremely hyped up. He was angry and frustrated over the defeat, and with energy still to burn, he shadow-boxed in the dressing-room for several minutes. Although everyone watched, not a word was uttered.

Andy Smith was very disappointed, but full of praise for Palomino. "It was a beautiful punch," he remarked. "It was a punch either of them could have thrown, but at that stage you need good fortune."

Although it was a practice not to reveal referee's scores in Britain, James Brimmell indicated that Palomino was ahead. "I thought for a while that Green's strength might do it," he told Graham Houston of *Boxing News*, "but Palomino picked his punches better."

Smith thought Green was ahead, and whilst Houston had the champion two rounds in front, he stressed that the turning point came in round 10 when Dave's left eye began to close.

American manager and trainer, Gil Clancey had sympathy for Dave. "If Green's eye hadn't gone he would have won," he told reporters at ringside. "He had Palomino out on his feet. With the crowd right behind him the way they were, there was no way Green could have lost if it had gone into the 12th round or so."

Whilst the critics differed over who was in front and who might have won, they were united over the fact that it had been a marvellous contest. In *Boxing News*, Graham Houston wrote:

> Sometimes, to give everything is not enough. This it was with Dave Green whose bravery and do-or-die fighting failed to dethrone world welterweight champion, Carlos Palomino.
>
> A near capacity crowd saw Green contribute to one of the greatest fights seen in a British ring....

The fight was shown on BBC television the following evening, but could not accurately convey to viewers the magnificent atmosphere inside the Empire Pool. That will remain in the memories of those privileged to be there. The thousands of rowdy, but extremely well-behaved Green supporters chanted, whistled, cheered and sang. It was like a massive country carnival as hundreds paraded in farm worker attire.

"They were really great," said Dave recalling the event years later. "They were wonderful people, and really pulled behind me when I had him in trouble."

Later that evening, accompanied by wife Kay, Green returned to Cambridgeshire and stayed at Andy Smith's house at St Ives. As usual after a fight, he craved for a large portion of homemade apple pie and ice cream. Ever since turning professional, it was the first thing he looked for whenever he got home, and Kay always made sure that an adequate sized luxury awaited him. What he didn't eat in the middle of the night was quickly devoured the next day.

Despite the exertions of the strenuous battle with Palomino, Dave and his manager sat up until after 3am going over events and clearing their heads. They relived every round, recalled the highs and lows, and even dared consider the probabilities. Both were convinced that had Dave's head not crashed against the canvas, he would have beaten the count and still been in with a chance of victory.

Green suffered no lasting effects from the dramatic defeat, and despite his disappointment, insisted that he wanted a return with Palomino as soon as possible. In the meantime, he needed a good night's sleep because in a few hours time the people of Chatteris planned to welcome him home in style.

✦ 11 ✦

WELCOME HOME

Green and Palomino spent the day after their incredible fight in vastly contrasting ways. Although both showed the scars of battle, Dave's swollen eye and cheek would heal naturally within a few days. Palomino, however, required specialist treatment for his injuries. With 13 stitches in three wounds around his eyes – six in one above the right and seven in two others over his left, he flew from Heathrow airport to Westminster, California later that day.

Talking to reporters over breakfast before leaving their hotel, the champion and his manager, Jackie McCoy, were full of praise for Green. Admitting that it was not the type of fight a manager liked to see his fighters in, McCoy said: "Green is a heck of a fighter and very effective in his own way. He is not orthodox, but he is very good, and gave my boy a hard time."

Nodding in agreement, Palomino said: "Dave Green is very strong and made it difficult for me. I tried to stop him with a left hook all the time, but mostly he managed to dodge it."

"It was one of my toughest fights," he added, "but when I noticed his eye had closed in the 10th, I started to pressure him and it paid off. It was a little too close for comfort, so I am glad it ended the way it did."

There had been emotional moments in the champion's

dressing-room after the fight as he told reporters how, at the end of round nine, he thought about what losing would mean to him. "I'd be unable to buy the ranch I want for my father, or fulfil all the plans I have for my son," he explained. "I told myself I would die before I let this title go."

At Chatteris, hundreds of people gathered outside Cromwell Community College to greet Dave when he arrived for a civic reception. Dark glasses covering the damage to his left eye, he showed clear disappointment at not returning home as world champion.

"Thank you for turning up," he said with a smile, but a touch of emotion in his voice. "For a loser, that's not bad, but I am very sorry I did not bring the title back."

If Dave thought he had let people down, nobody agreed with him, and his remarks were greeted with a spontaneous outburst of *"For he's a jolly good fellow."*

Miss Hilda Clarke, chairman of Chatteris Parish Council summed up the general feeling in the town. Addressing the gathering, she said: "I am sure you will all have felt disappointment for David, but we are still as proud of him as ever. As always, he gave his all."

Presenting Dave with a silver plated tea-caddy, Miss Clarke said: "He was loyal to his town, always ready to give his support as he did in the Jubilee, even during his training. All that matters now is that he is okay and not too badly hurt."

Being a celebrity in the town, Dave had attended and supported a number of local events during the build-up to the Jubilee, and made presentations whenever called upon. Even when in strict training, he still made himself available, and that support would continue throughout the year. He also showed his generosity by putting £25 into a bank account for a baby, Victoria Alexander, who was born over Jubilee weekend. It was his response to a gift of £2 he received from the Chatteris people when he was born on Coronation Day 24 years earlier.

Accompanied on the stage by Kay and Andy Smith, Dave was visibly moved as the speeches of praise and consolation continued. Chairman of his supporters club, Alec Dawson, drew massive applause when he said: "He is a credit to his family, his town, his country, to all of us. What more can we say?"

Alec had known Green a long time, having first seen him many years earlier when he stopped by King Edward School playing field to watch some young boys playing football. One lad who was much smaller than all the others, stood out as he quickly darted up the pitch skilfully beating much bigger players. It was his first glimpse of Dave Green.

After the reception, Dave was pursued by a posse of excited young fans as he left for a luncheon with members of the Parish Council, his family and close friends. That evening, he was guest of honour at a hurriedly arranged disco at The Palace.

Every effort was made to ensure the day was special. Although Jubilee bunting still decorated the streets of Chatteris, there were also other banners bearing the words "DAVE'S A KNOCK-OUT" and "GREEN SPELLS DANGER." These had been made by children at Cromwell School especially for the occasion.

Before attending the civic reception Dave had toured the town in a plush motor car loaned by wealthy local farmer, Arthur Munns. As the vehicle had a sun-roof, he was able to stand on the front seat and wave to his adoring fans along the route. It may not have been the procession of triumph everyone had hoped for, but despite cold weather people still gathered in doorways and on street corners to cheer him as he passed by.

In what would have been a wonderful achievement, Supporters Club committee member, John Salisbury, attempted to get Carlos Palomino to attend the civic reception. He telephoned the champion at his London hotel, and offered to send his Rolls Royce to collect him. Carlos said he would be privileged to attend, but explained that because his injuries were serious, he had already made arrangements to return to America that afternoon.

"I would liked to have shown him Fenland hospitality,"

John told a local newspaper reporter. "He is a thorough gentleman, and a homely sort of guy."

Green's popularity was incredible, and that weekend a barbecue was held at Whitworth Sports & Social Club, Chatteris. Two months earlier, members of the Supporters Club committee held a meeting and decided that irrespective of the outcome of the fight, an event should be staged to celebrate him fighting for the world championship.

It was massively successful, and although more than 600 people were in attendance, the organisers were convinced that had the venue been big enough they could have sold twice that number of tickets. The well-known Johnny Howard band were engaged to provide music for dancing, and Dave Green rosettes manufactured by a company at Norwich were given to everyone attending.

During the evening, Alec Dawson presented Dave with a silver tray and nine silver goblets. Andy Smith thanked everyone for attending, and for the unbelievable support they had received from the Fens. "I have been in boxing for 30 years, but have never seen people get behind a local boy like they do you," he remarked. "A lot of the success is because of that support."

The event required tremendous dedication and determination, but there were plenty of volunteers. An advantage to the committee was that members, John Salisbury and Greg Feast, had lorries available from their businesses. These were used to transport extra chairs and tables from the Working Mens Club, Church Hall and Boxing Club to the venue. There was no need to employ anybody or hire anything. It was all free of charge.

The Supporters Club Committee had organised a number of previous events since formation in 1976. On 4 June that year, 'The Dave Green Appreciation Dance' was held following his victory over Joey Singleton, and a homecoming party staged at The Palace following his defeat of Jean-Baptiste Piedvache.

Formation of the committee originated from a friendship forged over several years between Green and Gordon Palmer, a local man who worked as a insurance agent. He first knew Dave as a small boy, basically because in a small town like Chatteris everybody knew everyone else.

The friendship between the two developed when Dave was about 16, and Gordon read about his boxing successes in the *Chatteris Advertiser.* He collected insurance money from clients on a weekly basis by calling door-to-door, and quite often when he went along Tithe Road, Green stood at his front door with a copy of the paper. "Come and look at this Mr Palmer," he said, "I'm in it this week – go on, read it."

Warmed by his enthusiasm, Gordon read every word whenever Dave thrust a story at him. He showed genuine interest in the likeable youngster, and had many chats with him as his boxing career developed over the next few years.

One evening, Green called at Gordon's house at York Road and asked: "Would you like to come and watch me Mr Palmer – I'm boxing tonight." Because his work often involved evening calls, Gordon had to decline, much to Dave's disappointment. This happened on several occasions over a 12-18 month period, and although he hated letting the lad down, he needed more notice.

Dave never gave up, and Palmer eventually watched him box for Eastern Counties against Home Counties in the ABA zone finals at Luton in March 1974. Green had called on him the previous evening, and finding himself free from work commitments, Gordon telephoned his close friend, John Salisbury, who agreed to accompany him.

Both were impressed by Dave's workmanlike performance as he outpointed Mickey Ryce of Abingdon in a great contest at the Vauxhall Motors Club. Within four weeks he had progressed to the ABA semi-finals at Hull, so Palmer and Salisbury went around Chatteris telling people how good the local lad was. They, together with Philip Wool, who worked as a lorry driver for John, travelled to Hull to support Dave, and also went to Belle View, Manchester, for his fight with Terry Waller.

The Supporters Club started soon after Green turned

professional. More and more interest developed in Chatteris, and he often asked Gordon Palmer if he would help him sell tickets. Posters advertising Dave's fights were displayed in local shop windows giving Gordon's telephone number.

Between 15 and 20 tickets were sold for each of his early professional contests, but the numbers accelerated rapidly as he progressed. For each fight, Andy Smith ordered a quantity of tickets from the promoter, passed some to Green, who in turn handed them to Gordon. In order that sufficient quantities could be ordered, he and his wife Celia, gradually built up a list of those people wanting tickets for Dave's fights. They came from all walks of life, and for the contests with Alan Salter and Billy Waith, sales reached almost 200.

Once the fight with Joey Singleton was announced, the demand became even greater. Palmer had by this stage become heavily involved, but found the situation too much for him to handle alone. Apart from selling tickets, he had also started to organise a 'Dave Green Appreciation Dance' to be held at Cromwell College on Friday 4 June 1976, three days after the Singleton fight.

After discussions with Alec Dawson and other interested parties in the town, it was agreed that a Supporters Club Committee should be formed. The first meeting was held at Craven's Garage, Huntingdon Road, Chatteris, on 10 May 1976, and officers duly elected. Dawson was appointed Chairman, Palmer agreed to the role of Secretary, with Dennis Hall as Treasurer. Other committee members were Philip Wool, Greg Feast, son of Dave's employer, Jimmy Allen, a builder, and Dave's father, Ken Green, to maintain close liaison between boxer and committee.

Although Alec Dawson had seen Green as a talented young footballer, his interest in him as a boxer began the night he went to Luton with Gordon Palmer. "Even then, he had that killer determination," recalled Alec. "I think he would die rather than lose."

Dave's victory over Joey Singleton ensured that the 'Appreciation Dance' was a huge success. With tickets priced at £3, all expenses were covered. There was a grand buffet, music by the George Kay band, and the committee agreed that any funds left over would be donated to Chatteris Amateur Boxing Club.

Gordon Palmer met Dave on a regular basis to discuss fights and proposed events. Following the victory over Piedvache, more than 200 people attended a 'Homecoming Party' at The Palace on 13 December 1976. There was dancing to the Carl Roper band, a buffet, and St Raphael's, a charity organisation which supplied wheelchairs for the disabled, were invited to conduct a raffle to raise funds for their work. The charity were also involved at the barbecue after the Palomino fight, and received a donation from the proceeds.

Events organised by the Supporters Club were given massive publicity, particularly by local newspapers. Dave was incredibly popular, and whatever he did was good for a story. He was what the public loved – a local boy who had grown from humble surroundings to become a national hero.

Yet with Green it was not just about success. He was extremely likeable, which went a long way to explaining his popularity. That high regard led to the setting up of the Supporters Club Committee, and as it developed everyone got great pleasure from being involved. They were proud to do what they could for a local champion.

Fame did not change Dave one iota. At functions organised in his honour, he circulated with his fans, neighbours and folk he had grown up with. He was still one of them, and if anything, became slightly embarrassed by all the attention he received.

Alec Dawson always believed that memories of Eric Boon kept the interest in boxing alive in Chatteris. It flared again to massive proportions as Green went from success to success. By the time he faced Palomino, he had thousands of fans in the Fens alone, and the 600 tickets for his celebration barbecue sold out within days. The fact that he lost made no difference whatsoever – everyone still turned up to see him.

* * *

Dave quickly overcame the disappointment of his defeat to Palomino, and within a few days returned to work at the carrot farm at Southery. Although Andy Smith told him to take a well-earned break and forget about fighting again until September, he was back in the gym within a week. He had only one thing on his mind – a return with the world champion. "I thought the longer I left it, the harder it would be to get back," he remarked.

Meanwhile, offers of fights were received from all over the world because Green's exciting style was a certain winner at any box-office. There was even talk of a re-match with John H. Stracey in London later that year.

Andy Smith, however, was an extremely astute man who would only act in his boxer's best interests. Dave was at the top of his game with massive earning potential, particularly at international level. After considering all the options Smith advised the boxer to relinquish the European light-welterweight title in order that he could concentrate on working towards a return with Palomino.

Whilst the British Boxing Board of Control were more lenient, the EBU had given him a deadline of 16 July to defend the European title against Primo Bandini of Italy which was an impossibility. There was nothing sinister in the demand because it had long been the practice of the European body to require champions to defend their laurels every three months.

Although it was generally thought that Dave could beat any man in Europe at his weight, Smith decided it was more professional to relinquish the title than have it taken away. Green was a genuine world class fighter, and European title defences were unlikely to progress him at that level.

Smith was, nevertheless, far from happy with the general situation. "The EBU are the most bloody unco-operative people in the world," he told the press. "All they want are Italian and Spanish champions – they did the same with Joe

Bugner. The deadline was just ridiculous and I told them so. By relinquishing the title and not being stripped of it, David now automatically becomes number one contender."

"It is not in David's interest to take second-best contests," Smith continued. "At this stage it is vitally important that the decision who he boxes is mine. It is to our advantage that he should be unhampered by titles."

It was not until mid-August, however, that Green relinquished the British title. On doing so, the Board of Control immediately nominated his stable-mate, Des Morrison, to meet Colin Powers for the vacant title.

Dave's success and popularity brought invitations to attend prestigious events all over the country. In July, in the company of Andy Smith, his wife Valerie, and Jimmy Harrington, he travelled to Newcastle where they were guests at a four-day event aimed at raising £70,000 for the National Association of Boys Clubs at Tyne & Wear. The principle attraction was Muhammed Ali, but invitations were also extended to top British boxers, past and present, to join the world heavyweight champion at a number of special events including a Parade of Champions.

Although they stayed at the same hotel as Ali and his entourage, Smith still kept Dave on a tight rein. Boxing remained his business, and it was hoped that he would be back in action during the autumn. He therefore went to bed early each evening, and along with Harrington, did his roadwork in the mornings around the streets of Newcastle.

The Parade of Champions was staged in the Mayfair Ballroom, and despite the high price of tickets, drew a huge crowd of boxing enthusiasts. The event included a seven-course banquet, and cabaret starring Frankie Vaughan with supporting acts. Other boxers present included Terry Spinks, Bobby Neill, Chris and Kevin Finnegan, Richard Dunn, Alan Rudkin, Terry Downes, John Conteh, Howard Winstone, Vic Andreetti and Vernon Sollas.

During the evening, Ali and his party, which included wife Veronica and their baby daughter, Hanna, sat at a massive table on the stage. He delighted the audience with his familiar act of shadow-boxing and dancing, entwined with frequent shouts of *"I am the greatest."*

The following day the boxing personalities joined Ali aboard an open-top bus for a ride to South Shields. The trip had been well publicised, and the cheering crowds that lined streets along the route were five and six deep. The turnout was much greater than two weeks earlier when the Queen visited the City with American President, Jimmy Carter.

"Ali must have been the best known man in the world at the time" said Dave fondly recalling the event. "He was a fantastic speaker, and we all had an incredible time."

After a civic reception at the Town Hall, the party returned to Newcastle for the Muhammed Ali Talk-in hosted by Reg Gutteridge. During the evening the boxers attended an event at Washington Sports Centre where a crowd of more than 1,500 watched Ali box a series of exhibition bouts in aid of charity. Supporting contests included Green against Harrington, Spinks v Neill, and Kevin Finnegan v Albert Hillman.

On the Sunday morning Ali and wife Veronica attended a mosque at South Shields to have their recent marriage blessed at a special muslim ceremony. Because of Andy Smith's involvement with Joe Bugner, Dave was one of the few guests boxers to receive an invitation to attend. Whilst it was a completely new experience to him, he attended out of respect for Ali.

The following month, Dave was one of many boxing personalities to attend a grand reception and dinner at the Grosvenor House Hotel at London's Park Lane to honour Ali. Andy Smith and Eric Boon were also guests.

Despite the Board of Control requesting him not to, Green also acted as referee during an exhibition arranged by Smith at Birmingham between Ali and his sparring partner, Jimmy Ellis. Afterwards they went to Ali's suite which was guarded by two large minders. Suddenly, a boy aged about 13 walked in and said: "Please Mr Ali, can I have your autograph?"

"How did you get in here?" asked Ali.

179

"I just walked through the door," replied the boy.

"You must be some kind of kid to get into this place," said Ali who had been wearing a robe with his name emblazoned across the back. Without further ado, he signed it beneath the name and gave it to the boy in front of everyone.

It was an incident which stuck in Dave's mind because of the attitude shown by the best known fighter in the world. "It was typical of Ali," he remarked, "and showed what a warm human being he could be."

✦ 12 ✦

BACK TO WINNING WAYS

During late August 1977, Andy Smith told Green he believed he had found the right opponent for his return to the ring. Andy 'Hawk' Price had outpointed Carlos Palomino over 10 rounds at San Diego in August 1974. He had also beaten Pipino Cuevas on points just six weeks before he won the WBA title in 1976.

Harry Levene had a verbal agreement with Palomino and manager, Jackie McCoy, for a return with Green early in 1978, provided Dave kept winning. Consequently, a great deal of thought went into selecting his next opponent.

Green was at the crossroads of his career, and his connections knew he had to have a fight of status, not only to satisfy his mind, but also that of the public. It was important, therefore, that he faced, and beat, somebody of world class. During lengthy discussions between Smith, Levene, and matchmaker, Mickey Duff, a short-list was drawn up. It contained good quality fighters including Price, former world champion Billy Backus, and Jorgen Hansen.

Once Price had been selected, agreement was quickly reached between parties. Billed as a world championship eliminator, the fight was set to take place at Wembley on 27 September over 10 rounds at 10st 7. The St Ives camp were determined there should be no slip-ups, and paid £85 for a film of Price in action to be flown from America.

"Price will be a very, very difficult man to beat," said Smith. "He is an opponent who will create interest, and give Dave satisfaction in fighting."

Some critics believed Price was the wrong type of opponent for Green because they doubted if he would be the same after the Palomino defeat. Dave was under no illusions about the task he faced, but insisted on taking the fight to maintain his momentum at world level.

"I was at the top of my game, and all I wanted was a return with Palomino," he recalled. "To knock over some unknown Yank or continental in a couple of rounds would have proved nothing."

The 23-year-old Price was backed by a film syndicate headed by 'Bionic Man', Lee Majors, Burt Reynolds and James Caan. He was an educated man who had been a full-time professional since graduating in business studies at West Los Angeles College, California.

With a record of 27 wins and three draws from 34 contests, he had solid credentials. His only defeat in four fights during 1977 was on points to world-rated Harold Weston in June. He carried the nickname 'Hawk' in honour of his idol, Kid Gavilan, who was known as the 'Cuban Hawk'.

As usual, Dave was well supported by his faithful army of Fenland fans, and Wembley was packed for what promised to be a great night of boxing. Apart from Green, Kevin Finnegan, Maurice Hope and John L. Gardner all faced American opponents in 10 round contests.

Dave knew this was a fight he had to win to stay in the world rankings and hopefully secure another shot at Palomino. In the opening round, however, things did not look good as the flashy Price displayed dazzling footwork to match the patterns weaved by his crimson gloves.

Under orders to jab, Green was too static, and was repeatedly caught by the American's sharp, but relaxed punching. Left hooks whipped through his guard, and whenever he did attack, Price counter-punched with ease and accuracy.

It was a poor start for the Chatteris fighter, and there was more of the same early in round two as his face became reddened by a flurry of sharp hooks. A graze appeared on his left cheekbone, and he winced as the American scored with a good right uppercut.

EMPIRE POOL, WEMBLEY

TUESDAY, SEPTEMBER 27th, 1977

DOORS OPEN 7 p.m. COMMENCE 8 p.m.

HARRY LEVENE Presenter   **MICKEY DUFF** Matchmaker

THE GREATEST FIGHTING BILL EVER STAGED AT WEMBLEY

GREAT BRITAIN v U.S.A.

ELIMINATOR FOR THE WELTERWEIGHT CHAMPIONSHIP OF THE WORLD
(Awaiting W.B.C. approval)
10 (3 min.) Rounds at 10st. 7lbs.

Dave 'Boy' GREEN v Andy 'Hawk' PRICE

(Chatteris). Contender for the World Title. Britain's most exciting fighter

(California, U.S.A.). Contender for World Title. Defeated W.B.C. Champion Carlos Palomino and W.B.A. Champion Pipino Cuevas

10 (3 min.) Rounds International Light-Middleweight Contest at 11st. 2lbs.

MAURICE HOPE v TONY LOPES

(Hackney). Light-Middleweight Champion of Europe. Uncrowned World Champion!

(Brockton, Mass., U.S.A.). New England Champion. Winner of 20 out of 25 contests

10 (3 min.) Rounds International Middleweight Contest at 11st. 8lbs.

Kevin FINNEGAN v Karl VINSON

(Iver). Middleweight Champion of Great Britain. Europe's finest boxer

(California, U.S.A.). Known as "The Middleweight Joe Frazier". Lost only 5 of 28 contests

10 (3 min.) Rounds International Heavyweight Contest

JOHN L. GARDNER v DALE 'SAILOR' ARRINGTON

(Hackney). Undefeated in 24 contests. Now challenging for British and European Titles

(Seattle, U.S.A.). Winner of 20 of 23 contests. Has defeated Pat Duncan, Joe Roman, Terry Daniels

10 or 8 (3 min.) Rounds Lightweight Contest at 9st. 9lbs.
Awaiting reply to offer of £5,000 Challenge to

CORNELIUS BOZA-EDWARDS v CHARLIE NASH

(Harrow). World's outstanding light-weight prospect

If not accepted, Edwards will meet a leading E.E.C. opponent

Prices (inc. VAT): £3.50, £6.50, £8.50, £12.50. Ringside £15.50

To HARRY LEVENE   87 WARDOUR STREET. W.1 (01-437 2304)

Please reserve .... seats at .... Empire Pool, Wembley, on Tuesday, September 27th, 1977. Please enclose stamped, addressed envelope for reply. Cheque/Postal Order herewith. TOTAL VALUE

£   :   p.

M ....

Poster advertising fight between Green and Andy Price

Suddenly, Green reverted to his more familiar snarling agricultural style. Wading forward, he banged away heavily to the body, and pinned Price against the ropes for long periods. Although the clever American slipped, parried and blocked many of the shots, plenty more got through to give Dave at least a share of the round.

Boxing intelligently, he stayed on top throughout the third and most of the fourth. Cleverly cutting down the ring space, he worked his slippery opponent along the ropes and into corners where he thumped him heavily about the body. An occasional 'muck-spreader' found the target, although many others finished behind the neck.

Price was looking decidedly unhappy and disorganised, but when a cut appeared beneath Dave's left eye midway through round four, he regained his enthusiasm. He attacked fiercely, throwing uppercuts, hooks and body punches as he chased Green across the ring. From looking a certain winner, the Chatteris man was suddenly in dire trouble, and very relieved to hear the sound of the bell.

The big effort took a lot out of Price, and he allowed Green to get back on top in the fifth with solid accurate jabbing. The sixth was also a good round for Dave as his heavy body punching had the American looking flat-footed and in some pain.

The seventh was a tremendous round in which fortunes fluctuated. Once again, Price appeared on the verge of defeat, but pulled himself together to set up a blazing counter-attack. Green met him halfway, and the crowd roared with excitement as they stood toe-to-toe trading heavy punches throughout the final 30 seconds of the round.

Although his cut cheek had become considerably worse, Green's aggression was the telling factor during the early part of the eighth. Yet as the round wore on he appeared to tire, and there were concerns that his earlier work-rate may have taken its toll.

The fight again swung dramatically in round nine when Green was in terrible trouble as Price hammered him with explosive hooks and uppercuts. Dave reeled about the ring under intense pressure, but somehow managed to stay upright.

Andy Smith frantically yelled for him to hold on as Price unleashed wave after wave of vicious shots. Green wobbled badly, and was close to defeat as big punches continued to find the target. Referee, Sid Nathan, watched closely, and must have contemplated stepping in.

Green, however, showed untameable spirit and sheer guts to hang in there, and by the end of the round was punching back. Although the sound of the bell was a huge relief, he raised his arms in a defiant salute as he walked to the corner. He showed incredible durability in a round where he absorbed more punishment than anything inflicted by Palomino.

Going into the final round, ringsiders and newsmen were divided as to who was in front. It was extremely close, but using his tremendous powers of recuperation, Dave showed real fighting heart and gave it everything he had. His aggression throughout the session, and Price's failure to hold him off, swung it in his favour. At the final bell, Sid Nathan walked straight to him and raised his arm. The score of 96-95 indicated Green had won by five rounds to four with one even.

Sheer guts and determination propelled Dave to a magnificent victory much to the delight of the packed house. Writing in the *Daily Mail*, veteran boxing correspondent, Peter Moss said:

> I have seldom heard such a sustained applause during a match at Wembley, certainly never in a non-title fight.

When considering the terrible knockout Dave suffered at the hands of Palomino three months earlier, it was an incredible triumph. Many fans thought it was, in fact, his best ever performance. Matchmaker, Mickey Duff, said it was even better than his performance against Palomino.

A genuine world class opponent, Price proved strong and elusive, and the Green of old would probably have become frustrated at not being able to knock him over. By this stage, however, he was a much more mature fighter who stuck to his task by using the left jab brilliantly. He constantly forced the American to retreat, and despite some desperate moments, generally denied him room to work to the full.

Dave didn't emerge from the fight unscathed. He had damage around both eyes, and three stitches were inserted in the gash on his left cheek which was also badly swollen.

Paying tribute to his opponent, Green said: "He was very clever – I would have to say that as far as classical boxing goes, he was more difficult than Palomino."

Andy Smith agreed. "He was a counter-puncher of the highest calibre, and more difficult to hit than Palomino," he remarked. "Dave needed a win over a quality opponent, and he achieved it."

One reporter asked Green if he had been concerned about returning to the ring after losing his unbeaten record by a knockout. "No, not a bit," he replied. "The way I figured it, there was nothing in it with Palomino for 10 rounds – then the lights went out."

"I learned from Palomino," he continued. "When I got cut this time, I didn't go mad – I just stuck to what I was doing because I always knew I could win."

Not all the critics agreed with Sid Nathan's decision, and as always with a close fight, there was discontent in the loser's camp. Price's trainer, Walter Tyler, was convinced his man had done enough. "Anywhere else in the world we'd have got it," he moaned, "but when there's just one point in it in the other guy's home town, you can't expect favours."

"Andy needed just one more punch to finish Green in the ninth, but couldn't find it," he continued. "He was never in any kind of trouble, and he's unmarked. Go look at Green."

Dave was absolutely exhausted after the fight, and Andy Smith told the press that he would not box again until the New Year. "He needs a really good rest," he insisted. "Two fights like that in the space of three months is enough for any man."

Victory over Price kept Dave well up in the world rankings. Only Pete Ranzany, Wilfredo Benitez, Angel Espada and Harold Weston separated him from world champions, Carlos Palomino (WBC) and Jose 'Pipino' Cuevas (WBA). The EBU installed him as the number one challenger to new European champion, Jorg Eipel of Germany, whilst at home he was the leading contender to welterweight champion, Henry Rhiney.

* * *

Although Dave enjoyed his well-earned rest, there was still plenty of talk about a possible return fight with Carlos Palomino. The stumbling block however, was American television. They would have to become involved because without world-wide coverage it would be virtually impossible to raise the sizeable purse needed to tempt the champion to meet Green again. For their first contest, it was reported that Carlos received £93,000, but would demand considerably more for a return.

Although the fight in June was televised, it was not shown in Britain until the following evening. American viewers had to wait 14 days to see an edited version, yet by November the World Boxing Council had named it 'Fight of the Year'.

Andy Smith saw this as a carrot to dangle because he knew Harry Levene could not afford to bring Palomino back to England. "The only source of revenue not exploited last time was American TV," Andy told local reporter, Pat Ringham. "If they buy the fight it will be worth a lot of money."

Smith dismissed suggestions of a return in London in March 1978 as speculative. "It would be an easy job to take Dave to Los Angeles, but I want Palomino to come to Wembley," he remarked. "As I have said before, money is the problem."

By the end of 1977, Palomino was well established as WBC champion, and could afford to dictate the terms. Since beating Green, he had successfully defended his title on two occasions, both in Los Angeles. In September, he outpointed Everaldo Costa Azevedo, and three months later knocked out Jose Palacios in 13 rounds. He was already lined up to make his fifth defence against Ryu Sorimachi of Japan at Las Vegas in February 1978. All were well below Green in the world rankings, and regarded as relatively safe fights for the champion who was being exceptionally well paid.

187

In less than two years, Carlos had become probably the biggest welterweight money-spinner in boxing history, yet Green, who remained the greatest attraction in British boxing, came so close to beating him. With a little bit of luck it could have been him and not the Mexican who banked those huge TV cheques.

Meanwhile, Dave's carrot-packing days were over. His overalls and a fork-lift truck were replaced by pin-striped suits and a high-performance company car as a smart sales-manager with Tony Powell Sportswear.

The company, situated at the Honeysome Road Industrial Estate, Chatteris, was started by Tony Powell in May 1975, and founded on the manufacture and sale of football shirts and track-suits, but expanded into skateboard outfits. Branches at Sutton, Warboys and Wisbech were closed at Christmas 1977 in order to concentrate business from the Chatteris premises.

The opportunity was created for Dave by Andy Smith who was already a Director of the company. He first became involved when he placed an order for the infamous Fen Tiger T-shirts prior to the Joey Singleton fight. With the company being local, and offering considerable potential, he became a Director and shareholder when the Chatteris premises were expanded in January 1977.

A cocktail reception marked the opening of new premises where more than 60 women were to be employed. Visitors, who included representatives of Cambridgeshire County Council, were shown around and given demonstrations in the modern stencil and printing rooms. Green and Smith joined them, and there was speculation that Dave was to become involved in the business. Exactly one year later that speculation became reality.

An engineering consultant by trade, Smith was an exceptionally good businessman. He was also a Director of Andy Smith Enterprises Limited, an engineering company, and set up Aqua Sports, a prominent fishing and leisure interest at Chatteris Marina.

With an eye to the future, Andy was determined that when

Dave left boxing he would have another career to turn to. He therefore created the opportunity for him within Tony Powell Sports, but would not allow him to risk investing his own money. Instead, he became involved in the development of the new factory.

The move attracted the attention of local newspaper reporters who contacted Smith. "David is the type who will be successful in a business venture," he told them. "I am sure it will give him something to do and enable him to build himself a future outside boxing."

Dave learned his new trade by leaving home at 7am, and even swept the factory floors and helped with the packing. As with everything he did, he put in maximum effort from day one.

He travelled a lot, particularly to London, and the long-term plan was for him to eventually have his own branch. Although boxing remained his main trade, the press continued to show keen interest in his business development. "David Green is a damned good salesman as well as being a super-honest kid," Tony Powell told them. "It is a bonus that he is so well known. He is our insurance policy because he never really has to go looking for business."

* * *

Meanwhile, *Boxing News* made Green's fight with Palomino it's Fight of the Year. Dave was also ranked number three in the publication's top ten boxers of 1977. Editor, Harry Mullen, wrote:

> He was the champion crowd-pleaser of 1977, and is one of only a handful of British pros who could fill a major venue. He might have been placed higher had his win over Price been more decisive.

Although the fight with Andy Price was stirring stuff for the fans, it was also physically demanding. By taking Green out of circulation for a while, Andy Smith again showed that he was more than just a manager to him. He was caring and compassionate, and refused to succumb to Dave's repeated requests for a fight. A manager of lesser morals would have cashed in on his popularity and had him back in action by November or December.

Dave, however, did not remain idle. During his spell out of the ring, he kept in condition by working out in the gym and doing his roadwork. By the New Year, he was fresh and desperate to get back into action. "I love training," he remarked one evening in the gym, "but what drives me through it is the thought that I must be 110 per cent fit for every fight. I never want to lose because I am not fit."

He went on to describe how he was often accompanied on his early morning runs by another local lad who wanted to get himself into shape. "He's coming on a bit now, but I'll never let him beat me," he remarked. "If he gets close to my shoulder, I have to go a bit harder."

"I always wanted to be active," he recalled years later, "but when you are fighting blokes like Palomino, Stracey and Price, you can't expect fights every month. I soon got to realise Mr Smith had my best interests at heart."

The period of inactivity also gave Smith the opportunity to reflect on certain aspects of Green's style. Dave had always been a naturally aggressive fighter, but since turning professional he had gradually developed good boxing skills, particularly with the left jab. Having reached the top level of the sport, Smith knew that further changes were needed if he were to beat fighters of Palomino's calibre. Over the ensuing months he therefore tried to convince Dave of the need to adopt a 'preservation period', particularly during a 15 round contest.

Smith was convinced that had the fight with Palomino been over 10 rounds, Green would have won. "Dave tends to start off in third gear, then change to top," said Andy. "I am trying to instil into him the need to go up through the gears."

It was a delicate balancing act because the last thing Andy wanted to do was curtail Dave's aggression. After a period of

190

concerted effort, however, the manager felt real progress had been made and that Dave was exercising more control.

"He's maturing and beginning to sort out his punches before he throws them," said Smith when local reporters made one of their frequent visits to the St Ives gym. "You can't compare the Green of today with the Green who stopped Billy Waith, or even the Green who stopped Stracey. He's improved so much since the fights with Palomino and Price."

Despite the work they were putting in, Dave was utterly frustrated at not having had a fight for over four months. By the end of January 1978, however, Smith felt he was ready to return. "He's been on my back for months," he remarked. "Only the Christmas and New Year holidays allowed me to stave him off for a few weeks."

"He's like a terrier who fights an alsatian one day, gets bitten and still goes back the next day," continued the manager. "That's why he wants Palomino so badly again."

After discussions between Smith, Mickey Duff, Mike Barrett and Harry Levene, two fights were lined up for Green within the space of a fortnight. In the first, he was due to top the bill at the Royal Albert Hall on 21 February in a 10-rounder against Hipolito 'Zovak' Barajas of Mexico. Two weeks later it was planned that he would face Canadian, Clyde Gray, over 15 rounds at Wembley for the Commonwealth welterweight title.

It was an ambitious programme, but Andy Smith stressed that he only agreed to the Gray fight on the understanding that he was satisfied with the outcome of the contest with Barajas which was made at 10st 10.

Less than a week before the fight, Barajas pulled out with an injured hand. He was replaced by Roy Johnson, from Bermuda, but boxing out of Philadelphia. He had a record of eight wins and three draws from 14 contests, which caused some critics to question his suitability. A Board of Control spokesman, however, was quoted as saying that Johnson was considered a suitable opponent to enable Green to ease back.

At a press conference a few days before the fight, Andy Smith denied that Green's popularity had waned during his period of inactivity. "He has sold £9,000 worth of tickets for this fight," insisted the manager. "That speaks for itself."

Some critics believed Dave lacked the killer punch required to become a world champion. It was pointed out that George McGurk, in January 1976, was the last man he had knocked out, but again the manager sought to appease them.

"What people have to realise is that in this modern era, referees are so protective," he remarked. "When Eric Boon was boxing, the referee would stand back and allow him to finish the job. If Boon and Danahar had fought today, the referee would have stopped it in Danahar's favour."

The fight with Johnson was an awkward, bad-tempered affair which left Dave with a damaged right hand. Although he won by a knockout in round four, his performance did little to enhance his credibility as a world title contender. The press boys were not impressed, and in the *Daily Mail*, Peter Moss wrote:

> It was probably Green's worst performance since he came into world class.

In what was intended as a warm-up for his Commonwealth title bid, Dave was exceedingly slow to start, and his five months absence from the ring was apparent. Boxing strictly to orders from Andy Smith, he tried to find the range with his left jab, but the timing was out, and he didn't have his usual bounce about him.

With cries of; "Give him the muck-spreader" ringing in his ears, Green was the one caught wide open as Johnson launched one of his rare attacks. In reply, Dave was wild with his hooks, and his head-work was rough. Midway through the opening round there was a sickening clash of heads as they fell into a clinch, and the Bermudan emerged with an ugly gash by his left eye.

Referee, Sid Nathan, pulled Green aside and gave him a stern lecture for careless use of the head. He went to the corner at the end of the round and repeated his warning.

Green had more success in round two as a couple of

looping haymakers found their mark. Both men were covered in blood as the Bermudan's cut worsened, and he wobbled as Dave unloaded his power-packed hooks. Generally, however, it was a mauling affair as Johnson, who was awkward and courageous rather than talented, seemed intent merely on survival. His holding and spoiling tactics frustrated Dave who received further warnings from Nathan over use of the head.

In round three, the referee took time out to issue what appeared to be a final warning to Green after a particularly nasty butt. Moments later he winced with pain as a wild right bounced off the top of Johnson's head. Knowing there was an injury, he confined himself to left hooks and jabs for the remainder of the round.

He adopted similar tactics in the fourth, and weakened Johnson with a sustained body attack. With blood streaming into his eyes, the Bermudan eventually collapsed against the ropes from a left hook to the ribs. The blow badly winded him, and although he was fully conscious, he was unable to rise and was counted out as he lay with his head resting on the bottom rope. The official time was two minutes 35 seconds.

"I was a bit rusty, and it showed, but I've been out a while and expected that," said Green back in the dressing-room, his right hand immersed in a bucket of ice. "He gave me enough trouble, but I was glad to get back, and thought I did well."

Andy Smith was also satisfied with the night's work. "The left hooks to the body were David's best shots," he remarked. "Our intention was to do a little more boxing rather than go out there and take chances."

Despite some soreness and swelling to Green's right hand, an X-ray confirmed that no bones were broken. A metacarpal was badly bruised, and after three days he was still unable to punch the heavy bag. Insisting that he needed at least 10 to 14 days before facing an opponent of Clyde Gray's quality, Smith pulled him out of the fight, and Harry Levene cancelled the Wembley promotion.

When the contest was re-scheduled for 9 May, Smith was

quick to tell the press that if there was any re-occurance of the injury in training, he would pull Dave out again. "With a world title chance still in the offing, David will not fight again until he's capable of punching stone walls," he remarked.

* * *

Ever since losing to Carlos Palomino in June the previous year, all Dave thought about was a return. The proposed fight with Clyde Gray was intended as a serious warm-up because the Canadian was genuine world class. Ranked number 10 behind Green at five, it was hoped victory would enhance the Chatteris man's chances.

Much, however, depended on the attitude of Palomino and his advisers. He was cashing in on his title, and in February had knocked out Ryu Sorimachi in seven rounds. Five weeks later, he stopped Mimoun Mohatar of Morocco in nine, yet neither opponent was in the world top 15.

"Palomino says he'll fight me again and that's all I want," the frustrated Chatteris man told the press. "What matters most this year is getting him again, and beating him. That is all I am thinking about, all I'm aiming for. I just want the chance."

Although discussions had been ongoing, Andy Smith was convinced that the champion was reluctant to face Green again because he saw him as a very dangerous opponent. He was demanding £150,000 to return to London, which, as Smith pointed out, was more than any other boxer, including Muhamed Ali, had received for fighting in Britain.

"If I want Dave to fight him in the next two months, I will have to agree to a contest in Los Angeles," said Smith. "I don't want to do that, but I can't make him come to London. I can offer him the best part of the purse, but the money they are demanding is exorbitant."

In the meantime, Green concentrated on his preparations to meet Gray. His hand healed well, and he put in weeks of sweat, toil and dedication on the road and at the St Ives gym. He was so far ahead of his schedule that a week before the fight, Andy Smith gave him a two-day break from sparring on Friday and Saturday. He had completed 52 rounds, but when he returned on the Sunday morning to prepare for the final run-in, disaster struck.

In a routine session with Newmarket light-welterweight, Paddy McAleese, Dave injured his right hand again in another freak accident. As McAleese bent forward after being hit by a jab, Dave swung his right and caught the sparring partner on the top of his head.

Ashen faced and in terrible pain, Dave knew at once that he would be unable to go ahead with the fight with Gray. His mood changed to one of emotional anguish because he felt he had let everyone down, particularly his fans and the promoter.

Andy Smith took no chances, and arranged for his fighter to see a Harley Street specialist. The injury was diagnosed as a damaged ball and socket joint in the second metacarpal of the index finger. A piece of damaged gristle needed to be removed to enable the ball of the joint to slot back into the socket. An operation was performed at the Royal Free Hospital a few days later which Andy Smith described as "like taking a tooth out."

Although the operation was a success, Green was told that he must not punch for a least two months. Realising he would be out of action for a long time, he found it a difficult situation to handle. He took the news badly because although injuries are an occupational hazard in boxing, he had never experienced such set-backs before. Smith described it as the worst blow of his career.

* * *

On 24 April, Dave featured in an Anglia TV documentary entitled *"Lifestyle"* which told the story of Andy Smith's success in boxing.

The film began by showing a coach load of Chatteris supporters on their way to London for the fight with Andy

Price. A number of local people were interviewed because the documentary covered a wide spectrum involving the build-up to a big fight. Much of the filming was done at the St Ives gym, and aspects of Joe Bugner's career were also featured.

✦ 13 ✦

ANOTHER EUROPEAN TITLE

Although it would be almost nine months before Dave boxed again, he had plenty to occupy his mind and temper the frustration. Apart from keeping in shape by doing roadwork and light exercise, the period was also used as an intensive teach-in. It was the chance for Andy Smith and his fighter to expand on the work they had done in the period following the fight with Andy Price.

"Mr Smith told me straight that I'd never be a world champion fighting the way I was," Green recalled years later.

Although tremendous fitness, heart and determination helped Dave to 24 straight victories before he faced Palomino, Smith knew some fundamental changes were still necessary. They watched videos of the fight with Palomino, and others including those with Singleton, Piedvache, Guillotti and Stracey. Over many hours and many evenings they studied what worked and what didn't. They watched them over and over again until Dave was fed up with continuously seeing the same mistakes. Bad balance, poor timing and the inability to pace himself were all areas they worked on in the gym. "I couldn't tell him before the Palomino fight," said Smith in an interview. "How can you persuade an unbeaten fighter that he's boxing all wrong?"

Always a polite, eloquent and entertaining man, Andy explained in great detail the faults and steps taken to try and remedy them. "I was able to prove to David that he was too vulnerable, particularly in the matter of lasting the pace," he remarked. "Dave Green is one of the strongest boys I've come across in the game, but there is a limit to human strength, and he was trying to go beyond it."

Smith described how Dave generally rushed from his stool in a state of high tension and gave everything from the opening bell. "It was as realistic as a three-mile runner starting with an all-out 100-metre dash," he said. "Apart from using up energy, all the charging made a mess of his footwork."

"He was frequently accused of butting when in fact he was stumbling head first into opponents," continued Smith. "So we've been practising and practising to get those things right, getting David to roll on the back leg far more so he can miss the bad ones aimed at him, and always be positioned to punch."

The manager was at lengths to explain that his biggest concern was to avoid switching Dave off. The danger in controlling his impetuosity could result in something vital being lost. "He mustn't lose his drive and momentum," he added, "but he must apply it with greater control."

Green is fortunate that he has always been a good listener who can take constructive criticism. In all aspects of his life, he has always wanted to be the best, and would work tirelessly to achieve it. His relationship with Andy Smith was second to none, and whenever he was told that he was doing something wrong, he accepted it and set about correcting it.

"My poor balance brought me so many warnings about my head," he remarked. "I've never gone in deliberately butting opponents, but I kept falling into them when my punches missed."

"Mr Smith explained how I was staying too tensed up because I was so determined to bowl opponents over," he continued. "My animal instinct just seemed to take over – that's exactly what happened when Palomino knocked me out."

Dave was convinced that all the study, analysis and hard

work would make him a better fighter. "In my old style, I wouldn't have lasted more than two years," he said. "The way I've learned to pace myself I reckon I can now carry on for at least another four if I want."

Aside from boxing, Dave was again invited to compete in the British Superstars competition. John Conteh was originally selected as the boxing representative, but when he withdrew at short notice, Dave was a popular replacement.

He was entered in the third qualifying heat which took place at Harlow, Essex on 10 and 11 July. His fellow competitors were Trevor Brooking, Tony Currie and Gordon Hill (football), Peter Collins (speedway), Eric Hughes (rugby league), Ray Stevens (badminton) and David Wilkie (swimming).

The programme notes contained the comment:

> Andy Smith was proved right last year when he described his charge as a "competitor in the Kevin Keegan mould", before the competition. David finished third and impressed everyone with his sporting, but highly competitive approach. This time he has stepped in at the last minute as substitute for John Conteh, but even without training for the events, will be a tough competitor to beat.

It was an accurate prediction because with a total of 31 points, one ahead of Hill, Dave was the outright winner of the two-day competition, earning him prize money of £1,250. It was a tremendous achievement considering he had done no real preparation, and was sidelined from boxing. "But you know Dave, he always wants to compete," remarked Andy Smith.

Each competitor had to take part in six of eight events. Dave opted out of cycling and canoeing. He excelled on the first day with second place at swimming, and winning the weight-lifting by managing to lift six and a half kilograms more than his own body weight. In the gym tests, he tied for first place with Hill who won the press-ups while Green triumphed at squat thrusts.

He had a bad start on the second day, finishing only fifth in the crossbow because he failed to master the equipment.

After coming a disappointing fifth in the 100 metre sprint, everything depended on the final event – the 650 metre steeplechase. After a really gutsy performance, Dave finished third which was enough to make him outright winner of the heat.

Encouraging him throughout every event, Andy Smith regarded the two days as perfect training for the proposed fight with Clyde Gray which they still hoped would go ahead.

As winner of his heat, Dave qualified for the 1978 Superstars final at Bracknell, Berkshire, on 30 and 31 August. Determined to do well he commenced training almost immediately, and only eased up to spend a week's holiday with Kay in Malta. When he returned, he went to the Army Training Centre at Aldershot for the final stages of preparation.

Under the watchful eye of his exceptionally fit personal trainer, Lance Corporal Drummond, Green was on the road at 7am every morning for a week. After six miles of the most demanding running, he went to the gym where he underwent other torturous aspects of fitness training. "I thought I was fit," declared Dave, "but I've never met a man as fit as him. He really put me through it."

After two days of intense competition, Dave finished fourth in a top class field of eight competitors. His opponents were defending champion, Tim Crooks (rowing), Lynn Davies (athletics), Andy Irvine (rugby union), Brian Jacks (judo), Ian Neale (swimming), Brian Phelps (diving), and Gordon Hill (football) who qualified as runner-up in Green's heat. Jacks was the overall winner, and such was the quality of the field that 1977 champion Crooks, finished behind Davies, Irvine and Green.

Andy Smith accompanied Dave as his advisor, and after the competition was very supportive of his charge. "We should be very, very proud of him," he remarked. "He was competing in a world class field in events that were foreign to his training. He did remarkably well."

Ironically, Smith's advice probably cost Green a top three placing. Conscious that there was still a strong chance of securing a return fight with Carlos Palomino, he erred on the side of caution. Rather than risk injury, Andy persuaded Dave to pull out of the weight-lifting competition which he had won in his qualifying heat. It was a decision which undoubtedly cost valuable points, but the manager was terrified that over-exertion by Green could lead to a muscle or ligament strain which would seriously hamper his boxing training.

Despite his manager's caution, Green still put in stirring performances in the canoeing, gym tests and 100 metre sprint. Completing the 125 metre canoeing course in 41.8 seconds, he attributed his victory to training he had done with the Somersham Scouts over previous weeks on the river Ouse. Much of the preparation related to perfecting style with the paddle which he mastered by being made to work as hard as he could whilst the instructor held the end of his canoe to prevent it moving forward in the water.

He needed to call upon all his fierce competitive skill, instincts and reserves of energy to take second place in the gruelling gym tests. He completed 28 parallel dips and 83 squat thrusts, just one behind the winner, Brian Jacks. It was a mammoth effort, and an improvement from the qualifying heat of 11 dips and 75 thrusts.

Dave also put in a great performance to finish second in the 100 metres in 12.85 seconds, another improvement from the heat in which his time was 13.33.

In other events, he was fifth at swimming and crossbow, and fourth in the 650 metre steeplechase and soccer, in which he scored just one goal from three attempts. Because of his ability as a schoolboy, he was expected to do well in the soccer event which involved dribbling a ball around a slalom course and attempting to score past Ipswich Town goalkeeper, Paul Cooper.

* * *

By September, Dave was itching to get back into the ring. There was talk of a fight with Clyde Gray being staged at

Wembley later that month despite Gray's manager, Irv Ungerman, saying he would never agree to fight in England again.

When he returned to Canada in May, Ungerman was quoted as saying: "So far as we are concerned, we fulfilled our part of the contract. If Green wants the title fight when he's fit again, he's going to have to come here for it."

Andy Smith, however, remained optimistic. He believed Ungerman was being hasty and would realise there was nowhere else where his boxer could earn the sort of money he would for fighting Green.

"I thought it was a bit childish for him to say that Dave feigned injury to get out of the fight," Smith told Harry Mullan of *Boxing News*. "It's nonsense to even suggest he's scared of Gray."

Meanwhile, negotiations continued in an attempt to get Green the long-awaited return with Palomino. In mid-September, *Boxing News* reported that the fight looked set to take place in either Monte Carlo or Venice on 21 October. Italian impresario, Rodolfo Sabbatini, was in talks with an American TV network to screen the bout live.

It was later reported that because of a dispute with French television, the fight had been switched to Pessaro, Italy. American TV were still prepared to screen it live, and the Italian Television Service also agreed to specific coverage. Four weeks later, however, it was announced that the fight was cancelled because of technical hitches over TV transmission. Then it was reported that Palomino had damaged a back muscle whilst training, and would be immobilised for a week.

Despite the new setbacks, there was still hope that a return fight could be staged. As Harry Levene had the Empire Pool, Wembley, booked for 7 November, it was hoped that the champion could be persuaded to return to London. A New Year confrontation was also mooted, but Andy Smith was not optimistic. With the passing of time there were other obstacles.

When Palomino offered to fight Green at Monte Carlo, it would have been a voluntary defence. Even when contracts were exchanged, he and Smith knew the champion was committed to a mandatary defence early in 1979. The subsequent delays therefore made the fight less likely.

Carlos had become the highest earning welterweight in the history of boxing, and paying him the kind of money he wanted for a voluntary defence remained extremely difficult. Most of the Monte Carlo purse was to have come from American television, but to catch audiences in the States, the fight needed to be staged on a Saturday night which could have seriously effected live gate receipts.

Although every effort was made by Smith and the London promoters to get Dave the return he so desperately wanted, negotiations finally broke down in late October. With all the uncertainty spread over several months, it had been an extremely frustrating period for all concerned, but they had to move on.

With Green fit and raring for action, he was matched with Santiago Valdez of Ohio, over 10 rounds at Wembley on 7 November. It was the chief supporting contest to Alan Minter's European middleweight title defence against Gratien Tonna of France.

A few days before the fight, Valdez was replaced by Aundra Love from Texas who had previously beaten Valdez in three rounds. It proved to be a good fight for Green because, having been out of action for nine months, there was plenty of ring rust to shift.

Although Dave won by a stoppage in the eighth round, the American was dangerous early on with left hooks and a neat right uppercut. The Chatteris man was visibly shaken on occasions, and finished with a swelling beneath his left eye, testimony of Love's stiff punches.

Looking better as the fight progressed, Green's best round was the seventh when his punches suddenly had crispness about them. Looking like the Fen Tiger of old, stiff jabs to the face and left hooks to the body took the fight out of Love.

He kept up the pressure in round eight, and a constant stream of jabs and hooks sent Love reeling against the ropes on several occasions. Green punched non-stop, and with the American throwing nothing back, referee Larry O'Connell, called a halt.

Apart from some bruising and swelling the following day, Dave's right hand stood up well to the test. It was important that he kept busy, and four weeks later he faced Sammy Masias of Miami, over 10 rounds at the Royal Albert Hall. The fight shared top-of-the-bill with John L. Gardner and Charlie Magri also facing overseas opposition over 10 rounds.

Masias, a Mexican residing in Florida, was the State Golden Gloves champion in 1973 and '74. He had a professional record of 16 wins and a draw from 24 fights, with one no contest. With 14 stoppage victories to his credit, Dave was told his punching power was to be respected.

Green, however, was never a man to fear reputations, and recapturing his old form, smashed Masias to defeat in 85 seconds of the opening round. It was an impressive display in which Dave placed his shots precisely and accurately. Gone were the wild swiping punches of earlier fights, and his finishing was clinical.

Two powerful rights won Green the fight after he had imposed himself with a stream of solid left jabs to the face. A right to the jaw sent Masias to the floor for a count of eight. When he rose, Dave bombarded him with powerful punches from both hands before a hard right to the head followed by a perfect left hook to the body ended the fight. Sammy was in a bad way, and it was several minutes before he could return to his corner.

Although the result was announced as a knockout, referee, Larry O'Connell, did not bother to count because he realised Masias was badly hurt. "I thought it was important that the boy be seen to as soon as possible," he said afterwards.

Dave was delighted with his performance because it was the first time the Mexican had been knocked out, and only his second stoppage defeat. "I was a bit nervous about letting my

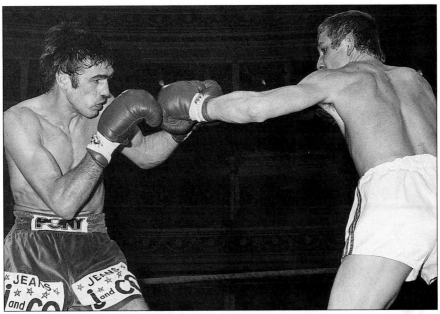

Green throws a jab at Jean-Baptiste Piedvache who retired after nine rounds in their European light-welterweight championship contest at the Royal Albert Hall on 7 December 1976.

Dave, with his parents and brother Michael (right), proudly shows his European championship belt.

Green and John H. Stracey sign contracts for their fight in March 1977. Terry Lawless (back left), promoter Harry Levene and Andy Smith are present.

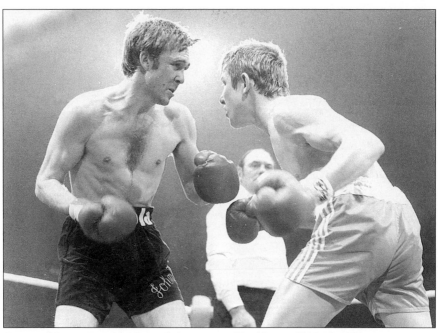

Green and Stracey in action during their contest at Wembley on 29 March 1977.

Dave and Andy Irvine contest the lead in the 1977 Superstars hurdle race. Trevor Brooking (left), Gordon Hill and Tony Currie are in hot pursuit.

Dave puts tremendous effort into the weight-lifting event.

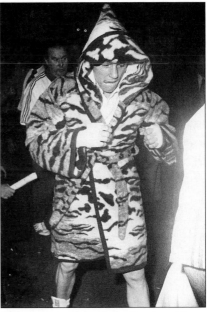

Dave 'Boy' Green in his familiar tiger-skin dressing-gown.

World welterweight champion, Carlos
Palomino, holds the cake as Dave blows out
the candles on his 24th birthday.

Green catches Carlos Palomino with a left hook during their world welterweight title contest at
Wembley on 14 June 1977.

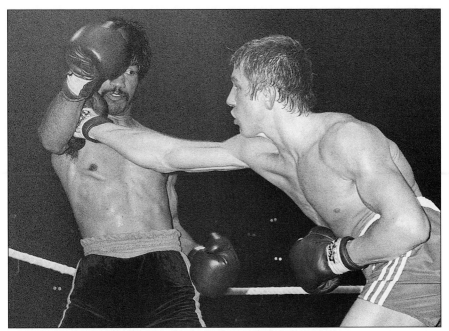

Green narrowly misses with a right in his contest with Carlos Palomino.

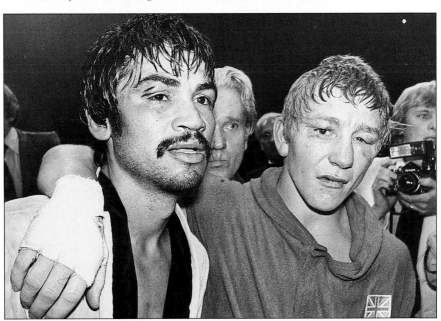

Green and Palomino show the signs of battle after their fight at Wembley on 14 June 1977, won by the Mexican in round 11.

Palomino sends Dave crashing to the floor in the 11th round of their world championship fight at Wembley.

Dave does a massive amount of charity work and is frequently invited to attend public houses in East Anglia to knock over piles of coins in the bars.

Andy Smith tries to console the distraught Dave 'Boy' Green following his shattering knock-out defeat to Carlos Palomino.

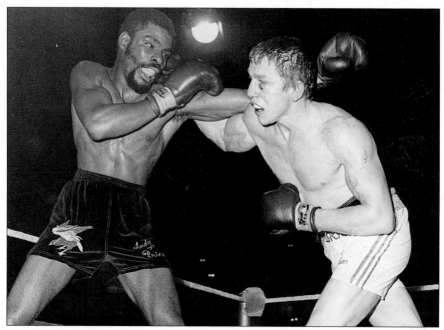

Green attacks Andy 'Hawk' Price whom he outpointed at Wembley on 27 September 1977.

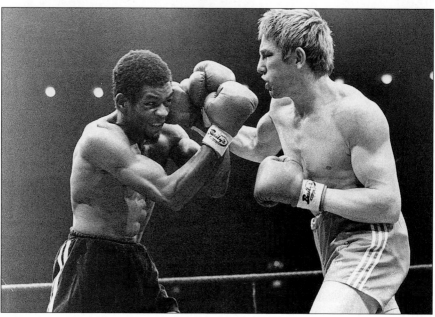

Green crashes a right hook through the guard of Henry Rhiney from whom he took the European welterweight title on 23 January 1979.

right hand go in my last fight," he said back in the dressing-room, "but tonight I just let it go without thinking. It was a proper short punch too."

It was a timely victory because three days earlier in Austria, Henry Rhiney had won the European welterweight title in sensational style by knocking out defending champion, Josef Pachler, in 10 rounds. It was the fifth time the title had changed hands within 18 months in what was a topsy-turvy division at European level. Yet despite his world title aspirations and prolonged period of injury, Green had been ranked as the number one contender throughout the entire period. With two good stoppage victories within a month, an all-British championship contest against Rhiney was mouth-watering.

Danish promoter, Mogens Palle, promptly offered Rhiney £20,000 to defend his newly-won title against former two-time champion, Jorgen Hansen, in Denmark. The champion, however, preferred to stay in England, and by mid-December accepted an offer from Mike Barrett to defend against Green at the Royal Albert Hall on 23 January 1979.

Announcing the fight at a press conference at Mayfair's Casanova Club on 21 December, Barrett said it had cost him £30,000, making it the most expensive championship contest he had ever staged in 16 years of promotion at the venue. It said much for Green's drawing power, that Rhiney's purse, said to be over £20,000, was reportedly more than he had earned in his entire career.

The fight looked to be one of the best between two British boxers since Green beat Stracey, yet 18 months earlier it would never have seemed likely. As Dave sat backstage receiving sympathy and admiration following his epic effort against Palomino, Henry was in the ring struggling in an eight-rounder against Pat Thomas. In his first appearance on a public show in London, he only just made it to the final bell, and lost on points.

The fight was an anticlimax to what had gone on before, but as British champion, Henry was expected to do better. His

205

stock sunk even further four months later when he was stopped in seven rounds by Joey Mack, but showing great character, he re-grouped, put the bad form behind him, and prepared to face Green with confidence.

ROYAL ALBERT HALL

General Manager: A. J. CHARLTON

TUESDAY, JANUARY 23rd, 1979

Matchmaker: MICKEY DUFF

DOORS OPEN 7 p.m. COMMENCE 7.30 p.m.

MIKE BARRETT proudly presents a 12 (3 min.) Rounds Contest for the

WELTERWEIGHT CHAMPIONSHIP OF EUROPE

HENRY RHINEY
(LUTON) WELTERWEIGHT CHAMPION OF GT. BRITAIN AND EUROPE

v

DAVE "BOY" GREEN
(CHATTERIS) FORMER UNDEFEATED LT.-WELTERWEIGHT CHAMPION OF G. BRITAIN AND EUROPE

10 (3 min.) Rounds Lt.-Middleweight Contest at 11st. 2lbs.	10 (3 min.) Rounds Flyweight Contest at 8st. 3lbs.
JIMMY BATTEN (Millwall) Lt.-Middleweight Champion of Great Britain	**CHARLIE MAGRI** (Stepney) Flyweight Champion of Great Britain
v	v
JUSTICE ORTIZ (New York, U.S.A.). Has fought Billy Backus, Robinson Garcia, Johnny Gant, etc.	**GARCIA TANIO** (Seville, Spain). Has fought the best in Europe. Lost close points decision for Spanish Bantamweight title

8 (3 min.) Rounds Light-Middleweight Contest at 11st. 2lbs.	8 (3 min.) Rounds Heavyweight Contest
DAVE PROUD v **COLIN WARD** (Penge) No. 1 Contender Lt.-Middle Title (Northampton) Beat Mickey Minter, etc.	**STAN McDERMOTT** v **GORDON FERRIS** (Basildon) (Enniskillen)

6 (3 min.) Rounds Light-Welterweight Contest at 10st. 2lbs.	6 (3 min.) Rounds Light-Heavyweight Contest at 12st. 2lbs.
SYLVESTER MITTEE v **SEAN McGARRY** (Bethnal Green) (Ballaghadereen)	**STEVE LEWIN** v **REG SQUIRE** (Streatham) (Swindon)

TICKETS: £3.50 ★ £5.00 ★ £SOLD ★ £SOLD ★ £12.50 ★ £15.00 ★ £20.00
Inc. V.A.T.

To: MIKE BARRETT   60-66 WARDOUR STREET, LONDON, W.1 (437 5956)

Please reserve . . . . seats at . . . . Royal Albert Hall, Tuesday, 23rd January, 1979. *Please enclose stamped, addressed envelope for reply.* Cheque / Postal Order herewith value £

M . . . .

Poster advertising European welterweight championship contest between Green and Henry Rhiney

Jamaican-born Rhiney boxed out of Luton, and turned professional in 1973. He was an experienced man who had boxed in France, Luxembourg, Holland, South Africa and Austria. From 51 contests, he had the respectable record of 32 wins and six draws, with 13 losses.

Rhiney became Southern Area welterweight champion in October 1976, stopping Mickey Ryce in eight rounds. Two months later he won the British title by stopping Pat Thomas, also in eight rounds. His only defence had been in February 1978 when he outpointed Billy Waith over 15 rounds.

The fight was of tremendous importance to Green because defeat could mean the end of his career. Rhiney, who had the habit of proving the critics wrong, was a big step-up in class from Johnson, Love and Masias. When he took the British title from Pat Thomas, he was the outsider, having already lost twice to the Welshman. Against Billy Waith, he was not expected to keep the title, and was given little chance in his European title challenge because he lacked a punch. Yet against Thomas and Pachler, Henry won inside the distance.

His manager, Johnny Barclay, was confident of the outcome against Green. "It's a psychological thing," he remarked. "Henry always seems to raise his game when a title is at stake."

By the time the fight was made, Rhiney had already been ordered by the British Boxing Board of Control to defend his British title against official contender, Kirkland Laing, by 31 March. That title was not at stake against Green because British titles were still contested over 15 rounds. History, however, was being made because Henry was the first European champion to defend his title in Britain over the new EBU limit of 12 rounds. The European governing body reduced the championship distance from 15 rounds following the tragic death of Italian boxer, Angelo Jacopucci, following his 12th round knockout by Alan Minter in July the previous year.

The contest was also the first for a European title to involve two British boxers which did not involve a British championship. Furthermore, it was the first time that two British judges and a British referee had been appointed to officiate in a European championship fight.

Green embarked on an arduous and demanding training schedule. It included 90 rounds of sparring using five partners, each with a different style, to prepare him for anything Rhiney could throw at him.

Leading up to the fight, Andy Smith was frequently interviewed by local reporters at the St Ives gym. "It's really a world championship," he insisted, "for if we don't pull this off, there won't be a world title fight."

He said Rhiney would be put under pressure he had never experienced before. "Joey Singleton was supposed to be a master boxer, Stracey was a master boxer, but Dave didn't have any trouble with them," he remarked. "We aren't making any special preparations for Rhiney, but if he's thinking about out-jabbing Dave, he's in for a surprise."

Having sold over £11,000 worth of tickets to his Fenland supporters, Dave showed what a great box-office draw he still was. Despite snow and transport strikes, there were no empty seats at the Royal Albert Hall, and many of his loyal fans were unable to get in.

The only setback to the contest was that appointed referee, James Brimmell, telephoned the Board of Control stating that due to adverse weather conditions, he was unable to make the journey from Cardiff. His place was taken by Sid Nathan, with Harry Gibbs and Mike Jacobs acting as judges in accordance with EBU rules.

Green was always the betting favourite for the fight, and many modest wagers were laid on him. When one single bet of £1,080 to £600 was laid on the day of the fight, bookmakers William Hill, shortened his odds to 7-4 on.

It was a crucial fight for Dave because Wilfredo Benitez had taken the world title from Carlos Palomino on a split decision at San Juan nine days earlier. He had reportedly been contacted by the London promoters and expressed a willingness to meet Green. After all the disappointment over Palomino, defeat against Rhiney was therefore unthinkable, but Dave also needed a crowd-pleasing performance to interest American TV into backing a contest with Benitez.

A few days before the fight, however, one of Green's former sparring partners, Mickey Laud, dropped a real bombshell by saying he believed Dave would retire after only another couple of fights. In a letter to Frank McGhee, boxing correspondent for the *Daily Mirror*, he said he was convinced that Andy Smith believed it would be better to retire as a champion than a former champion.

"He would never allow Dave to absorb any serious punishment, and would always put the health of his boxers first – and money last," wrote Laud.

Whilst Laud's remarks about Smith's morals and compassion were absolutely correct, he and Green dismissed any suggestion about retirement. "I cannot understand it," Dave told the *Cambridge Evening News*. "I am just as enthusiastic as I ever was."

Endorsing his man's remarks, Smith added: "There is no figment of truth in what Mickey Laud says. What people are reading is the imagination of an ex-fighter."

At the weigh in at The Horseshoe, Tottenham Court Road, at 1pm on the day of the fight, Green scaled 10st 7, an advantage of three quarters of a pound over Rhiney. He looked in magnificent condition, and was really pumped-up by the time he got into the ring. He snarled at the champion with arrogant confidence as they faced each other in the centre of the ring for the referee's final instructions. Rhiney looked tense and edgy because as one reporter later put it; "he was facing a tiger about to be unleashed."

The bout was fought at a terrific pace, and the excitement was breathtaking. In an absorbing opening round, the atmosphere generated by the capacity crowd made it a memorable occasion.

Green, predictably started quickly, throwing the punches he hoped would bring about a swift victory. Rhiney, however, settled well, and began to look positive and confident. Standing his ground, he pumped accurate left jabs into the challenger's face, frequently made him miss, and put him on the defensive. Yet as always, the Chatteris man's answer was to go toe-to-toe and hit back. Grimly determined, he forgot about niceties as he sought to take control, and was twice warned for careless use of the head as referee, Sid Nathan, asserted his authority early on.

Neither showed the slightest respect for the other at the start of the second round. Two good uppercuts gave Rhiney the confidence to go toe-to-toe with Dave early in the round, but the challenger's strength quickly became apparent.

Heavy punches from Green made Henry hold. Then, as he attempted to fight back, Dave hammered him with powerful accurate left jabs. More big rights in the final minute again made the champion hang on desperately.

"The fella's knackered," Green told Andy Smith as he returned to his corner. He knew it was just a case of being patient and not taking risks.

At the bell for round three, Green strode purposefully across the ring to resume hostilities. Rhiney had barely left his stool when he was clubbed by a right to the head. The champion took it well and hit back with hooks to the ribs to which Green had no defence, but again his strength was decisive.

Remaining focused, he let Rhiney have his fling, then went back on the attack. Three swift counter-punches had the champion's defences in tatters. It was see-saw stuff in which neither man gained real advantage, but it was brilliant for the crowd.

Another big attack from Green shortly before the bell left Rhiney part way through the ropes. The action was so intense that neither man heard the bell, and Dave landed two left hooks in extra time before being ordered away. The feeling at ringside was that the power of his punches was becoming the dominant factor, and it was just a matter of time before he ended it.

Although Rhiney had some success by getting inside Dave's left jabs in the fourth, he could not match his power or strength. Whatever the champion did was short-lived because having worked up a tremendous rhythm, Green was in almost complete control. Henry's composure had gone, and when he slipped to the floor near the ropes, the end looked in sight.

Green hammered away mercilessly from the bell to start round five, and the champion, his nose bleeding badly, looked weary. Heavy punches at the end of the previous round had taken all the fight out of him.

"Body, body," they shouted from Green's corner, and the challenger responded with a vicious right hook to the ribs. The reaction from Rhiney confirmed the corner advice, and Dave steamed in tigerishly looking for the finish.

The end came suddenly, albeit in somewhat confusing fashion. A solid right to the head was the start of the champion's downfall, and although he ducked and tried to cover up, his strength had gone. He was forced back against the ropes, desperately bobbing and weaving as Green hammered away relentlessly with both hands. Never giving an inch, he smashed big punches to the hapless champion's head until Mr Nathan jumped between them.

Thinking he had won, Dave leapt into the air, only to learn that the third man had imposed a standing count. There was confusion among the crowd, most of whom didn't realise such a situation was permissible under EBU rules. Yet another piece of boxing history had been created because it was the first time that a standing count had been issued in an all-British championship contest.

Mr Nathan counted to eight before waving them back into action, but it was all academic. Rhiney was still clutching the top rope when Green pounced, forcing him into a corner with a stream of punches. When a full-blooded right spun his head to one side, it was enough for Nathan to signal the end. Henry's six-week reign as European champion was over after one minute 59 seconds of the fifth.

Despite taking some good shots from the champion, Green fought a smart technical battle. Using non-stop tactics, he out-jabbed Rhiney with stiff lefts to the head, and weakened him with cruel body blows throughout the contest. He was never in trouble, and with typical ruthlessness, finished the fight when the opportunity arose.

Modifications which had been made to Dave's approach really showed in round three. He covered up well, then went on the attack with accurate forceful punching. Whilst there was plenty of the old Green fire about his work, his patience and control laid the foundation for victory.

As Andy Smith was quick to point out, Rhiney didn't have too many options in the bout. "He found he couldn't out-jab David, couldn't out-box him enough to dictate the fight, so he showed his courage by trying to storm us into trouble," he remarked at a post-fight interview. "But it was never on. From the early minutes David was breaking him in half with the body shots. After the third round, the desire had left the boy's eyes. He didn't chuck it, but he knew he was a loser."

Green was ecstatic over his victory. "This is everything I've dreamed about – being a dual-European champion," he enthused. "I out-boxed Rhiney, out-jabbed and out-fought him. Now I am ready for Benitez, but the one I really want is Palomino. He's the only guy to beat me, and I want to put the record straight."

Dave's performance was unquestionably one that amounted to complete rehabilitation after some lack-lustre performances since Palomino. It was appropriate that he achieved it on a night when Mike Barrett had only his fourth complete sell-out in 98 promotions at the Royal Albert Hall. For the first time since Billy Walker fought Ray Patterson in 1966, there was not a ticket of any description to be had. Staff at the venue even had to open up the gallery to accommodate 300 late-comers.

The immediate talk was of a fight with Benitez which Smith described as being "99.5 per cent certain." He had a provisional agreement with the champion's manager, Jim Jacobs, but before making a full commitment they wanted a film of the fight with Rhiney.

Harry Gibbs, who was a judge at the Benitez-Palomino fight 11 days earlier, believed Green would be too strong for the brilliant 20 year old champion. Although there was talk of a possible date in March, most reporters felt Dave had no chance of home advantage. Andy Smith accepted that they would have to go abroad and even conceded that he would do a good job just to get the fight outside Puerto Rico.

For several days the press heaped praise on Green for the way he beat Rhiney. Writing in the *Sunday People*, former featherweight boxer, Frankie Taylor emphasised the skill shown by the Chatteris man:

> Not many people realise how much Dave 'Boy' Green out-thought Henry Rhiney. There was more to it than his superior strength and punching power. He cleverly forced Rhiney to stand and fight by cutting out the room he needs for his normal boxing.
>
> Green's fourth round was the best I've seen by a British boxer for years. He weaved half a dozen Rhiney leads and then timed a right hand to perfection. He let Rhiney tire himself and that set him up for the stoppage.

It was a great night in the ring for Dave because his victory made him the first Briton since Ted 'Kid' Lewis in 1920, to win European championships at two weights. Furthermore, the ring rust had gone, his punching power was as good as ever, and most importantly there was no reaction from the right hand which caused him so much trouble over previous months.

Outside the ring, however, it was a night of mixed emotions. Kay was about 12 weeks pregnant at the time, but had been having difficulties.

Because Dave was staying at Andy Smith's house, which he always did for a period prior to a big fight, Kay went to stay with her mother who by this time lived at Cambridge. A couple of days before the fight, she began haemorrhaging. She returned to Chatteris and saw her doctor who immediately referred her to the RAF Hospital at Ely. She was kept in overnight, but lost the baby on the day of the fight.

When Ken Green climbed into the ring immediately after the fight to congratulate his son, the first thing Dave said was: "How is Kay?"

Quietly, and with a comforting arm around the shoulder, Ken told him the distressing news. Whilst it was a terrible shock which dampened the joy of his championship success,

Dave hid his emotion well. Only Andy Smith and people very close to him became aware of what had occurred.

"I always believe there is a reason why these things happen," said Green when recalling the event. "You never know, if the child had been born it might have had serious problems which would have been even more heart-breaking."

Despite their disappointment, Dave and Kay did have something to look forward to. A new house which they were having built, was almost complete, and being a true romantic he had chosen Valentine's Day, 14 February, for them to move in.

On Andy Smith's advice, Green had purchased a quarter-acre plot of land on the Eastwood Estate in Chatteris 12 months earlier. He was earning well from boxing, and with his manager's guidance invested wisely in order to provide a quality lifestyle for his family.

Wanting their freedom by not being penned-in by surrounding properties, Eastwood was the perfect area for Dave and Kay. On the edge of acres of flat arable farming land, there was a view almost to Ely 12 miles away.

The couple worked out exactly what they wanted, and the house was built to their design and specification by property developer, John Bailey, from Bury St Edmunds, who played football for Chatteris Town. They had met in January 1977 on a flight to Tenerife. John and his family were sitting three rows in front of Dave and Kay, and during the flight he turned and said: "Are you Dave 'Boy' Green?"

It transpired that they were all staying in the same hotel. They got on well together, and at one stage Bailey told Green that if he ever wanted a house built, to let him provide a quote.

A good friendship developed, and once he had purchased the plot of land Dave engaged John to build the house. It was of Georgian style, with four bedrooms, open-plan kitchen, a full-sized snooker room, large living room, double garage and drive, with spacious front and rear gardens. John persuaded Dave to have oak doors, each costing £115, throughout.

Due mainly to poor weather conditions, the property took

about a year to build, but in some respects completion came at a fortunate time. Choosing new curtains, carpets and household essentials kept Kay occupied during her period of difficulty, and helped the couple through it.

✦ 14 ✦

SHATTERING SET-BACK

The victory over Rhiney made Green more sought after than ever. Talks with Jim Jacobs, were on-going, and it was hoped to stage a fight with Benitez by the end of May. Money, however, was again the main obstacle because, as with Palomino, the purse needed to lure the champion away from Puerto Rico could only come from a television deal which would enable the fight to be screened live to the United States.

Tentative efforts were also made by northern promoter, Manny Goodall, to stage a re-match between Green and John H. Stracey. There was some confusion amongst the press as to what was planned, prompting both Stracey and Andy Smith to contact *Boxing News* editor, Harry Mullan, to put their points.

According to Stracey, the initiative for the fight came from Smith who he claimed approached him at the Boxing Writers Dinner in January saying: "When are we going to make some money – you're the only one Dave can earn with in Europe." John said he was interested in the fight, but would insist that it took place either at a neutral venue or for another promoter in London. His dispute with the major London promotional network had become long and bitter.

A couple of days later, John read that Goodall had offered Green £30,000 to fight him, but had been turned down. He stressed to Mullan that he was not chasing Dave because he had other possibilities.

216

Andy Smith told Mullan that Goodall telephoned him and offered £25,000 for Green to meet Stracey at Belle View, Manchester, or Liverpool Stadium. "I explained that I wasn't in a position to accept because we were already committed to a fight at Wembley on 6 March, and were also negotiating to meet Benitez in May," said Smith. "Stracey wasn't part of our immediate plans."

Smith added that on 6 February he received a letter from Goodall offering £30,000, but replied that the position remained unchanged.

"Of course Green against Stracey would be a good money fight," said Andy, "but for that reason, I can't see the commercial sense in matching a cockney with an East Anglian in the Midlands or North. If this fight is worth £45,000 there, it must be worth £100,000 in London."

Although Dave had been matched with Dum Dum Pacheco of Spain at Wembley on 6 March, Harry Levene cancelled the show when the EBU refused to recognise it as a European title defence.

The problem arose because in November the previous year, the governing body passed a ruling compelling champions who win titles in a voluntary defence, as Green did against Rhiney, to make their first defence against the official challenger. Former champion, Jorgen Hansen of Denmark, was the EBU nominee, although contracts for him to face Green were not due to be lodged until 6 April.

Board of Control General Secretary, Ray Clarke, contacted the Danish Boxing Federation and secured their agreement for Green to make a voluntary defence against Pacheco. Hansen had no objection provided he was given first shot at the winner. The EBU, however, refused to relax its ruling.

Meanwhile, Dave got a surprise call to replace judo champion, Brian Jacks, as a British representative in the World Superstars competition at Freeport, Grand Bahama, between 9 and 11 March. Jacks, who won the British event very impressively, had to pull out with a blood disorder, but being very patriotic, insisted on helping Green prepare.

217

Every day for a week, Jacks and his team of instructors put Dave through strenuous fitness and event training at Crystal Palace sports complex. Brian's parents even invited him to stay with them to avoid travelling to and from Chatteris each day.

Dave set off for the Bahamas on the day he should have fought Pacheco. He was accompanied by Andy Smith, and Lynn Davies who qualified for the competition by finishing runner-up to Jacks in the British event. "It's a wonderful consolation for Dave," Andy Smith told *Boxing News*. "The competitive edge he will acquire over three days of competition will do him as much good as a warm-up fight."

The party flew from Heathrow to Miami and then on to Freeport where they stayed at the luxurious Princes Hotel. The first two days were spent sight-seeing and making final preparations for the individual events.

World Superstars was a massive event worth $25,000 to the winner, $15,000 for second, and $10,000 for third. Each of the 12 competitors would receive an extra $300 for every point scored.

Green faced strong competition from the field which included high-jumper, Dwight Stones, American football stars, Greg Pruitt and Jim Taylor, water-skier, Wayne Grimdich, Peter Snell (athletics), Emerson Fittipaldi (motor racing) and eventual winner, Brian Budd, a Canadian soccer player. Having had only five days specialist training, he did remarkably well to finish equal sixth with Stones, and take home approximately £3,000 in prize money.

Whilst he performed exceptionally well in the squat-thrusts, Dave's most memorable event was the football slalom in which he scored three goals from three attempts in a world record time. It was an unforgettable all expenses paid trip, but on returning home he went straight back to his daily routine in the gym.

Andy Smith was full of praise for Dave's performance, but because of TV rights was unable to give details of how he fared. With the event due to be screened by BBC television on

21 April, all he would say was that Green and Lynn Davies both did very well.

Within a few days of his return from the Bahamas, it was announced that Dave would challenge Wilfredo Benitez for the WBC welterweight title at Monte Carlo on 26 May. Andy Smith had earlier rejected an offer for Dave to face the champion in Puerto Rico, but felt the neutral venue was of greater advantage to his man.

Instead of facing Green, Benitez made the first defence of his title against Harold Weston at San Juan on 25 March. Smith decided it was important that they were at ringside, so they spent a week in Puerto Rico during which time they watched Benitez train on a number of occasions.

As the champion's next proposed opponent, Dave was invited to work with American television, and during the contest give expert opinion on its progress.

The fight took place during the afternoon, and the sweltering heat of the Hiram Bithorn Stadium was further proof of Andy Smith's astuteness in refusing to allow Dave to fight there.

Benitez won by a unanimous decision, but Green said he thought Weston had played into his hands by not throwing enough punches. He declined to comment on how he would tackle the champion, but remarked: "With my style against Wilfredo's, it's going to be a cracking fight."

Dave returned to Britain full of confidence and believing he had a better chance of beating Benitez than any of the other top welterweights. He resumed training immediately, but in mid-April received disappointing news that his fight with the champion was off. Although there was talk of it taking place at the end of July, the frustrations experienced when chasing Palomino reared up again.

When John Conteh pulled out of a fight at Wembley scheduled for 1 May, Green readily stepped in. "It's very convenient for us because it's a good chance for Dave to keep active," said Andy Smith. "He was sick after going all the way to Puerto Rico and seeing Benitez, to be told he wasn't getting the fight as soon as he thought."

Originally matched with Tony Daniels of America, Dave faced former Canadian middleweight champion, Lawrence Hafey from Nova Scotia, over 10 rounds. Hafey, a veteran of over 60 fights, had been outpointed by Benitez in 1975, which gave Green the incentive to do better.

Sharing joint top of the bill with Charlie Magri who captured the European flyweight crown, Green turned in a clinical performance to secure a fifth round victory. Throwing his famous wild right very sparingly, he relied on a hefty left jab which rammed into Hafey's face time and time again.

After a quiet opening round, Dave became more aggressive in the second, landing good left hooks to the head off the jab. He went up another gear in round three, hurting Hafey with right uppercuts and left hooks, and causing slight damage above the right eye.

Green kept up the pressure in the fourth with jabs and hooks to the head. Then, in response to Andy Smith's shouts from the corner, switched his attack to the body. Heavy hooks from both hands really took the fight out of Hafey who showed great courage to stay on his feet.

The Green camp had been expecting a distance fight because not many men had stopped Hafey who was renown for his toughness. Yet on this occasion he was relentlessly ground down by one of the fittest and strongest welterweights in the world. Dave was so clearly in charge that as the bell sounded for the start of round five, Smith ordered him to go out and finish it.

Hardly wasting a punch, Green punished the Canadian freely, and drove him to all sides of the ring. Short hooks to the head were sickening, and people from all sides of the ring were calling for it to be stopped. Dave didn't let up, and poured it on until referee, Mike Jacobs, eventually stepped in after two minutes 50 seconds of the round with Hafey exhausted and bleeding heavily from the nose.

It was a sensible, controlled display by Green who was ruthless when he knew his man was on the verge of defeat.

His reward was a top of the bill 10-rounder against Rafael Rodriguez at Wembley Conference Centre two weeks later.

Meanwhile, there was still a lot of speculation about the Benitez situation. Following the cancellation of the Monte Carlo fight, there was talk of it being staged at Madison Square Garden, New York, in late July. Andy Smith remained sceptical, but again emphasised that because of the climate there was no way he would allow Dave to fight in Puerto Rico. He was mindful of what the humidity did to Joe Bugner when he fought Muhammed Ali at Kuala Lumpa in 1975. It was clearly becoming a stalemate situation because, prompted by his father, Benitez insisted that he was not prepared to fight in Europe.

Packed with talent, the welterweight division was the hottest of all at world level, and Green was right up there with some of the greatest names in boxing. Benitez was WBC champion and Pipino Cuevas held the WBA title. *Boxing News* rankings for May put Dave at number four behind Palomino, Roberto Duran and Thomas Hearns. Behind him came Harold Weston, Sugar Ray Leonard and Pete Ranzany, making him the only non-American in the top seven.

Leonard was the rising star, and even at this stage, Andy Smith recognised his immense talent and drawing power. "This Sugar Ray Leonard is doing for the welterweight division what Ali did for the heavyweights," he remarked. "He is injecting the same type of magic."

Although Top Rank promoter, Bob Arum, had Green under contract, such agreements in boxing have always had the habit of being broken under pressure from big money, which is exactly what happened.

During mid-May 1979, Dave's hopes of ever fighting Benitez were finally dashed when the champion signed for a bonanza fight with Leonard. The combined purse was said to be $2.2 million, and the fight scheduled to take place in the autumn. Benitez was not prepared to take any risks, so the promoters shelved any plans for him to face Green. Andy Smith was furious, and sent letters of protest to the Board of

Control and WBC, while Mickey Duff contacted Bob Arum. It was all to no avail.

* * *

Rafael Rodriguez, a 32-year-old Mexican boxing out of Minneapolis, USA, was known in boxing circles as one of the toughest and gamest welterweights around. A pro since 1970, he had been stopped only once back in 1972, despite having faced some of the best men in the world including Hedgemon Lewis (twice), Denny Moyer, Clyde Gray, Billy Backus, Harold Weston, Bruce Curry, Pete Ranzany (twice) and Sugar Ray Leonard.

A week before the fight, Andy Smith received a telephone call from his close friend Angelo Dundee who warned that Rodriguez was; "a tough devil with a concrete jaw." It was a view shared by most newspaper critics who predicted that Dave would have to travel the full distance.

Green, however, loved a challenge. Bursting with anger and frustration following the let-down over Benitez, he duly proved the critics wrong by becoming only the second man to stop the tough Mexican.

Again, he fought an impressive yet controlled fight, very similar to that against Hafey two weeks earlier. He opened quietly, even allowing Rodriguez to take the initiative and possibly the round. In the second, Green settled down and had the Mexican in trouble from a solid right to the body and left to the head combination.

Although Rodriguez was an old pro who knew how to fiddle his way out of danger, Dave would not be denied. He kept control throughout the third and fourth with solid jabbing, worked his opponent into corners and forced him to trade punches. Towards the end of round four he really cut loose, and in a sustained attack had the Mexican in all sorts of trouble, and holding on to avoid going down.

Referee, Harry Gibbs, checked the Mexican's condition before the start of round five in which he was again on the receiving end. Dave got right on top by jabbing well and slamming energy-sapping rights below the ribs.

The sixth was a rough round in which Green was warned for illegal use of an elbow, and Rodriguez for careless headwork. Although it was quieter, the Mexican looked tired and flat-footed, and was in trouble when Dave cut loose just before the bell.

He also controlled the seventh by patiently and systematically breaking up his tough opponent with solid accurate left jabs. It was one-way traffic.

"This is it, Dave – the last round," called Andy Smith as Green left his stool to start round eight. The European champion duly obeyed and went to work. Rodriguez was swamped as the Chatteris man doubled his punch-rate and hammered away furiously until Harry Gibbs stepped in after 50 seconds of the round. Although the Mexican made a token protest to the official, it was done so through pride. Despite still being on his feet, he had taken a lot of punishment, and his defiant, but largely ineffectual counter-attacks had ceased.

It was an impressive performance by Green, and a perfect tune-up for his European title defence against Jorgen Hansen in Denmark on 28 June. Describing him as a young, eager and sharp opponent, *Boxing News* editor, Harry Mullan wrote:

> Andy Smith has been as good as his promise to reincarnate Dave Green. The 1979 model is a mature calculating box-fighter, nothing like the rumbustious tearaway of the 1976-78 period… He works carefully for his openings, jabbing hard and in bursts.

* * *

After a two week holiday in Corfu, Dave commenced training for the fight against Hansen. Danish promoter, Mogens Palle, won the bidding, substantially beating that submitted by Harry Levene. The fight was originally set for Copenhagen, but when Danish television failed to meet the promoter's terms, it was switched to Randers.

Accompanied by Andy Smith, his son Robert and Danny

Holland, Dave travelled to Denmark a couple of days before the fight. They stayed at Aalberg about 30 miles from Randers where he kept loose at a local gym. A sizeable contingent of Fenland fans also made the trip by chartering a plane from Norwich. They included Dave's parents and members of his supporters club committee. Another group flew from Heathrow.

The 36-year-old Hansen was vastly experienced. After an eight year amateur career in which he won 136 of 157 contests, 82 inside the distance, he turned professional in 1969. In the paid ranks he had won 59 of his 72 fights with 28 victories coming inside schedule, but nine of 13 defeats had been by stoppage.

Hansen first boxed for the European championship in 1972, but was knocked out in 10 rounds by Roger Menetrey of France in what was his first defeat after 22 victories. He did, however, become a two-time European welterweight champion. In June 1977, he knocked out Italian, Mario Scano in five rounds, only to lose the title to Jorg Eipel of Germany on a 13th round disqualification. He regained it in April 1978, knocking out Alain Marion in six rounds, only to be disqualified again four months later in eight rounds against Josef Pachler. Going into the fight against Green, Hansen was unbeaten in four contests, the last being an eight round points decision over Billy Waith.

Despite his set-backs, the Dane was a proven puncher with a reputation of having a thunderous right cross. In a pre-fight interview, Andy Smith said: "Don't write Hansen off as a has-been. Other people have made that mistake and paid for it. He may be getting on, but he is still very dangerous with that right hand."

There was a lot of talk before the fight about Green struggling to make the weight. When pressed by Danish reporters, Smith insisted the rumours were untrue, and even invited them to watch Dave on the scales. Some expressed disappointment when he scaled half a pound under the championship limit because it meant they had no story.

"That's okay lads," said Smith with a smile. "You tell your readers, and Jorgen, that we've got real problems."

In the hours before a fight, Dave was normally very calm, but this time he was unusually on edge. He had been unable to sleep the night before, and in the dressing-room, couldn't keep still as he anxiously awaited being called to the ring.

"For Christ sake, calm down," said Andy Smith as he paced back and forth. "This man is dangerous, but after a few rounds you'll be alright. Just be sensible and keep your guard up."

Hansen entered the ring to thunderous applause from the packed Raudershallen, but stood stiffly in his corner as Green climbed through the ropes to some booing. The British contingent countered the discourtesy by giving their champion a massive cheer, and some Union Jacks were waved at ringside.

Weighing exactly on the welterweight limit of 10st 7, Dave had an advantage of just eight ounces. He made a good start, boxing calmly and picking his punches well, just as he did against Hafey and Rodriguez the previous month. Stiff jabs rammed into Hansen's face, and he also had some success with solid right crosses.

Looking to take early control, Green forced the Dane to retreat, and staggered him with a vicious right swing. To the delight of the British fans, a two-fisted attack had the challenger covering up on the ropes. The atmosphere was electric because the Danish fans roared with excitement whenever their man threw a punch, and there were a couple of early danger signs when he let his famed right hand go.

A solid right to the chin at the start of round two sent Hansen reeling into the ropes. Hooks to the head from both hands had him rocking as Green was quick to follow up. Another right to the head sent him crashing to the floor in a neutral corner. Although he was on his feet at 'two', the Dane looked decidedly unsteady as German referee, Kurt Halbach, gave him the mandatory eight-count.

Determined to finish it, Green strode forward at the order to 'box-on', but was wide open. A left-right combination from

Hansen caught him flush on the chin as he abandoned caution. A stream of left jabs and a good right hook all found the target as the local crowd screamed with excitement. The challenger was right back in the fight, and although Dave did not appear to be in any trouble, he had taken far too many head punches. It was thrilling stuff, and anybody's fight.

Knocking Hansen down was the worst thing that could have happened to Dave because it gave him a false sense of security. "I've got him, I've got him," he snarled as he returned to the corner brimming with confidence. "I'll knock him out in the next round."

"Calm down, calm down," yelled Andy Smith as Green slumped on his stool. "You've got all night to do this." Dave wasn't listening – he was too fired up, and couldn't wait for the bell.

In the opposite corner, the Danish camp were planning Green's downfall. "It's now or never," trainer Boerge Krogh, himself a European champion in 1966-67, told Hansen as he left his stool for the start of round three. He knew he had to win quickly, and Dave made his task easier.

Recklessly abandoning defence, Green went looking for a quick finish. Hansen stood his ground against the wild punches thrown at him, and hit back with a fast combination. The pro Danish crowd erupted as heavy punches from both hands followed.

A big grin across his face, Dave appeared to be relishing the punch-up, but looked more sullen when two hard rights dumped him in a heap beside the ropes. It was impossible to hear the count, but the champion was on his feet at eight or nine only to meet more trouble.

A solid professional, Hansen knew his man was going. Another two-fisted attack had Dave covering up before a vicious right flush on the chin sent him crashing face downwards to the canvas. Although he bravely struggled to his feet at eight, he lurched alarmingly as referee Halbach counted him out and led him to his corner. After just 44 seconds of round three Green was an ex-European champion.

226

Because of the noise, there was so much confusion at the end that it was not clear whether Green had been counted out or stopped. Determined there should be no misunderstanding, Herr Halbach, who spoke very little English, told the press: "Not referee stopped fight. Ten-out."

Always a true sportsman, Green joined in the applause as Hansen was presented with the championship belt. His only consolation was that as defending champion, he received 60% of the purse for what was his first professional contest abroad.

As he left the ring, the crestfallen Chatteris fighter paused to speak to British fans seated nearby. "I'll be back," he told them. One fan attempted to cheer him up by remarking that at least it wasn't for the world title. "It was for me though," said Dave.

The result of the fight was a terrible disappointment to the group of East Anglian fans who had made the trip to cheer on their idol. Rod Marriner, who was wearing an imitation tiger-skin jacket made especially for the occasion, quickly made his way towards the dressing-rooms to see Dave. On reaching the door, however, he decided it was not a sensible thing to do. Instead, he went to Hansen's dressing-room.

"Ah, the Fen Tiger," said the jubilant new champion as he popped his head out of the shower cubicle. Rod congratulated him and said he wanted him to have the jacket on condition he gave it back after Green had beaten him in a return.

"I do not think so," said Hansen with a smile. "I think I will have this for good."

Being without his jacket, Rod became cold later in the evening. He also suddenly realised that he had left his plane ticket in the pocket. Fortunately, Hansen was staying at the same hotel, and early the next morning Rod found him before he checked out. He gave him the ticket, but remarked: "You are not having the jacket."

The defeat was a major set-back for Dave who, by throwing caution to the wind, seemed to have forgotten all the lessons of the post-Palomino era. Andy Smith pulled no punches in the dressing-room because the fight was supposed to be a well-paid warm up against a man thought to be past his prime. Although neither he nor Green attended Mogens Palle's post-fight party, a few selected journalists were granted interviews.

"I don't know what David was thinking about by just walking towards him like he did," remarked the angry and thoroughly disappointed manager. "We had told him before he left the dressing-room to jab and double jab, keep his gloves up, and box for four or five rounds."

"He treated the man with contempt and took the consequences," added Smith. "It was going too easily for him in the first round. He gave the title away by his own foolishness. Hansen must have thought it was Christmas."

Typically, Green made no excuses, and agreed with his manager's assessment. "I was stupid. I was too cocky and too clever," he sobbed. "Things have been going too well, but now I have to get back up off the ground."

Even Hansen admitted being surprised at beating Dave so easily. "I had watched five films of Green's previous fights," he remarked, "and in every one of them he was bobbing and weaving, making himself a difficult target. But he came straight at me without attempting to cover up, and made himself so easy to hit."

Green's pride was always an important part of his tremendous fighting personality, and he felt he had let down the British fans. He had planned to stay in Denmark for a couple of days, but defeat changed all that. After raging unconsolably long into the night, he told Andy Smith there was nothing to stay for. The manager wasted no time, and ordered a private plane to fly them from Copenhagen the following morning. "I was so disgusted with my performance that all I wanted to do was go home," remarked Dave when recalling events.

Before leaving Denmark, Smith and Green gave interviews to reporters at their hotel over breakfast. Smith, who was more reflective than the previous evening, was adamant that Dave's own fighting heart proved to be the most decisive factor in his defeat. "He had the fight won, but threw it all away," insisted the manager. "He became over-eager to finish the job, and was getting caught by right hands. All the hours spent in the gym were lost in a matter of moments."

Dave knew he had to put the defeat behind him, and having had a few hours sleep, was in a more positive frame of mind. "If he will give me an immediate chance to get my title back, I won't want any money," he remarked. "Sorry, Mr Smith, I mean it. I'll fight him for nothing because I deserve nothing. I threw my title away and I want it back."

Negotiations for a return had, in fact, already commenced. Immediately after the fight, Mickey Duff spoke to Mogens Palle about the possibility of staging it at Wembley in September. The Danish promoter said it was possible provided the money was right, but made it clear that Hansen would want a huge pay-day to fight in London. One newspaper quoted the amount as being half a million kroner, (about £45,000).

Whilst Duff conceded that they would probably have to let Hansen name his price, Smith remained adamant. "We have got to get Hansen again, anywhere," he insisted with a hint of desperation. "I have got to get David another shot at that title. It's priority number one."

Board of Control General Secretary, Ray Clarke, who had been at the fight, was less optimistic. "Mountains have got to be moved to get them into the ring again," he remarked at a press conference.

Despite all the efforts, Dave never got a return contest. Plans to stage it were thwarted by an EBU ruling which prevented immediate return contests as had been the case three months earlier when efforts were made to match Green with Pacheco in a voluntary defence.

Although Hansen was deprived of a massive pay-day, he cashed in on the title by making seven defences before retiring in late 1981. He had home ground advantage on each occasion, and two of his defences were against British boxers, Joey Singleton and Horace McKenzie. He never showed any real interest in facing Green again.

Dave's powers of recovery, both physically and psychologically, were incredible. He had a very positive outlook, and within a few days of the defeat was back in the gym as though nothing untoward had happened.

✦ 15 ✦

SUGAR RAY

Although the defeat by Hansen was a serious set-back to his plans, Dave was honest enough to admit his mistakes. He made no excuses, but was quick to point out that both his professional defeats were basically one shot knockouts. "It's different to being battered for three or four rounds," he insisted. "I got over the Palomino defeat, and I'll get over this one."

After a three months break, he eased back with an undemanding task against Steve Michelarya, a 27-year-old schoolteacher from Pennsylvania at Wembley on 25 September. The fight was made over 10 rounds as the chief support to Maurice Hope's WBC light-middleweight title defence against Mike Baker.

Dave was itching to get back into action, and in the days leading up to the fight, was very keyed up. He knew he had to pick up the pieces and prove he had learned lessons from the Hansen fiasco.

As expected, the Chatteris man scored an emphatic victory inside three rounds, but still received criticism from some members of the press. Having been beaten on six occasions in 18 contests, the American was not in his class, but at this stage the quality of the opponent was not the priority. Despite Dave's confidence, the Hansen defeat was bound to have left a psychological scar. It was therefore important to take things steadily.

Green attacked from the opening bell and didn't let up until the job was done. There was one moment in the second round when he was caught by a hard right to the chin, prompting frantic screams from Andy Smith. "Box him, box him," yelled the manager from the corner. Dave responded well, switching his attacks to the body to have the American looking distinctly uncomfortable.

Strength and power took their toll in round three. Walking through Michelarya's jabs, Dave hooked heavily to the body. Accurate jabs and uppercuts forced the American into a neutral corner, and as Green piled it on, the fight was stopped after two minutes four seconds of the round.

Despite the set-backs against Palomino and Hansen, and adverse comments in the press, Dave's popularity remained as high as ever. He was constantly in demand to make public appearances throughout the United Kingdom, and he rarely let people down.

In November, he was Guest of Honour at the Jersey Dinner & Sporting Club at St Helier. The club were staging the Young England international trials at the Hotel de France, and among the cream of young boxers was Andy Smith's son, Robert.

A few months earlier, Dave had agreed to take part in a 'Fix-it' contest involving star motorcycle riders. His 'opponent' was British speedway champion, Michael Lee, who faced him over one three-minute round at the St Ives gym.

A member of King's Lynn speedway team, Lee was one of the heroes of the British Lions side which had recently thrashed Australia 7-0 in a test match. In the boxing ring, he found the going even tougher, especially when Green accidentally caught him flush on the nose.

Dave really struggled in his next contest, at Wembley on 4 December 1979. At the end he was greeted with boos and jeering for the only time in his career. Although he comfortably outpointed New England State champion, Dick

Ecklund, over 10 rounds, it was a disappointing affair, with many fans siding with the underdog.

Best known for taking Sugar Ray Leonard the distance at Boston in July 1978, Ecklund had been a professional since 1975, winning 12 of his 16 contests. After losing on his debut, he won the next 10 before travelling to London in early 1977 at the age of 19 where he trained at the Wellington gym, Highgate, under the guidance of former world middleweight champion, Terry Downes.

"After another six or seven fights, he could be ready for Dave Green," Downes told Graham Houston of *Boxing News*. The former world champion's assessment was spot on because, showing great courage and a fair amount of skill, Ecklund gave Dave a remarkably tough fight. Referee, Mike Jacobs score of $98^1/_2$-97 indicated that Green had won six rounds, Ecklund three, with one even.

Dave entered the ring to the usual rapturous reception from his fans, but many became almost silent as the bout progressed. Although the American was floored for a count of three in the second round, it was the only time he appeared to be in any trouble.

Unbeknown to the fans, Dave damaged his left thumb in that round, and the extent of the pain convinced him it was broken. For the remainder of the fight, he used his left sparingly, thus limiting his attack and making his performance appear somewhat pedestrian.

Technically, Green was the better fighter, but Ecklund attracted more attention with his mickey-taking antics. He did exercises in his corner during the intervals, and taunted Dave with the occasional remark of "that didn't hurt", when caught with a hefty blow. Even when floored in round two, he got up smiling.

Despite all the showboating, Green, always a true professional, quietly got on with his job. While many people in the crowd lapped up the American's antics, he piled up the points, but always had to be on his guard. Ecklund, however, had no respect for his reputation, and shook him a few times with good left hooks and right crosses. Despite being cut over the right eye in the fourth, and bleeding for the rest of the fight, the tough American never looked like being stopped.

No matter what the crowd thought, Andy Smith was unperturbed and remained as loyal as ever. "I was delighted with Green's performance," he remarked. "Ecklund was a mighty tough cookie. I didn't give him a round, even though Dave thought he had broken his thumb."

After X-rays at Doddington Hospital, it was found that the left thumb was partially dislocated. Requiring regular treatment, Dave attended out-patients every day for a fortnight for ultrasound treatment designed at getting deep into the bone to speed recovery.

* * *

On 30 November 1979, at Las Vegas, Sugar Ray Leonard took the WBC welterweight title from Wilfredo Benitez by stoppage with just six seconds of the fight remaining. Although the ending was described as controversial, all three judges had the challenger ahead.

In Britain, Kirkland Laing, whom Green beat three times as an amateur, had captured the welterweight championship from Henry Rhiney, and Colin Jones from Gorseinon, was emerging as a tremendous prospect. He had won a final eliminator for the right to challenge Laing. The fact that no attempt had been made to match Dave with either man, was a clear indication of his determination to pursue world honours.

Shortly after Leonard became champion, representations were made on Green's behalf. Negotiations went well, and on 10 January 1980, it was confirmed that he would challenge Sugar Ray at Las Vegas or Maryland in March on a date still to be finalised.

Some critics expressed concern at the WBC's agreement to the contest. The governing body's normal ruling called for any boxer winning a championship from a voluntary defence, as

Leonard had done, to make his first defence against the official number one contender. Yet with Sugar Ray, the WBC appeared to be turning a blind eye. Not only was he making a voluntary defence against Green, but planned another against Roberto Duran during the summer.

Boxing politics being what they are, Dave was fortunate to have excellent connections, especially after having seemingly been eliminated from the world title scene by Hansen. He had been relegated to number eight in the world rankings which no doubt helped his cause because the Leonard camp saw him as an undemanding first defence. He also struggled with Andy Price in 1977 whom Sugar Ray stopped in the opening round two years later.

Andy Smith, however, was unmoved. "It would be wrong to turn down the chance," he remarked. "There's no doubt that Leonard is a great fighter, but it's styles that make fights. Dave feels very confident about the job."

Although it was originally planned for the fight to be staged at Las Vegas, it was eventually set for Landover, Maryland on 31 March. Green and Smith had preferred Vegas, but agreed to the change because the stadium held 19,500 and was set some 15 miles from the US capital, Washington.

Once agreement was reached, Dave was called to America for promotional purposes. Early on 6 February, he and Andy travelled to Heathrow and flew to Washington. On arrival they were taken to the Capital Centre, Maryland, for a press conference at which contracts were signed, and Dave met Leonard for the first time. He also had the opportunity to watch films of the champion in action against Pete Ranzani and Armando Muniz.

As with most meetings with the press, Andy Smith was their spokesman. "Leonard's obviously something special, but the people he's met haven't pressured him the way Green will," he remarked. "Dave knows he will be the underdog, but wasn't favoured against Palomino or Stracey either. His mental attitude is just right, and he's going to surprise a lot of people."

235

Some American reporters were critical of Dave as a challenger, making particular reference to his defeat by Hansen. "Everyone loses," said Smith calmly. "The great Joe Louis was knocked out by Max Schmeling, the incomparable Ray Robinson lost more than a dozen fights, and Willie Pep lost a few too. Dave made a mistake against Hansen and was punished."

The state of British boxing also came under fire, but Andy stood his ground and gave as good as he got. "You do know Britain has three current world champions, don't you?" he asked one journalist who made derogatory remarks.

"Oh," was the response of the man who hadn't done his homework.

When asked by another individual why the British did not win many battles abroad, Smith again had the perfect answer. "There's one guy who wouldn't agree with you," he said tersely.

"And who is that?" enquired the journalist.

"Adolf Hitler," snapped Smith.

Back home after the demanding three-day trip, Dave immediately resumed training. He was well into his schedule when called to America, having commenced as soon as the fight was confirmed in early January. He started by running four miles each morning during the first week, increasing it to six the next. By the end of the month he was pounding between six and seven miles a day around the Fenland lanes to Setchfield and Langwood, and on his father's farmland. By the end of the month he had done 162 miles which he meticulously logged each day in a diary.

Early sparring was done with his brother-in-law, Steve Hopkin from Ely, who was also managed by Andy Smith. He held the Southern Area light-middleweight title, and had lost just one of 16 professional starts. He was very much the quiet man of the camp whose career had progressed almost unnoticed while the media focused on Green. Although Steve had the same fiery enthusiasm, there was no rivalry between him and Dave. They were quite close, having sparred hundreds of rounds and done much of their early morning roadwork together.

As the training intensified, Dave also had regular sparring sessions with Des Morrison, Jimmy Harrington, and Andy Smith's son, Robert, a national schoolboy champion in 1978. Weight training was introduced into the demanding daily schedule which also included other strength-building exercises such as squat-thrusts and pull-ups, work on the speedball, heavy bag and with a medicine ball, and also periods of shadow-boxing.

In order to sharpen-up, Dave also travelled to the Royal Oak gym, at Canning Town in east London in early March. There he did five round sessions with Kirkland Laing who was also helping Jim Watt prepare for his world lightweight title defence against Charlie Nash.

Throughout the training period, members of the press made frequent visits to the St Ives gym, and Andy Smith was always pleased to accommodate them. Having been in Brian Curvis' corner when he challenged Emile Griffith for the welterweight title in 1964, and assisted Joe Bugner and Green against Ali and Palomino in 1975 and '77 respectively, it would be his fourth world championship contest as a manager or trainer. Yet in his opinion it was the most formidable challenge.

"Everyone agrees Dave has the hardest task of all British fighters trying to win titles," he told a reporter from the *Cambridgeshire Times*, "but if I could wish a world title upon anyone in the world, I would wish it on Green."

"He's the most dedicated boxer in the world," he added. "I have no worries about him at all. He does as he is told, and I know he won't pull any punches either in the ring or in training."

Smith believed Dave was the best of the British boxers currently in the hunt for world titles. "If he was in the same weight division as Alan Minter or John Conteh, then he would already be world champion," insisted Smith. "This lad is terribly unlucky to have been born when he was. At no other

237

time in the history of the welterweight division has there been such strength in depth."

Despite his intense training schedule, Dave still found time to perform other tasks. At the end of February, he was best man at the wedding of his pal, Jimmy Harrington, at Biggleswade Registry Office. On 12 March, he and Des Morrison travelled to London and collected their work permits from the American Embassy. Morrison was also boxing on the Maryland bill against Ortis Hooper in what was essentially a warm-up for his British light-welterweight championship eliminator against Sylvester Mittee on 27 April.

By the time he left for the United States on 15 March, Green had sparred a total of 83 rounds and completed over 350 miles of roadwork. His dedication and enthusiasm were incredible, and even on the eve of his departure, watched by a crowd of reporters, he sparred 15 rounds with Morrison, Hopkin, Harrington and Smith.

"There is not a more dedicated fighter anywhere in the world than Dave Green," insisted Andy Smith. "I shall go to bed tonight a very happy man after watching him spar those 15 rounds. If I had as much money as he has stamina and determination, then I would be a millionaire twice over."

Green, Smith, Morrison and Danny Holland left for the United States on 15 March. They flew to Washington, then on to Knoxville, Tennessee, where Dave shared a training camp with 'Big' John Tate who was preparing for his WBA heavyweight title defence against Mike Weaver.

Dave got a great send-off from Heathrow, particularly from three young supporters from Hurlington School, Fulham, wearing Fen Tiger T-shirts and waving Union Jacks.

Karen Poulter, a former Chatteris resident, was an avid Green fan when she lived in the Cambridgeshire town. On moving to Fulham, she maintained her interest and formed a Dave 'Boy' Green fan club. When she discovered that he was to fly from nearby Heathrow airport, she and two friends decided to be there to see him off in style.

A party of 25 loyal Fenland supporters made the trip to

America abroad an Air India flight. They included Dave's mother, father and brother. Before leaving Chatteris, they hung 'Good Luck' banners across the main street.

Kay was not allowed to travel because she was expecting their first child in June. Her doctor advised that the extensive travel, high altitude and strain from the pre-fight build-up, should be avoided.

At Knoxville, Dave ran four miles each day and continued routine training which included sparring with Des Morrison. For relaxation, he played table tennis with John Tate, went shopping, and one afternoon visited the local zoo.

By the conclusion of his preparations, Green had done 120 rounds of sparring, and laboured hard in an attempt to prove his doubters wrong. By fight-time, he was sharp, fit and remarkably confident. He couldn't wait to get to grips with the man whose popularity was becoming almost as great as that of Muhammed Ali, and made it clear he had no wish to become a good loser.

Despite most critics giving him no chance, Dave remained positive. "Let us hope that Leonard treats me with as much contempt as I treated Hansen," he remarked. "I didn't like getting stopped, and it was a terrible blow to my pride. But I stuck my chin out and got hit. No one was to blame except myself."

Whilst in America, Dave was also committed to a busy pre-fight promotional schedule. Early on the morning of 24 March, he and Andy Smith flew from Knoxville to Washington for a television interview. They were also taken on a sight-seeing trip which included a one-hour visit to the White House. The following day, they attended a press conference at Baltimore, and on 26 March did a radio interview in Washington. The next day, Dave underwent a pre-fight medical examination and check weigh. He scaled 10st 9 and Leonard 10-10½.

The British party moved from Knoxville to Maryland the weekend before the fight. There they faced a glut of press interviews, and at each one Andy Smith emphasised that Dave must keep out of trouble during the early rounds. The incentive for victory was massive because Smith claimed to have a contract guaranteeing that if Green took the title, negotiations for his first defence would open at $1 million.

During the build-up to the fight, it was well known that Leonard wanted to rile Dave. It was claimed that at one press conference he even asked a British journalist what he could say that would be derogatory towards him. The writer refused to get involved.

"I know he would like to get me angry," said Dave when he was told, "but I'm not going to oblige."

Taunting opponents had become almost an accepted part of championship boxing ever since Muhammed Ali invaded Sonny Liston's training camp in 1964. In many ways Leonard was similar to Ali, and had taken over from him as a boxing cult figure in the States.

Like Ali, Sugar Ray could be charming or cruel and irritating. When he and Green passed each other in a corridor at the Capital Centre, Maryland, where they were attending a press conference, not a word passed between them, but their looks could have been a flashpoint.

Despite his gamesmanship, Sugar Ray expressed great respect for Dave. "I know it's going to be a dynamite fight," he remarked. "If Green throws as many punches as he says he can – 72 a minute – my strategy will be to wear him down. Any challenger is capable of beating the champion, given the time and the right moment."

"Green's determination impressed me," added Leonard. "He really seems to want my title. That's why I've been working and developing my left jab."

Dave became somewhat irritated by members of the American press, many of whom were confused by his East Anglian accent. Consequently, he was often misquoted, while others wrote him off as a no-hoper. "I didn't come here for a bloody holiday," he snapped at one reporter. "I'm going to let the American public know I've got hands and feet."

According to the press, the Leonard camp were confident Dave didn't have the speed or power to bother the champion.

They said he was slow, and attacked with his chin in the air. In other words, he was a 'face-fighter'.

"Does this look like a face that has taken a beating," he asked. "I've got Danny Holland, the best cuts man in the business, and he hasn't had to work on me yet."

Despite the efforts of the press and promoters, Dave flatly refused to a get-together with Leonard before the fight. "I didn't come to America to befriend the guy," he snarled.

Whilst the schedule was demanding and often tense, there were moments of relaxation. A couple of nights before the fight, Green, Smith and Holland unexpectedly showed up at one of Towson's more unpretentious pubs. They went there to meet fellow Britons because the establishment was the haunt of a group of former Royal Air Force officers residing at Baltimore.

Bill Langston, an 84-year-old Londoner, who was custodian of British graves at Lorraine Park Cemetery, presented Dave with miniature replicas of the Union Jack and St George's Cross.

Before leaving, Andy Smith, with a small scotch in his hand, toasted his fighter, the RAF, and: "to a hell of a good fight gentlemen."

* * *

An Olympic gold medallist at light-welterweight in 1976, Sugar Ray Leonard had become a huge box-office attraction in America. A measure of his popularity was that his contest with Benitez drew the largest television ratings for any fight which did not involve Muhammed Ali.

With sharp reflexes, fast hands and a good punch he was a great exponent of boxing technique. Going into the fight with Green he had won all his 26 professional contests, 17 inside schedule. His opponents had been carefully selected by his veteran adviser and cornerman, Angelo Dundee, and as a result had overcome all conceivable styles. Almost faultless performances against Pete Ranzany, Andy Price and Wilfredo

Benitez confirmed his class. Consequently, all $100 ringside seats for the Green fight were snapped up within days of going on sale.

The humidity in Maryland made it easy for Dave to make the championship limit of 10st 7. Back home he always had to work hard to shift the final few pounds. At the official weigh in ceremony at noon on the day of the fight, he was right on the limit, as was Leonard. At 5ft 10, the champion was the taller by two inches.

Green had arrived at the Capital Centre wearing a kashmir coat, cowboy boots and a stetson hat which had been signed by 'Big' John Tate. Whilst he had little to say other than to express his confidence, Leonard was quite vocal. "Green is a puncher, so this is going to be a great fight," he said likening it to the first contest between Muhammed Ali and Joe Frazier. "I am the champ, I have the quickness of hands and the ability to defend by dancing. Green, like Frazier, has the strength, the durability and endurance. There really is a perfect blend of styles."

* * *

There was a full house at the Capital Centre. Preceding the main event, Des Morrison stopped Otis Hooper in the third round of a contest cut from eight rounds to four to accommodate television requirements. The WBA heavyweight title fight between John Tate and Mike Weaver was then beamed live from Knoxville on a huge 12 by 16 foot telescreen.

Green entered the ring in a confident mood, and during pre-fight preliminaries, glared at Leonard as he gave an interpretation of the Ali shuffle. There was also the customary eyeballing as referee, Arthur Mercante, issued his final instructions.

Urged on by a small, but noisy group of flag-waving British supporters, Dave began positively, throwing stiff left jabs behind a high guard. Shuffling purposely forward, he bobbed and weaved in an attempt to get inside and work to the body, but found the champion relaxed and elusive.

Leonard, who had predicted that Green would fall in the opening round, started as though he was doing a public workout before the capacity crowd. Hands at his sides, he appeared content to let Dave make the running. He backed away and threw very few punches until late in the round when he scored with two stiff jabs. At the bell Green returned to his corner with a slight cut on the side of his nose.

The pace quickened at the start of the second. Green scored with two good jabs to the head, and Leonard replied with a couple of flashy uppercuts, both of which were out of range. He did score with two hooks to the body, but when Dave threw his 'muck-spreader', Sugar Ray got inside and scored well to the body.

Although Dave gave ground whenever the champion opened up, he was not overawed by the task he faced. He produced the higher work-rate, but Leonard's silky skills made him a very difficult target to hit cleanly. Sugar Ray was also more accurate, and when forced to the ropes, counter-punched well with both hands.

Dave went straight on the attack at the start of round three, pumping out jabs, but ran into a good left to the body. When he threw a wild right swing, Leonard ducked underneath and worked to the body.

Oozing confidence, the champion looked intent on dictating the pace. At times, he ambled away from Green's attacks, and gave the impression that he believed he could end the contest whenever he liked.

Two lefts from Green in the opening seconds of the fourth shook Leonard and stung him into action. Standing his ground, he countered with a left and began putting together hurtful combinations. Showing his true class, he upped the pace and shook Dave with a right uppercut. A flurry of accurate shots followed, ending with a thunderous left hook to the chin which ended the fight.

The speed, power and accuracy of the blows were

incredible. Green was sent crashing backwards and fell into unconsciousness before his head struck the canvas with a sickening thud. As the referee stooped to take up the count, Andy Smith was already kneeling at Dave's side tugging out his gum shield. Realising the British boxer was badly hurt, Mercante immediately dispensed with the count and signalled the end.

The sudden and dramatic ending caused great anguish to Dave's mother sitting at ringside. She desperately tried to hold back her tears, then tried in vain to enter the ring to be near her stricken son. She had seen the crushing left hook smash against his jaw, and watched with alarm as his head thudded against the canvas.

Dave lay motionless for almost five minutes, and even after he had regained consciousness, it was a further 10 minutes before he could dispose of support from Andy Smith. Once he had recovered, the result was announced as a technical knockout, but at the insistence of the referee, corrected to a clean knockout at two minutes 27 seconds of round four.

Leonard feared the worst as Dave lay on the floor. "For the first time in my 10 years of boxing, I felt frightened after knocking somebody out," he admitted later. "When he lay there and they checked his eyes, I got a very funny feeling that I can't explain. I was scared."

One of the bravest professionals around, Green gave it all he had, and his defeat was no disgrace. In Sugar Ray, he was facing a man who was rapidly establishing himself as an all-time great. Against Dave, he showed devastating hand speed, and seemed able to land punches from the most acute angles.

Following a wave to his small army of supporters at ringside, some wrapped in Union Jacks, he hugged his sobbing mother. "I don't like losing," he said emotionally. "I've let all my fans down. They came all the way over here and I've let them down."

Back in the solitude of his dressing-room, Dave was distraught. Tears streaming down his face, he still asked what happened. When he tried to stand up almost an hour after the fight, he was still unsteady from the effect of Leonard's wonder punch.

Only after undergoing stringent medical checks was Green given the all-clear, but doctors still advised him to take it easy for a few days. Instead of attending the post-fight press conference, he was taken back to his hotel room where he promptly retired to bed.

Meanwhile, Sugar Ray was generous in his praise of Dave. "He caught me with a couple of good shots to the body, and was an awkward type of fighter to deal with," he remarked. "He reminded me of a mini Ken Norton the way he bobbed and rolled with the punches, always looking to work downstairs."

"Green has the will and qualities of a champion," he added. "Unfortunately, he ran into me." Leonard insisted that the left hook which ended the fight was one of the heaviest punches he had ever thrown. "Some people still say I can't punch," he said, "but maybe after tonight they will start changing their minds."

Despite his disappointment, Andy Smith acknowledged the sheer class of Leonard. "Gentlemen, you have just witnessed a young man who may be the greatest welterweight champion ever to have stepped into the ring," he gracefully told the press. "I have been around boxing a long time and seen some of the best, but he tops them all."

"I was proud of Dave tonight," continued the manager. "He gave everything he had, and you can't ask for more than that."

When the inevitable questions were asked about Dave's future, Smith refused to speculate. The debates went on into the early hours, but the manager flatly refused to announce his fighter's retirement. He recalled how the press urged Henry Cooper to retire years before his time, but he went on to prove them wrong.

The reporters, most of whom were from British newspapers, reasoned that their main concern with Cooper was that he was cut-prone. It had nothing to do with punishing defeats. With Green it was through compassion for a man who had excited the fans from his early amateur days.

Standing his ground, Andy Smith argued that every boxer should be allowed time for thought, and undergo extensive medical checks before making any rash decisions regarding his future. "That is what will happen with David," he insisted. "If, and only if, these tests show a deterioration, will the question of his retirement be raised."

"I will know when it is time for Dave Green to retire," added the manager. "I will advise him, and when he has reached a decision I will tell you. Until that time comes, the matter is closed."

The question of Green's welfare was not only a matter of concern for members of the press. Immediately after the fight, the Maryland State Boxing Commission suspended him from fighting for *'at least 60 days'*, twice the normal period imposed on a fighter following a knockout. "It was such a bad knockout that we had to take extra precaution," said Jack Cohen, executive secretary of the commission. "Green was already floating in the air unconscious before his head hit the floor."

* * *

Two days after returning home, Dave was the guest of Chatteris Parish Council at a special event in his honour at Cromwell Community Centre. Despite the defeat to Leonard, his faithful fans turned up in droves and gave him a tremendous welcome.

"We all share in your disappointment, but in no way at all did we feel let down," said Parish Council Chairman, Rita Goodger. "We are all very proud of our Chatteris lad. It was no disgrace to lose to such a great champion."

Roger Heading, the town's County Councillor, congratulated Green on bringing honour to Cromwell College where he had been a pupil. He said that such sporting achievements confirmed his belief that a high quality sports hall should be built at the college.

Fenland District Council were represented by Vice-chairman, Councillor Freddie Grounds, who told the gathering that Dave had set a wonderful example by giving a sporting lead to the region.

Huge cheers greeted the Chatteris fighter as he took the microphone. "I did my best, and think I was as fit for this fight as I have ever been," he said. "I don't think I could have done any more." He thanked the councillors, members of his supporters' club and townsfolk for their incredible loyalty.

The following evening, more than 200 fans attended a 'Welcome Home' buffet dance at the Palace, organised by Dave's supporters' club committee.

Meanwhile, several leading sports journalists were calling for Green to retire. Writing in the *Daily Telegraph*, Donald Saunders said:

Green would be wise to call it a day even though he is only 26. Three defeats in 36 contests is an honourable record.

Colin Hart of *The Sun* had similar thoughts:

Predictably, all Andy Smith would say was that it was too early to make any decisions about Green's future. I say enough is enough.

Along with other members of the press, Hart was extremely concerned about Dave's health, fearing that he could have lasting injuries. So too did Green's father, and when the journalist spoke to him some days later, Ken admitted: "I thought he had killed him."

Despite the feelings of the press boys, with whom he had an excellent relationship, Dave kept an open mind and remained very positive about the situation. "When you get hit by a punch as perfect as that, it doesn't hurt at all," he told Ian Wooldridge of the *Daily Mail*. "You don't feel a thing – it's goodnight, that's all."

247

"Listen, there is danger in everything you do," he continued, anxious to get over his point of view. "If something happened to me in the ring, at least I'd go out doing something I enjoy."

Green knew that his future depended on a meeting with a Harley Street specialist scheduled for 2 June when he would be given a brain-scan. "If that surgeon says there's some damage, I'll finish," he remarked. "If he doesn't then I'm going to continue."

Although the knockout had caused great anguish to his mother, Dave was back in the gym sparring just four days after returning home. The following day, he went for a four mile run, and continued on a regular basis. In the absence of Andy Smith, who was on holiday in Israel, he also helped Des Morrison prepare for a British title final eliminator against Sylvester Mittee, set for 22 April.

✦ 16 ✦

ONE LAST FLING

Although his career was on hold throughout the summer, Dave had plenty to occupy his time. At very short notice, he was invited to replace European middleweight champion, Kevin Finnegan, in a heat of the 1980 Superstars competition being staged at Orton Bushfield Sports Centre, Peterborough, on 3 and 4 June. Kevin had withdrawn after sustaining an elbow injury defending his title against Georg Steinherr at Munich on 14 May.

The suddenness of the invitation meant that the medical examination planned for 2 June had to be postponed. Andy Smith took the view that Superstars would confirm Dave's fitness level, and keep him in the public eye. "However well he does, it will be a tribute to how well the lad keeps himself in shape," Smith told the press after receiving the invitation.

Green had been in training for six weeks and shown no ill effects from the Leonard fight. Having put the defeat to the back of his mind, he had adopted the attitude that it was just another setback. His brother-in-law, Steve Hopkin, was preparing for an official British light-middleweight title eliminator against Charlie Malarky in Glasgow on 7 June. Each morning Dave accompanied him during roadwork, and sparred with him most evenings at the gym.

Without any special event training, Dave faced tough competition in the two-day Superstars event from footballers, Mike Channon, Gary Owen and Frank Gray, table tennis star, Desmond Douglas, skier Conrad Bartelski, and Roger Uttley and Andy Ripley from Rugby Union. Although he won the weight-lifting ahead of Channon and Bartelski, he did not perform as well as in previous years. Third place at swimming, fourth in the gym tests and canoeing, fifth at cycling and cricket, and sixth in basketball put him in overall seventh place with 19$^1/_2$ points. Winner of the competition was Uttley.

Green also proved his fitness by playing the full 90 minutes in a charity football match against a Tottenham Hotspur team at Soham. It helped raise £200 for the family of Bobby Skinner, manager of Cambridgeshire League Division Five champions, Ely AWA, (Anglian Water Authority) who had recently passed away.

* * *

On the morning of 28 June, at Ely RAF hospital, Kay gave birth to a baby boy, David Andrew, who weighed 8lb 14oz. It was a difficult birth because the baby was very broad across the shoulders, and lying face up instead of down. Dave was present throughout, and although he found it very distressing to see his wife in such discomfort, always maintained he wouldn't have missed it. Three days later, a photograph of the family appeared in the *Cambridgeshire Times.*

Kay had to stay in hospital for five days, and because of staff shortages Dave had to bath her and run errands. Once she was home, he was willing to do anything. He was gentle, com-passionate and loving, and quickly adapted to the role of being a father. He got up during the night to change his son's nappy and feed him, and during the day took him out in the pram.

Dave was thrilled at having a son. "Fantastic, just what I wanted," he told a local newspaper reporter.

* * *

Green's medical examination was re-scheduled for 7 July 1980. Accompanied by Andy Smith, he saw a neurologist at Addenbrookes Hospital, Cambridge, and underwent a brain scan. Three days later he attended Wellington Hospital, St John's Wood for a second opinion. The results from both hospitals confirmed that he had sustained no permanent damage.

Copies of the reports were sent to the British Boxing Board of Control and subsequently put before a meeting of the Southern Area Council on 6 August. It was agreed that Green and Andy Smith should attend an emergency meeting at the Board headquarters in London on 18 August.

Reports of Mr M.F.T. Yelland, Consultant Neurologist at Addenbrookes Hospital, Dr Ira Bletcher of Maryland, USA, Dr Jorgen Huusom of the Danish Professional Boxing Association, and Dr Adrian Whiteson, Chief Medical Officer of the British Boxing Board of Control, were read. Witnesses were also called on Green's behalf.

Addressing the Stewards, Andy Smith said that Dave had in the past, experienced difficulty making the welterweight limit. He was therefore considering moving up to light-middle.

Smith said that whilst he understood and appreciated the Board's concern following Dave's defeat against Leonard, he nevertheless felt the stewards may be influenced by the Willie Classen affair.

Classen, a 29 year old Puerto Rican journeyman, had been battered to defeat in 10 rounds by unbeaten middleweight prospect, Wilfred Scypion, in New York on 23 November. Five days later he died of his injuries. The previous month, as a late substitute, he had been knocked out in two rounds at the Royal Albert Hall by Tony Sibson. Immediately after the fight, he had been taken to Moorfields Eye Hospital suffering from double vision. Following his death, serious questions were raised in the press regarding his licensing and medical condition prior to those fights.

In answer to questions, Smith stated that Green's natural weight was 10st 10. He added that if permitted to continue boxing he would not perform at world level again, but concentrate on attempting to win British and European titles. Attending Addenbrookes Hospital had been for peace of mind of boxer and manager. Smith assured the stewards that he would never put Dave's health at risk. "I promise you that not only will I take responsibility for his career, but if he looks like going downhill, I'll pull him out," he remarked. It was an agreement they had anyway because Smith would never take a chance with any of his boxers.

After considering all of the evidence, in particular that of independent medical consultants, the Stewards decided that they were not justified in revoking Dave's licence. He would, however, remain suspended until 1 October after which date he could resume boxing, preferably at light-middleweight.

"He's delighted, I'm delighted, and I'm sure everybody is delighted at the news," said Andy Smith to a small group of journalists waiting outside the Board offices. "We have really got to play it by ear. He will have a fight in October, see how it goes and take it from there. After one or two fights we should know where to aim ourselves."

Given the all-clear, Green increased his level of training. He ran an average of five miles each day, and sparred on a regular basis, mostly with Steve Hopkin. By moving up from welterweight, he would resist the temptation of several money-spinning fights, including a return with European champion, Jorgen Hansen, and new British champion, Colin Jones, who had expressed a willingness to meet him.

Promoter, Harry Levene, planned to ease him back with an eight round contest against American, Earl Lyburo, on the Alan Minter – Marvin Hagler bill at Wembley on 27 September. Andy Smith wrote to the Board seeking permission, but even though matchmaker, Mickey Duff, had announced the contest, the Southern Area Council refused to sanction it. Smith even travelled to London and attempted to persuade the Stewards to change their decision, but to no avail. The Board subsequently issued a statement to qualify the decision:

Mr Smith and Mr Green were advised in April that we were

suspending the boxer's licence until 1 October. The Council are not prepared to let Green box before that date in his own interests. Although it is only a matter of a few days, we have made that decision. The majority of Council members felt that was the best period of time.

Although he was annoyed at the decision, Andy Smith accepted that the announcement of the fight was premature. "David has been training all summer," he insisted. "If he is not ready now, he never will be."

The ban still wrangled with Dave years later. "Other boxers are floored and they are cleared," he remarked angrily when recalling the situation. "I get knocked out by the greatest man ever, and look what they did. What else did they expect?"

Despite Dave's appetite for boxing, the sport had come under close scrutiny by the time of his proposed return. Apart from the Willie Classen affair, Welsh bantamweight, Johnny Owen, was in a coma at a Los Angeles hospital following a shattering defeat at the hands of WBC champion, Lupe Pintor. That tragedy added weight to the opinion of some leading sports writers that Green should not be permitted to fight again.

Writing in *Boxing News*, Frank Butler, Sports Editor of the *News of the World*, was particularly critical of the Board of Control:

> Dave had been concussed in three rounds when losing the European title to Jorgen Hansen, a fighter of 36 years. He held no British crown when he signed to fight Leonard, so the Board could have, and should have, intervened.
>
> We know there were problems. Green was offered £50,000, but surely nobody in boxing honestly believed he had a chance of beating Leonard. It was a bad match without justification because there could be only one winner.

Butler, a great writer of many years experience, insisted that if Dave continued he should be carefully monitored:

> Green must be watched if he again becomes too ambitious. He

is a gutsy fighter who wants to give good value, but his defence has always been poor and his jaw suspect against a good puncher.

Dennis Lehane in the *Sunday Times* was also extremely critical of the Board for sanctioning the contest. He made reference to the Classen affair, and stressed that people looking at boxing were still very sensitive.

Dave eventually returned to action against southpaw, Mario Mendez, at the Royal Albert Hall on 14 October 1980. Mendez, from Tijuana, Mexico, but boxing out of New York, claimed a record of 25 wins and two draws from 35 fights. Having faced world rated fighters, Alexis Arguello and Monroe Brookes, he was considered an ideal opponent to ease Dave back.

Although financially secure through boxing, Green fought for the love of it rather than need. Yet he still believed he had enough left to give it one more shot. For what was probably the most critical test of his entire career, he showed all his old menace as he climbed through the ropes. He glowered at the Mexican, and engaged in the customary eyeballing when they were called to the centre of the ring by referee, Sid Nathan.

Looking in peak condition, Dave used the opening round to size up his opponent. When he let go the occasional right swing to the head, it became clear that Mendez lacked the strength or know-how to keep him off.

Although the Mexican scored with good punches early in the second, he was soon looking for a way out once he felt the power of Green's hooks to the body. A vicious left hook made him wince, and he looked appealingly at referee Nathan claiming he had been hit in the kidneys.

With typical aggression, Dave increased the tempo, thumping home a solid combination to the head. The end was not far away, and when Mendez collapsed spectacularly to the canvas from a barrage of punches, the Fenland supporters went wild. Although he was up at five, the Mexican's legs dipped badly. As he grabbed the ropes for support, Green piled in, forcing Nathan to step in at two minutes 20 seconds of the round. Both men scaled 10st 10¹/₄.

Green's army of fans gave him a tremendous ovation as he left the ring, proof that even without a title he was still a tremendous box-office attraction. Some critics, however, felt that his victory was a hollow one because he was up against a poor quality opponent. In fact, the promotion was a disaster, becoming known as '*The Night of the Mexican Roadsweepers*'. Whilst Mendez lasted only two rounds, it was longer than three other Mexican's who were swiftly beaten by Charlie Magri, Cornelius Boza-Edwards and Jimmy Flint.

The plan was to keep Dave busy with a fight every six to eight weeks, and to assess his progress after each one. He was next matched with Everaldo Costa Azevedo of Argentina over 10 rounds at Wembley on 25 November, but for financial reasons the fight fell through. Efforts to match him at the Royal Albert Hall in December were also unsuccessful.

The comeback eventually got back on track at the Albert Hall on 27 January 1981 with a sixth round stoppage victory over Gary Holmgren of Minnesota, USA. Victories over Jose Roman Gomez (points) and Danny Long (rsc.4) followed on 24 February and 2 June respectively, also at the Royal Albert Hall.

Although the critics continued to call for his retirement, Green always believed he could win another championship. Andy Smith wholeheartedly supported his fighter, who despite being out of action for three months prior to fighting Holmgren, remained in constant training. "People don't realise the intense desire within David Green," he remarked. "The loss to Leonard was no disgrace, and now he is eager to re-establish himself."

Holmgren, a professional since 1974, confirmed his reputation of being an aggressive hit or be hit type of fighter. The contest was a bruising affair and not one for the purists, with neither man concerned about the niceties of the game. Both were careless with the head, and as a result Holmgren sustained a vertical cut between the eyes, and Green a gash over the left eyebrow.

Despite looking fleshy at 10st 11¼, his heaviest ever, Dave's victory was convincing enough. He used his left jab well, thumped plenty of heavy rights to the ribs, and was always in control. By the end of round two, the American was bleeding from the nose, and had a graze above the left eye.

Holmgren was, however, a good test because despite not being world class, he showed plenty of aggression and landed his share of full-blooded shots. Yet Green took them well and was never in trouble at any stage of the fight.

Both men were cut in round four following head clashes. An inch long gash on Green's left eyebrow caused some concern to his fans, but good work by cornerman, Danny Holland, stemmed the flow of blood.

The American bravely stood his ground and punched it out during the fifth, but was wide open to the 'muck-spreader'. His left eye completely closed, he couldn't see them coming, and big punches repeatedly crashed against his chin. Green relished the challenge, and when Gary scored with two hard rights, he slammed back with two-fisted attacks to have the American in trouble at the bell.

Dave kept up the pressure in round six, and although Holmgren never went to the floor, he was being overpowered by surging aggression. Green never let up, and with the American bleeding badly from his injuries and unable to throw anything back, referee, Mike Jacobs, did the humane thing and called a halt after two minutes 38 seconds of the round.

Holmgren had no complaints and was full of praise for Dave. "The way we bored into each other, there were bound to be head clashes, but they were all accidents," he remarked sportingly. "Everyone says Green is a slugger and brawler, but he is a good boxer. He is a world class fighter. I couldn't land that big punch and couldn't take the heat away from him. He was in fantastic condition."

* * *

The following afternoon, Dave was among a number of

former boxers to attend the funeral of Eric Boon at Chatteris Parish Church. The former British lightweight champion died at Newmarket General Hospital on 19 January following a heart attack at his Soham home. Affectionately known as the first *Fen Tiger of the Ring*, he had done a massive amount of charity work during the later years of his life. Like Green, he had always lived in the Fens.

Dave never forgot the encouragement given to him by Boon. "He gave me my enthusiasm for the job when I first started boxing," he told the *Chatteris Advertiser*. "He was the person I set out to try and emulate. He was there for my first professional fight, and was there when I won the British title. He gave me plenty of inspiration, and I'll never forget that."

* * *

Within a week of beating Gary Holmgren, it was announced that Dave would face Spanish welterweight champion, Jose Ramon Gomez Fouz, on 24 February. A former European light-welterweight champion in 1975, Fouz was a definite step-up in class. In a nine year professional career, he had a record of 68 contests, losing six with five draws. He had been beaten only twice since 1976, and had a reputation of being a classy performer capable of showing what Green had left.

The fight was originally made for 10 rounds, but cut to eight on the instructions of the Board of Control who were continuing to monitor Dave's performances. He still had his critics, some of whom made negative comments regarding his victories over Mendez and Holmgren.

Although Green outpointed Fouz, he was made to work desperately hard. At the end, he looked far the worse for wear with blood gushing from his mouth, a small cut above his left eye, and swelling on the left cheek. Fouz had a nasty gash on his left eyebrow.

Looking fit at 10st 9½, Dave started confidently from the opening bell. When heavy punches thudded into the Spaniard's ribs, it looked as though he would secure an early victory. In round two, however, the fight swung dramatically as the tall Fouz rammed counter-punches through the British fighter's guard. It was the start of a difficult period for Green, and he had to dig deep and battle hard to survive.

Having weathered Dave's early aggression, Fouz, an elusive, classy boxer, began to show neat skills. Heavy punches put Green under real pressure in round three, and he was badly shaken in the fourth which the Spaniard dominated. He was cut on the bottom lip and marked around the face, and many onlookers feared he was heading for a humiliating defeat.

Realising his career was in jeopardy, Dave bravely hung on, and in the fifth showed all his old desire for victory. Drawing on all his courage and raw aggression he intensified his attack to the body and drove Fouz to the ropes. Two fisted attacks swung the fight back in his favour, and sustained pressure put him on top. In the sixth Fouz was badly hurt, and looked anxiously to his corner for advice.

It was a big round for Dave who swarmed all over the Spaniard. He smashed away at close quarters, threw long heavy punches to the head, and attacked the body with venom. Fouz emerged from one melee on the ropes with blood streaming from a cut above his left eye. The injury became a target for Green's left jab, and at the end of the seventh referee, Harry Gibbs, asked the Spaniard if he wanted to continue.

The final round was fought at an incredible pace. Fouz made a last-ditch attempt to take the fight, but did not have the power as Green ripped in punches from every angle. It was a tough uncompromising battle, always hard, and often exciting. At the final bell, the crowd rose to both men, and the Spaniard received warm applause as he left the ring. Harry Gibbs score of 79$\frac{1}{2}$-78 indicated that Green had won by four rounds to one with three even.

Dave was ecstatic about his victory because he knew he had outboxed and outfought a tough opponent. In doing so he hoped he had silenced some of his critics.

"Well, I'm Spanish welterweight champion now," he said with a grin as he slumped into a chair in his dressing-room. Everyone laughed, appreciating the humour of a tough man who had the character to wisecrack after such a gruelling fight.

"It was just what I needed," he continued. "Different styles make good fights, and our styles blended well."

Andy Smith was delighted at his man's showing. "We are moving back to championship class," he remarked. "Fouz lived up to his reputation. You can see why he's never been knocked out. He was so fit and strong – it was unbelievable".

Yet Smith refused to look too far ahead. "I think David needs another six to 12 months at this level before we start thinking about anything else," he continued. "We are not going to rush him, but just go from fight to fight. His performance tonight was not the David Green I want to see in six months time. But it showed he is getting back to his old self."

Green had done everything that had been asked of him since returning to the ring. The plan was to keep him busy, but there was a set-back when he was matched with American, Al Fletcher, at the Royal Albert Hall on 28 April. What was intended as the chief supporting contest to the Colin Jones - Kirkland Laing welterweight championship fight, was suddenly called off because the Board of Control ruled that Fletcher was an unsuitable opponent.

General Secretary, Ray Clarke told the press that although the American was a 1974 Golden Gloves champion, details of his professional record were too sketchy. His only fight in 1981, was a draw against Roy Johnson who Green knocked out three years earlier, and in 1980 he boxed only twice.

The Board's examination of Fletcher's record was a clear indication of the way Dave was being monitored. Whilst his bouts were being restricted to eight rounds duration, he was not being allowed to take on inadequate opponents.

At short notice, Mickey Duff flew to America to try and find a more suitable opponent, but to no avail. When he put forward Sean Mannion of Massachusetts, he was also rejected by the Board.

With no immediate prospect of a contest, Dave accompanied Andy Smith to Italy to support Steve Hopkin who was fighting Rocky Mattioli at Rimini. It had been hoped that another leading Italian light-middleweight could be persuaded to fight Green at the Albert Hall, but the Easter holidays hampered negotiations.

Somewhat surprisingly, the Board of Control accepted Sean Mannion for a proposed fight with Green at the Royal Albert Hall on 2 June. It was to have been over 10 rounds, but when Mannion pulled out, he was replaced by Danny Long from Boston.

On what was his 28th birthday, Dave boxed better than in any of his fights since Leonard. The American, who boasted a record of 20 victories from 22 contests, never looked like lasting the distance, and was pounded to defeat in four rounds. He was hopelessly outclassed, and by the end of the opening session was marked under the left eye.

Wearing his familiar red boots and trunks, Dave opened cautiously, but attacked relentlessly throughout rounds two and three. Hurtful body punches drove Long backwards and had him covering up. A left-right combination sent him to the floor for a count of nine at the end of the third.

His right eye badly bruised, the American looked in a bad way at the bell, and during the interval, referee, Sid Nathan went to his corner for a close inspection. After a lengthy discussion with the seconds, he surprisingly allowed Long to continue.

It was all Green in the fourth as he hammered the American unmercifully. A savage barrage of body punches hurt and put him under severe pressure. With nothing coming back, Nathan sensibly stepped in and called a halt. It was a good display by Dave who kept his aggression under control and opened his man up with a series of stiff jabs.

It said much for his character that despite a background of public pressure for him to quit, he had still chalked up four consecutive victories. In most cases the calls were out of respect for a man who had been one of the biggest box-office attractions in Britain for years. In reality, he was unlikely to reach the heights of a few years earlier, but nobody wanted to see him hurt or humiliated by a moderate fighter.

Despite the concerns, Dave continued to draw the crowds, and his fights were still big news. Consequently, many of the journalists who had called for him to quit, still crowded into his dressing-room after the defeat of Long. Tape recorders and notepads at the ready, they digested every word that was said. It would still be tomorrow's news.

"I have never known a boy who is so well liked in my life," Andy Smith told them. "People who know him are over-protective, and that includes sports writers and the Boxing Board."

"My heart goes out to this kid," continued the faithful manager. "He has achieved more with his limitations as a technical boxer than any other man I have ever known. And he has done it through sheer passionate desire – he does everything with passion. If he was not that type of person, he would have allowed himself to be written off."

Green believed he had done enough to be considered for a shot at Herol Graham's British light-middleweight title. "It's the sensible progression for him," added Smith. "I had reservations about letting him fight tonight because he had a slight temperature and wasn't feeling 100 per cent. But allowing for that, I felt he boxed well enough to show that he's worth a shot at the title without having to go through an eliminator."

"He's had four comeback fights, and the last two have been against decent opponents," continued the manager. "We've built him up to the right level, and the light-middleweight title is the goal."

"Dave Green's the big draw," insisted Smith. "Graham's the champion, but he's not exciting, and people do not pay to watch him. If he wants to make some money out of the title, who can he fight apart from Green."

The following day, Graham issued a challenge to Green on a winner-take-all basis. "I will tell my manager to get in touch with Green's manager," said Herol. "Let's make it winner-take-all with a side-stake too – how about £5,000?"

Graham insisted, however, that such a contest would have to take place in Sheffield. "I am the champion, and I can say where I want to fight," he remarked.

Herol had won the title 10 weeks earlier by widely outpointing Pat Thomas, who in his previous title defence, stopped Steve Hopkin on cuts. "Green was a brilliant fighter in his day, but time is telling now," continued Graham. "He is still dangerous, but is not the same as he was before that terrible defeat by Sugar Ray Leonard."

Once the fight with Long was over, Dave enjoyed his belated 28th birthday celebrations, followed by a holiday in Jersey. On his return he got down to serious training for a fight in the autumn which he hoped would be against Graham.

Away from boxing, he took part in the first Great Cambridge Fun Run organised to raise funds for the British Heart Foundation. Joining him were the Mayor of Cambridge, round-the-world yachtsman, Shane Acton, and novelist, Jeffrey Archer. The event, promoted by the *Cambridge Evening News*, attracted 1,000 runners and over 5,000 spectators.

Dave was also in great demand for personal appearances, particularly at boxing club dinners. Being one of the most popular sporting personalities in the country, requests for his attendance came from many fields. On 25 October he made presentations at the England v Norway ladies soccer international played at Abbey Stadium, Cambridge.

✦ 17 ✦

END OF THE ROAD

Despite knowing he was unlikely to reach the heights of previous years, Dave always remained optimistic. He was still burning with desire and enthusiasm, and instead of feeling inclined to relax more at his luxury home, he often fretted over time spent out of the ring. "You are always better if you can get in say one fight a month," he told local journalist Mike Finnis. "Long lay-offs don't do anybody any good."

Since the Leonard defeat, he had fought his way back to the brink of a British or European championship fight at his new weight, and hoped to have another three or four contests before June 1982. "I want to make my mark again this season," he remarked. "I just hope to keep beating the fellows Mr Smith puts in front of me. I don't care which title I go for – whatever comes along."

Dave's comeback was scheduled to continue at the Royal Albert Hall on 13 October, but was put back to 3 November after he injured his right hand in training. He suffered bruising of a metacarpal after accidentally catching a sparring partner on the top of the head.

Veteran Spaniard, Jose Luis 'Dum Dum' Pacheco was announced as his opponent, and represented another step up in class designed to assess how far he could progress. Some critics, however, thought the Spaniard was an unwise choice and could bring the curtain down on Green's career.

Such comments annoyed Andy Smith. "The people who criticise don't know the real Dave Green," he snapped. "They don't see the depths and desire in his gym work."

A few days before the fight, however, the Spanish Boxing authorities refused Pacheco permission to face Green. Having boxed only 11 days earlier, he would have breached Spanish rules which required a break of 28 days between fights. It was the third time a proposed contest between the two had failed to materialise.

At short notice, the promoters engaged Reg Ford, a New York based Guyanan who had been a sparring partner to former world welterweight champion, Thomas Hearns for his defence against Sugar Ray Leonard in September. It proved to be an unfortunate choice.

Weighing 11st to Green's 10st 11¼, Ford was too big and too quick. Dave's wonderful ring career effectively ended when Andy Smith retired him at the end of the fifth round. Although it was officially announced that a badly swollen left eye brought about the ending, it was in truth a humane decision by an astute manager and close friend. Smith saved his fighter from the possible humiliation of a more conclusive defeat.

There had been some laughter when Ford stripped off his colourful dressing-gown to reveal a pair of striking vermilion and white chequered long-john trunks. The laughter died away once the fight got underway because it soon became obvious he meant business. He had been in with some of the best men in the world including Marvin Hagler, Ayub Kalule and Kenny Bristol, and although all had beaten him, he was well respected.

As always, Green went forward from the opening bell throwing long solid jabs, but for once lacked the tools of his demanding trade. Ford moved well and replied with classy left counters, most of which found their mark. Although Dave stuck to his game plan and worked to the body, it soon became clear that he had a real battle on his hands. Ford found him easy to hit and appeared to shake him with every right which landed.

Green kept up the pressure in round two, and although Ford was forced to cover up, he still scored with good counter-punches to head and body. Despite the stream of blows coming his way, Dave knew only one way to fight, and with tremendous heart, went after his rival.

Ford, however, was relaxed under pressure. A stiff left jab opened a cut under Green's right eye, and a left hook sent him tumbling to the floor. He quickly indicated to his corner that he was okay, hauled himself up at the count of five, but backed away rapidly as the Guyanan stormed after him. Only the bell saved him from further punishment.

Typically, it was Green who made the running in the third, throwing heavy rights and trying to deny Ford the room he needed. Although he boxed well on the retreat, Reg looked uncomfortable when the Chatteris man worked at close quarters. Ford though, was a good professional who had an answer to most situations, and shook Dave with a solid right uppercut at the end of the round.

A large swelling appeared over Green's left eye at the start of round four and worsened as the session progressed. Despite the handicap, he never stopped trying to press forward, and Ford was bulldozed to the ropes and forced to cover up. Again he fought back, and damaging combinations to the head rocked Green. By the end of the round his left eye was almost closed, and blood gushed from his mouth.

The fight could have been stopped at that stage, but Dave still had the intense desire for victory. With customary bravery, he stepped up the pace in the fifth to have his best round of the fight. Shrugging off his injuries he attacked viciously with scything hooks to the body, pinned Ford against the ropes and never relaxed the pressure. The non-stop attack took its toll, and as the crowd yelled encouragement, the flashy Guyanan suddenly looked tired as good head punches made him cover up.

"I won that round didn't I?" said Dave returning to his corner at the bell with a look of triumph. They were the last words he uttered as a fighter.

Although it had been a typical Green round, it was a last-ditch effort to try and save a great career. Andy Smith had seen enough, and as he climbed into the ring he put his hand on Dave's shoulder and said: "That's it son – I'm pulling you out." Without further ado, he called referee Harry Gibbs to the corner and signalled his man's retirement.

Despite Green's protests, the fight was over, and so was his career. A cut on the bridge of his nose, another beneath the right eye, and his left eye almost closed, were testimony of Ford's accurate punching. As Green buried his sobbing face in his gloves, Smith took the MC's microphone and said: "Ladies and gentlemen, that is the last time you will see the Fen Tiger."

Dave was stunned and heartbroken. He had no idea his manager was going to make such a dramatic announcement. Having battered his opponent almost continually throughout the previous three minutes, he could not understand the logic in the decision. Whilst they had always agreed that Smith would pull him out the moment he believed there was nothing left to offer, he was convinced he would have stopped Ford within the next two rounds.

The manager, however, was not prepared to take that chance because despite his big effort in round five, Green had looked a shadow of the great fighter who twice challenged for world honours. When he went forward with both fists pumping, he looked good. The problem was, he was wide open to counter-punches from his speedy opponent who time and again found a way through an inadequate defence.

Fighting back the tears, Dave took the microphone from his manager and said: "Thanks for supporting me – it's been fun. They were great years and I loved every minute of it." He wanted to go on, but the words wouldn't come out. He turned and embraced Smith because deep down he knew the decision was correct.

The sight of Green weeping openly once he knew his ring career was over, prompted the most spontaneous and emotional standing ovation ever seen at a British boxing arena. As he left the ring for the last time, hardened fans wept, and applauded him all the way to his dressing-room. It was a fitting salute to one of the country's most popular and exciting fighters.

"A wonderful response for a wonderful man," remarked Andy Smith to a group of reporters who crowded into the dressing-room. "There are not many Dave 'Boy' Greens in this world so we have to look after him."

In typical fashion, Smith took centre stage and gave an insight into the circumstances which led to his decision. He admitted having made up his mind during round three to pull Dave out. "I told him at the start of the fifth, and he agreed," said the manager. "What he didn't know was that it was the last round, not only of the fight, but his career. I could see it wasn't there. That fellow should never have been in the same class."

The reporters listened intently and noted every word of Smith's detailed analysis. He was, after all, the only man who could demand that Green surrendered whilst still on his feet. Yet he had to bide his time because stopping him fighting was like stopping another man breathing. Watching him struggle against Ford, however, was too much to bear, so he did the compassionate thing.

Andy explained that Dave had problems with his right hand before the fight and didn't really throw it during the opening two rounds. He conceded that his man may well have gone on to win the contest "But how far away was the glory again?" he questioned. "Probably beyond his reach. So what is the point of becoming an ordinary fighter after what he has had? I love him too much to let him go on any longer."

"David went out like he came in – like a tiger," continued Smith. "What a wonderful round to finish his career on. And what a wonderful place to finish at – a place where he has thrilled thousands of people."

The Royal Albert Hall was always special to Dave. It had been the scene of so many of his triumphs, and his only regret was that he did not leave the famous arena as a winner. He had 20 fights there including his championship successes over Singleton, Piedvache and Rhiney. Ford was his only defeat.

Regulars loved his exciting barn-storming style, and whenever he was on the bill, excitement and a full-house were guaranteed. Green was a rarity – a fighter who never gave less than his best because he genuinely didn't know any other way. That is why he found it so distressing to say goodbye.

Once he had composed himself, however, Dave agreed that his manager had made the correct decision. "It came as a great shock to me I can tell you," he remarked, "but I think Mr Smith is right. He has made all the decisions for me, and made the right ones. He said I was below par tonight, and he has watched me for thousands of rounds. There is some excuse when you are beaten by people like Sugar Ray Leonard and Palomino, but not this fellow."

In boxing, there has always been the saying that fighters are the last people to know when it's time to quit. Although such a statement could well have applied to Dave, his case was in many respects different because in reality he had never taken a prolonged beating. Whilst the Palomino fight was gruelling, he sustained no real damage. Against Hansen and Leonard, the defeats were virtually one-shot knockouts. The only damage was to his pride.

During the fight with Ford, however, Andy Smith realised the effects of 41 professional fights had suddenly caught up with him. The spark was no longer there, so it was time to go. The problem was how to do it.

Knowing Dave better than anyone, Smith was convinced that if he went on to beat Ford, which looked a real possibility after his good fifth round, persuading him to quit the sport he loved, would be difficult. His reaction to a lack-lustre performance would be: "It was just a bad night at the office." The manager therefore made an instant decision, taking the

Dave and Kay celebrate Christmas 1982 with twin daughters, Suzanne and Emma, aged two weeks and David aged 2½ years.

End of the road. Green is floored in round two of his fight with Reg Ford at the Royal Albert Hall on 3 November 1981.

Dave, Kay and their children dressed up for a fancy dress party.

Dave works in the corner of Robert Smith who turned professional in May 1981.

In Las Vegas with Andy Smith (left), former world heavyweight champion, Joe Louis, Bill Bugner and Joe Bugner

Sugar Ray Leonard meets Dave and his son at their Chatteris home in September 1982.

Leonard punches the heavy bag at Andy Smith's gym at St. Ives.

Dave with Chatteris resident Patricia Alexander and her daughter Victoria who was born during Jubilee weekend in June 1977, and for whom he opened a bank account.

Dave and Kay's three children, Suzanne (left), David and Emma.

With business partner, Bob Emerson, at Renoak Ltd premises, Honeysome Industrial Estate,
Chatteris.

At a charity golf event with former British and European bantamweight champion Alan Rudkin (right) and former world flyweight champion, Walter McGowan.

Dave (right) with his greatest fan Rodney Marriner, former world champions Charlie Magri and Alan Minter at a charity function.

After joining Renoak Limited in 1981, Dave is now Managing Director.

Kay and Dave relax at their Chatteris home with children, Emma (left), Suzanne and David in April 2004.

view that by having a good round, it was the right moment to go. With the fight lost, there would be no turning back. Green would accept the situation, albeit reluctantly.

"I would have fought until I dropped," said Dave. "That's the way I am. The biggest enemy Dave Green has got is Dave Green. I needed somebody like Mr Smith to say that is it. We had always agreed that when he thought the spark was gone, that would be it."

"I am not going to come back as a trial-horse for young boys," he continued. "I have no regrets because I have been 120 per cent fit for all my fights and done everything to the best of my ability."

At his home at St Ives the following morning, Smith admitted to his son Robert that he was relieved it was all over. He loved Dave and was not prepared to see him hurt or humiliated. They were sensible people and there would never be any talk of a comeback.

Some people criticised Andy for retiring Green the way he did. They thought it harsh that such an emotional occasion should have been made so public. Yet they didn't know the true situation or understand the passion of the fighter. To have taken Dave home and try to persuade him to retire after a winning fight would have been pointless. It had to be harsh to make him accept it. The true depths of Andy Smith's decision were never made public – they were known only to members of the two families.

* * *

Boxing personalities were quick to acknowledge Dave's massive contribution to the sport. "If only we had a few more Dave Greens to take his place," Board of Control General Secretary, Ray Clarke, told the press after the Ford fight. "But we haven't got one. He was one on his own – a throw-back. He was a fighting man, and his heart more than ability, got him where he went. He was a credit to the sport. You had to knock him out to beat him – he never gave in."

Mickey Duff, who was matchmaker for most of Green's fights, said: "For me, Dave 'Boy' Green kept boxing going for at least two years in this country."

Although he had come to the end of his ring career, Green would never be forgotten, least of all by his adoring Chatteris fans. Pat Ringham, former Sports Editor of the *Cambridgeshire Times*, who covered many of his fights, endorsed the feelings of many people in a letter to the paper shortly after Dave's retirement:

> Well the day had to come when Dave Green quit the ring – bringing an end to an unforgettable era for local sport.
>
> And for me, like so many others from the area, it has been an experience of a lifetime. British, European and world title fights all created an electrically-charged atmosphere we will surely never see again.
>
> And how many of us really believed Andy Smith's bold prediction way back in November 1975, of Dave one day challenging for the world crown.
>
> At that time, the 22-year-old fighter was merely a carrot farmer following in the footsteps of a Chatteris legend – Eric 'Boy' Boon. But a clever press campaign by his manager and a string of explosive victories, suddenly made the Fen Tiger a nationally known figure.
>
> The rest is history. British and European light-welterweight championship wins made him the toast of the Royal Albert Hall and helped set up classic encounters with John H. Stracey, and finally world champion, Carlos Palomino. Both fights graced the famous Wembley Arena, and for the 3,000 plus supporters from the Fens, it was our cup final.
>
> There were more thrills and spills to follow, but one thing never changed – the professional attitude of manager and fighter. David remained as polite and reserved as ever, while Andy was simply a pressman's dream.
>
> Thanks to them, we've got a few colourful stories to tell our grandchildren.
>
> David 'Boy' Green, 'Golden Boy of Boxing', you did us proud.

Green and Ringham had a close professional relationship, their paths having first crossed during a school cricket match at March. Pat, who was captain of Hereward school, also played adult cricket and could bowl leg spin, a unique achievement for a 15 year old. Green, a year younger, had never heard of it, and when he faced Pat, promptly despatched the ball to the boundary three times in quick succession.

Their next encounter was in a school football match at Manea the following year. As Ringham received the ball from a throw-in, Dave clattered into him and raked his studs down the back of his legs. Pat was furious, and told a team-mate he was going to "sort him out," but was told it would be unwise because Dave had just won an amateur boxing championship.

They didn't meet again until Pat was Sports Editor of the *Cambridgeshire Times*, by which time Dave was a professional. He knew little about boxing, but after the Chatteris man's first few successes, rather naively telephoned Andy Smith and asked if victory in his contest would lead to a fight with John H. Stracey. "Are you a complete fool, or do you know nothing about boxing?" snapped Smith. Pat admitted he knew nothing about the sport whereupon Smith mellowed somewhat and had a short conversation with him.

In November 1975, he telephoned Andy again and asked if he could do a feature on Dave. The manager was accommodating and invited him to the gym. Smith was impressed by the article which appeared in the paper the following week, and from then onwards gave Pat tremendous help and encouragement. He telephoned him on a regular basis and provided up-to-date, behind-the-scenes information about everything regarding Green's career.

Ringham was an excellent writer, and Andy Smith eventually offered to get him a position as a sports writer for a national paper in London. Pat, however, preferred to stay where he was, and as a local reporter wrote about Dave as though he was a Manchester United or Liverpool footballer because that is how big he was in the Fenland region.

Green created an incredible impression on Pat, who from knowing nothing about boxing, was rapidly drawn in by the atmosphere and excitement he generated. He became a celebrity in March because of his connection with the fighter, and couldn't walk 50 yards along the street without people wanting to know the latest about the Fen Tiger. At parties and in pubs, all people wanted to talk about was Dave Green because he had become a cult figure.

Following Green's retirement, the *Cambridge Evening News* also published a moving tribute to the man who had been the subject of so many of it's sporting headlines over the years:

> Too many boxers have to get out of the game when they are at the bottom, or on the way down. Dave 'Boy' Green chose a more sensible exit last night, but one which called for more courage.
>
> Announcing an unexpected permanent retirement halfway through a fight takes some doing. Dave Green managed it, thanks to the intervention of his manager Andy Smith, who once again showed that his breed is not made up entirely of greedy, callous users of other men's flesh and blood.
>
> He pulled his man out of the fight, and from the game. Both deserve congratulations.
>
> The young Fen Tiger has earned himself much popularity as another example of a great fighter, in the proper sense of the word, from this area. As a result, he was loved far and wide, and will continue to be so. This is not to be his obituary; we hope we will have the pleasure and pride of seeing him making an equally great contribution to sporting spirit by his example.

Most national newspapers paid tribute to Green's massive contribution to British boxing. He may not have won a world title, but he had tremendous heart and personality. During the weeks following his retirement, hundreds of cards and letters arrived at his house from appreciative fans.

Boxing News editor, Harry Mullan, travelled to the St Ives gym and presented Dave with the framed original of a cartoon by Mick Davis which the paper used to preview his fight with John H. Stracey. "Dave gave us at *Boxing News* so much pleasure over the years that we thought it only fair that we should give him something in return to mark his retirement," said Mullan.

Local people, in general, agreed with Andy Smith's decision to retire Dave. "Two years ago Ford would not have been in the same class. David would have finished him off quite quickly," remarked Gordon Palmer, Secretary of Green's Supporters Club. "All good things have to come to an end, and David gave 100 per cent all the way through."

Rod Marriner, who had been at all of his fights, said: "It was definitely right. Dave didn't have that snap there."

Dave's father, Ken, had a similar view. "I was a bit surprised, but relieved in a way," he remarked. "David has had a really good career and has got as far as he is going I suppose. There might have come a time when he got hurt, and he is too nice a boy to get hurt."

It wasn't until after the Christmas break that Dave struggled to come to terms with the fact that he wouldn't be fighting again. Yet he still did his running and went to the gym on a regular basis. By having Andy Smith as his manager and close friend, he was luckier than most boxers when they reach the end of their careers. Smith had already set him up in business and planned to keep him in boxing as a trainer at the St Ives gym. "I will convey everything I know to him," Andy told the local press. "I think he will be a good trainer, and in time I hope take over the managerial reins when I pack up."

Green was granted a British Boxing Board of Control trainer's licence early in 1982. He became second in command to Smith, and worked on the pads with all the boxers just as Andy had with him. He went to the gym every Sunday morning, and Tuesday and Thursday evenings. If a boxer was in the final preparations for a contest, his attendance was more frequent.

Dave worked with Steve Hopkin, Jimmy Harrington, and John Bibby, a welterweight from Bedford who made his professional debut in May 1982. In particular, he worked with Smith's son, Robert, a national schoolboy champion at 57kg in 1978, who had won all four contests since turning professional in May 1981.

Like Green, Robert was an aggressive fighter and already

regarded as a good light-middleweight prospect. He had been going to his father's gym since he was a small boy, and known Dave since he turned professional. He watched him train for all his big fights, travelled with him to Denmark, and even sparred with him as a schoolboy, usually to help build speed.

In his last year as an amateur, Robert felt the full force of Dave's punching power. He had bought himself a new body protector which he proudly wore during a particular sparring session. Green, who could never take it easy with anyone, suddenly hit him very low, then smirked and said: "Does it work?" It was a situation which had turned full circle because when Mickey Laud hit Green low in 1974 whilst he was training to meet Terry Waller, Robert had found the incident amusing.

The pair had built a good relationship both inside and outside boxing, and Andy Smith saw Green as the ideal man to develop Robert. "If he can put into my son, the dedication he has got, he will be doing him a favour," he remarked.

Dave held a trainer's licence for several years, relinquishing it in 1987 when he was appointed as a member of the Southern Area Council of the British Boxing Board of Control. He was recommended by former British middleweight champion, Johnny Pritchett, himself a council member, and John Morris, later to become General Secretary of the Board, who had known Dave since his amateur days.

The council is made up of professional people from all walks of life, but the involvement of respected former boxers is essential in order to provide balance and understanding. Council members have a number of responsibilities including attending monthly meetings to deal with administrative and discipline matters. They also act as representative stewards at promotions throughout the area.

In his position as a council member until he resigned in May 1998, Dave attended numerous shows at venues throughout the Southern Area which stretches from Norwich to Southampton. As a highly respected businessman and former boxer he was able to settle most disputes with a minimum of fuss.

The one low point during Green's position with the Board of Control, was the serious injury sustained by 21-year-old Wisbech boxer, Mark Goult, at Norwich in March 1990. Dave was the Steward-in-Charge, and after Goult's exciting 10 rounds points victory over Danny Porter for the Southern Area bantamweight title, had climbed into the ring and strapped the championship belt around his waist. He made his way home immediately after the show, but unbeknown to him, Mark collapsed in the dressing-room shortly after leaving the ring. He was rushed to Addenbrookes Hospital, Cambridge, where he underwent emergency brain surgery.

It was not until the following morning that Dave discovered what had happened. He immediately telephoned the hospital to enquire about Mark's condition, and continued to do so on a regular basis throughout his confinement. Whilst Goult eventually made a partial recovery, he is still confined to a wheelchair. He is taken everywhere by his father, and Dave sees him quite often at boxing shows and always spends time talking to him.

Apart from his continued involvement in boxing, Green also competed in another Superstars event. On 3 and 4 August 1982, he was a member of a fighters team in the UK Superteams championship at Bath. Other teams were from Rugby, Soccer and Bat 'n' Ball. At the end of the second day, the two leading teams stayed on to compete for the title of UK Superteams Champions on 5 and 6 August.

The following month Dave was privileged to receive a visit from Sugar Ray Leonard who had been brought to Britain by television company, Film Sport Canada. It was a nine-day trip to film part of a documentary series on sporting supermen. When the itinerary was being prepared, Leonard was asked if there was anywhere special he would like to go, and he stated that he wanted to meet up with Dave again.

Since fighting Green in March 1980, Leonard had lost and regained the WBC welterweight championship in fights with

Roberto Duran the same year. He then made successful defences against Larry Bonds, Thomas Hearns and Bruce Finch. In June 1981, he also won the world light-middleweight title by defeating Ayub Kalule. Following the fight with Finch in February 1982, however, he was found to be suffering from a detached retina, and there were universal calls for him not to box again.

Already a multi-millionaire, Sugar Ray arrived at Dave's house in a huge limousine accompanied by two burly minders and a television crew. It was the first time they had met since their contest at Maryland, but greeted each other with warmth and great respect. In the comfort of Dave's living room, they chatted easily as good friends. Leonard was totally relaxed, and looked more like a film star than a fighter as he met Kay who was expecting twins at Christmas. He then knelt on the floor and faced up to two-year-old David junior in boxing pose.

They watched the film of their fight, and at the point where Green was knocked out, he grabbed his former opponent's arm and quipped: "Hold on Sugar Ray, I might get up this time." Framed photographs of the prestigious visit are among the massive collection which adorn the snooker room walls of the Green household.

During the early afternoon, they went for lunch at one of the County's oldest pub restaurants, the Pike & Eel at Holywell on the river Ouse. The team of television cameramen were in close attendance, and regular diners and local people at first seemed more interested in the film-set than Leonard, as he chatted with Dave for the documentary. Suddenly, people realised who he was. Word spread quickly and within a short time the two fighters were happily signing autographs.

Sugar Ray remained totally relaxed during the visit to the Pike & Eel, and was happy to discuss his future which remained in doubt due to his eye injury. "The rest has allowed me to re-evaluate my life and character, and to enjoy my life and family," he remarked to a fascinated audience. "When I knew I was coming to England, I insisted that I met up with Dave because he was a great fighter. He was an opponent I respected because of his guts and determination."

After lunch, the party visited Andy Smith's gym at St Ives where Green and Leonard posed for photographs in the ring. Dave was delighted that the former world champion had asked to meet him, and was pleased that local people had been able to get close to such a great star. The visit to Cambridgeshire lasted almost four hours before Leonard and his entourage made their way back to London.

The following evening, Dave was a guest at a huge function at the Grosvenor House Hotel in London to honour Leonard. He was seated at one end of the top table of 25, but within five minutes Sugar Ray had altered the arrangements to ensure that he was sitting next to him throughout the evening. In a moving speech Leonard paid tribute to Green's achievements in the ring, and before they parted company invited him to visit America as his guest.

* * *

Despite not having the rigours of a demanding training routine, life during 1982 remained extremely hectic for Green. Kay was expecting twins on 20 December, but experienced considerable difficulty throughout the year. The problems started during the spring while she, Dave and their son, were staying with friends, Rodney and Sheila Marriner, in Spain.

Kay was two months pregnant, and started to haemorrhage in a similar way to when she lost the first baby three years earlier. She was taken to hospital, and after examination was advised to stay there for a month. As Dave had to return to England for business, she didn't want to stay in a Spanish hospital, especially as she didn't speak a word of the national language. They therefore decided to take a chance and return home.

Dave's business partner, Bob Emerson, met them at the airport and drove them back to Chatteris. After seeing her doctor, Kay spent a month resting in bed during which time she was given injections. Everything settled down, but after undergoing a scan at the hospital, was told that she was expecting twins. She had no idea, but often thought that but for the heavy haemorrhaging, she may have had triplets.

Kay was told that at 35 weeks she should return to hospital for bed-rest because twins are often born early. Not liking the idea, she plodded to the hospital every week for check-ups, but eventually had to be admitted because the babies were both large. Although not due until 20 December, they were induced because of their size, and born at Ely RAF Hospital 10 days early.

Dave was present at the births, but was very agitated throughout. He kept pacing up and down, and at one stage dislodged a drip which was attached to Kay's left hand. The delivery room was very small, and apart from him there was a midwife, anaesthetist, two nurses and two assistants present.

Kay was more concerned about what her husband was doing than what was happening to her. Eventually, a nurse suggested he got a flannel and mopped her brow to try and cool her down. Instead of being gentle, Dave slopped the soaking wet flannel on her face as though he was refreshing a boxer in the corner during a fight. Water streamed down Kay's face and into her eyes, prompting her to suggest he left the room for a while. He flatly refused, and remained throughout the birth of his twin daughters. He later accompanied a nurse to see them weighed. Suzanne-Marie scaled 7lb 12 and Emma-Jane 7lb.

Shortly after Dave returned to the ward, his father arrived at the hospital to visit a friend who had been knocked down in a road traffic accident. It was sheer coincidence, but as Dave saw him through the window he called him into the ward to see his granddaughters within minutes of their birth.

Kay remained in hospital for five days, but shortly after returning home she developed gout in her foot. She was in extreme pain, even more so than when giving birth. Unable to walk or even hop, she spent two weeks in a chair with her foot raised. Throughout her period of incapacity, Dave did everything. He cared for his wife and son, prepared the babies food, winded them, did the housework and shopping, and even went to work whenever Kay's mother called to lend a hand.

The night after Kay returned home with the twins, Dave was bathing his son who suddenly started to cry. "Want you to take them back," he sobbed. It was mild jealousy, but Dave handled it well. The man who had been a vicious fighter in the ring, was gentle and caring at home. He loved his family, and after a few days of gentle persuasion, young David accepted his baby sisters and soon became extremely fond of them.

✦ 18 ✦

LIFE AFTER BOXING

By the time he retired from boxing Dave had already embarked on a new career by working as a sales representative for Chatteris based company, Renoak Limited. During discussions after the Ford fight, Andy Smith made it clear that a comeback was not an option, and his life needed to go in another direction. "I never want to see you in the ring again," he told him firmly. "You've done what you wanted, now get out there and do something else."

Smith knew the difficulties fighters faced when they left the sport, and being a father-figure to Green he had no intention of allowing him to fall by the wayside. As soon as he realised Dave was on the decline as a boxer, he began planning for his future. Some months before the Ford fight, Andy contacted Bob Emerson, a prominent local businessman he had first met at a social function a couple of years earlier. Bob lived at Needingworth, a village next to St Ives, and gradually got to know Smith by going to the same functions and parties. He was Managing Director of Renoak Limited which was set up in April 1978, and operated from premises on the Honeysome industrial estate. The company imported goods from abroad which were re-packaged and sold on to cash and carry outlets.

Although Dave was completely unaware of it, Smith told Emerson that he planned to retire him from boxing and ease him into business. He asked if there was a position within Renoak suitable for him. Bob knew nothing about boxing, and at first thought that the unlikely alliance of a former public schoolboy and a boxer was something which was unlikely to work. Smith, however, was persistent, and a few weeks later telephoned Emerson and invited him to lunch at the Pike & Eel. Although he had some misgivings, he agreed to go along, and after a long discussion agreed to give Dave a chance.

Smith convinced him that the boxer could become an asset to the company. His first experience in the commercial world had been with Tony Powell Sports three years earlier. He had also been involved in Noble Art Limited, an offspring company of Tony Powell Sports, which distributed sports and leisure wear, and operated from Andy's home address at St Ives. Company headed notepaper bore a tiger's head emblem.

Green and Emerson came from contrasting backgrounds. Bob was an orphan who had grown up the hard way in Barnado's Homes before being sent to a public school through an insurance arrangement. His educational qualifications were not exceptional, but being commercially minded and believing he could earn a lot of money, obtained employment on the M1 motorway construction. Shortly after starting as a labourer, however, he found that he was not physically strong enough. Instead, he became a clerk and tea-boy, and still managed to earn £20 a week when people in other walks of life were taking home less than £5.

At the age of 21, Bob joined Nestles as a sales representative, later worked for himself and travelled all over the world before setting up Renoak Limited with three other shareholders. Although business was good, there were several hundred cash and carry outlets in the United Kingdom, and it was never possible for Emerson and his sales staff to reach them all. He therefore considered that Green could be usefully employed contacting some of those companies.

Dave joined Renoak Limited as a sales representative about six months before he fought Reg Ford. His first trip was to Scotland where in a week he made 36 calls and obtained 35 orders. Nobody was available when he called at the other company. Bob was very impressed, and immediately arranged for him to make a similar trip to Wales. Again he was extremely successful, obtaining orders from every company he visited.

Dave has incredible energy and is gifted with a likeable and outgoing personality. Despite the fact that he was still boxing, he adapted well to the role of a salesman. He spent a week in the north of England, and made profitable trips to many other parts of the country. "You're making more money than me, and I'm Managing Director of this company," Emerson told him one day.

Gradually, over a period of time, Dave became more successful than Bob and his team of salesmen put together. He learned his business acumen from Andy Smith whilst he was at the peak of his boxing career. Whenever the manager negotiated a major purse, he involved him and explained the reasons for every decision he made. Dave put that experience into practice in his new role, and as a result the company began pulling in a tremendous amount of business from new outlets all over the country. Turnover therefore increased dramatically.

At the time, Bob Emerson owned 25% of Renoak Limited, and three other shareholders based in London owned the remaining 75%. Having been continually impressed by Dave's success, he felt the two of them could turn the company into a more profitable concern. They discussed the situation at length, agreed to make an offer and eventually bought out the other three shareholders in February 1983.

When they bought the company, Bob owned 75% and Dave the remaining 25%, although at the time Dave was told that he could purchase a further 24% over the next five years. Within three months, however, he had brought so much business into the company that Emerson told him: "Dave, never mind about waiting five years, you've already earned your money." He was then allocated the extra 24% of the company, and by 1993 they became joint owners.

In view of his trusted long-term relationship with Dave, Andy Smith was appointed as an Associate Director. He was an experienced businessman with a cool head, and was seen as an ideal man to sit at board meetings when difficult decisions had to be made.

Although they effectively started with nothing, Green and Emerson were extremely ambitious. They made good business decisions and as a result the company quickly made a gross profit. As it expanded they took over further units on the Honeysome industrial estate, including those used by Tony Powell Sports which had since closed down. They were cheap to rent, being only 65p per square foot as opposed to £2 elsewhere.

They made frequent trips to New York and Hong Kong to make bulk purchases of good quality goods such as Cartier watches and other brand name items which were then sold on to the cash and carry outlets. They also purchased substantial amounts of bankrupt stock and clearance lines. They were interested in any non-food items. On one occasion, 3,000 footballs had been left over from a consignment of 10,000. These were bought as a job lot for about 10p each and sold on at £1. Dave also shifted a consignment of 2,000 bird boxes at a substantial profit. At the request of a major sorting bank they obtained large quantities of leather goods such as pocket diaries.

At the time, the cash and carry businesses were denied brand name goods which Renoak Limited were discovering all over the world. They became the official agents for Fisher Price Toys which were purchased in bulk for distribution in the UK. During the 1980's, Bob and Dave also made purchases in China which was a daunting experience because the country had still not been westernised. They also had an interest in a manufacturing unit about 90 miles inside Southern China.

Despite the ongoing success, everything which was occurring dramatically changed the face of the company. It became less of an entrepreneurial sales driven outfit, and more contractual. During 1983, Bob met the head of purchasing for a major bank who at the time were about to launch their first ever marketing initiative which involved ceramic piggy banks. He was asked if Renoak Limited were equipped to package and distribute the items in bulk to individual branches throughout the United Kingdom.

The venture proved highly successful, and the company later obtained a contract for similar business with the then Midland Bank. The contracts brought in huge amounts of business, but whilst successful, were to the detriment of that with the cash and carry outlets.

Bank stock was all printed matter and promotional material which had to be packaged and distributed to branches in the form specified by head offices. Business was in fact growing at such a rate that at one stage the company didn't have enough storage room. In order that staff could work throughout the day, existing stock had to be moved outside each morning, covered with tarpaulins and then put back at night. The process was repeated daily for some while until additional units were acquired. Renoak Limited had to recruit more staff to cope with the new demands. Just eight were employed at the time of the change, but that quickly rose to 48 permanent employees and up to 200 part-timers to deal with packaging.

Despite the success of the company, the transformation of business became of great concern to Dave because his day-to-day work became very different. Consequently, he felt his input was far less than before. As a committed salesman he had become accustomed to visiting companies with a product in his hand and saying: "Look, this is £1," or words to that effect. After good sales talk he generally sold the client two dozen, 2,000 or whatever, and at the end of each week knew exactly how much money he had made the company.

Although Bob Emerson had similar feelings, he was more

adaptable to the change because he could see the profitability increasing rapidly thereby making Renoak an extremely successful company. He knew they had to look at the theory behind the business and how it would grow on the contractual arrangements they had got.

Over a three to four year period, Dave found the situation extremely frustrating because in his mind he was unable to make commitments as before. Much of the problem arose because of the type of person he was. Always hard working and conscientious, he wanted to be fully committed to everything he did and ultimately achieve the best. It had been that way ever since he was a child. Yet despite his concerns the growth of the company was highly successful due largely to the fact that it was well managed by him and Bob.

To get around his concerns, Dave basically had to rearrange his commercial life because it was pointless both of them making important day-to-day decisions. To help ease the situation Bob suggested that Green took over as Managing Director and dealt with all day-to-day matters involving the company, particularly those involving responsibility for staff. Emerson, meanwhile, concentrated on the strategic aspects to ensure that the company continued to expand and move forward.

With the passing of time, Dave's frustrations gradually eased especially once he came to terms with the fact that he no longer had to go out on the road each day to secure new business contracts. Once he adjusted, he accepted the change and became far more of a commercial businessman as opposed to a sales representative.

Over a period of years, Renoak Limited developed into an efficient and highly respected company. They created a computerised system which measured the individual strengths of all their client bank branches, and identified which would be good providers of specialist products such as mortgages and pensions. The company also analysed the entire branch networks of three major clearing banks in order that stock supplies could be streamlined thereby saving those banks substantial amounts of money. Instead of sending out 1.5 million advertising leaflets for one client, Renoak reduced the amount to 600,000, and each branch still had an adequate supply.

Overall, the partnership between Green and Emerson has worked well and flourished for almost 25 years. Both are extremely professional, with respect for each other's strengths, and have always worked hard to resolve any differences of opinion. Coming from contrasting backgrounds, it was inevitable that difficulties would arise, and in the early days there were a number of heated arguments.

Both well remember a particular incident one night during their first year together. They were travelling along the M11 motorway in the early hours when an argument developed and became so heated that Bob pulled off the road into a dark lay-by. "You obviously haven't got over your boxing," he snapped as he stopped the car. "Go on then, have a go at me."

"You don't turn me on," retorted Green, "only Sugar Ray Leonard turns me on."

The dispute was quickly resolved and they drove on, but it was an incident both always remembered with some amusement. It was a typical difficulty which arose largely because of the massive transformation Dave had to make when he went into business after being a professional fighter.

Although Green had been well advised by Andy Smith, who also looked after his welfare when he left boxing, the transformation into commercial life didn't come any easier. Even some years after his retirement, he still longed to fight again. "Every day I felt the urge to get back into the ring," he remarked, "but if I had in my condition, it would practically have killed me." It was a situation so typical of problems experienced by many sportsmen when they move away from something which has occupied their lives day in day out for so long. Whether it be boxing, football or any other high profile entertainment activity, such transformation is the most difficult thing in the world.

In boxing, only the most successful can avoid such a

transition. Whilst Dave was financially sound when he retired from the ring, he still needed to be fully active in life which was partly why Smith created the opening for him with Renoak. Apart from the early days when he was successfully selling, tremendous difficulties arose as the company expanded and moved into contractual work. At the beginning everyone wanted to know Dave Green the boxer because of his celebrity status. Many didn't know he had retired, and when it came to getting the right people to make commercial decisions, it proved difficult. He was a sporting hero walking into a commercial environment, and people wanted to talk about his fights with Stracey, Palomino and Leonard rather than devote time to business matters.

Only during recent years has Dave fully realised his commercial worth. At the beginning he missed boxing to the extent that the business was a secondary thing even though he knew he had to do it. Despite that, he was very astute, and his business acumen was such that he was able to make far more money than he ever did from boxing. He invested his profits into property at the right time and ensured that he and his family would be set up for life.

His experiences, particularly those regarding transformation over a long period, made Green realise the plight of others. He learned so much and felt he could do a great deal to help those faced with similar difficulties. His personal success became well documented, and suggestions have been made that he set up an advisory agency to help sportsmen and women take the right avenues and invest wisely.

Dave's development within the commercial world often aroused the curiosity of the media. "Yes, I love being in the business world," he told a national newspaper reporter in 1990 at a time when Renoak Limited employed 150 staff and had an annual turnover of about £3½ million. "I really love the cut and thrust of this world. The fact is, business and boxing are very similar, and I certainly invest as much effort into this as I did when I was in the ring."

Despite the stresses, strains and frustrations over the years,

Dave coped well, and maintained his high energy level and contact with people. Even when he was out on the road selling to cash and carry outlets, he still got up early each morning and went for a run despite not having gone to bed until the early hours. Constant fitness kept him focused and alert.

Accompanying Green on business trips was often a fascinating experience for Bob Emerson, and none more so than one Saturday morning when they were returning home from a business trip to Yorkshire. Not realising that it was the rugby league cup final at Wembley, they stopped at a motorway service area on the M1 for breakfast. The place was packed, and within minutes Dave was surrounded by people wanting autographs. The pattern continued as more coaches kept arriving, and it was more than two hours before he and Bob were able to leave and continue their journey.

Although Bob was familiar with Dave's achievements in the ring, he never ceased to be amazed at his popularity which went way beyond boxing. The only time he saw him fight was when Andy Smith invited him to the contest with Reg Ford. Some while after the contest, Bob left the Albert Hall and walked across the road into Hyde Park where he found Green in a sad and confused state. He was unsusceptible to sympathy, and said he had gone out on his own to try and get his head straight.

Green and Emerson have also had some amusing experiences over the years, often because Dave is very much a creature of habit. During the early stages of their business relationship they did everything possible to keep company costs and expenses to a minimum. Consequently, whenever they were travelling around the country to visit clients, they booked twin rooms at hotels. This arrangement, however, soon became unacceptable to Bob because, unlike Dave, he preferred to be in bed by midnight. Whilst he was fast asleep, Green remained in the bar chatting and drinking, playing snooker, pool or darts. He loved socialising, and often didn't retire to their room much before 4am. Then, being wide awake, he woke Bob to talk about business.

In order to get some sleep, Emerson resorted to booking separate rooms whenever they were away on business trips. Even then, he was often woken by Dave knocking on his door in the early hours wanting to discuss the rights and wrongs of the company. Bob eventually resolved the problem by putting cotton wool in his ears when he went to bed. By the time Green knocked on his door, he was fast asleep and oblivious to his presence.

Dave's antics were often amusing, none more so than one night when they stayed at a Posthouse Hotel at Haydock during the 1980's. They were booked into separate rooms opposite each other on the ground floor, and as usual Green spent the evening socialising in the bar and didn't return to his room until about 3am. He got undressed, but suddenly remembered Bob was in the room opposite. Completely naked, he crossed the corridor and knocked on his colleague's door. As he did so, his own door shut tightly behind him with the keys inside.

Emerson was sound asleep and failed to hear Dave's persistent knocking and pleas to open up. Left with no alternative but to seek help, the naked former boxer sheepishly made his way towards the reception area. Doing his best to cover himself with his hands, he explained his predicament to an amused night porter. "That's not a problem Mr Green," he remarked with a smile, and immediately accompanied him back to the room and let him in by using the master key.

Despite his inconvenience, Dave was still up at 6.30am. He shaved and showered, and after packing his overnight bag, knocked on Bob's door. "Are you ready to go?" he asked as the door was opened. With a busy schedule ahead of them, Bob suggested they had breakfast before setting off. "Not on your Nellie," said Green explaining the events of a few hours earlier with extreme embarrassment. "I'll see you by the car." Without further ado, he opened Bob's window, threw his bag outside and climbed into the car park.

Emerson went to reception, paid the bill and left the

building through the main entrance. By this time, most of the hotel staff had heard about Dave's misfortune and knew his identity. "Come on, let's get away from here as quick as we can," he remarked when Bob joined him by the car. Breakfast was taken at the first motorway cafe.

Renoak Limited has been very much part of the local economy, which from Dave's point of view is very satisfying because he has lived in Chatteris all of his life and is unlikely to move. The company has been extremely successful and provided work for thousands of local people over the years. At the beginning it gave many of those working in fields, the opportunity to move to a more comfortable environment with heated premises.

The company remains sound and highly respected, it's major clients being sorting banks, building societies and catering companies. With Bob Emerson as Chairman and Dave Managing Director, it currently employs 45 permanent staff and about 100 part-timers who are called upon as required according to the volume of work undertaken.

During the 1980's and 90's, Renoak had premises at Norwich, Warboys, Swaffham and Fakenham, but all business is now concentrated under seven large warehouse units at Chatteris. Transportation of goods to and from the company is carried out by Securicor.

Since formation, the company has had only one bad debt, that being for £25. Bob attributes that success largely to Dave's persistence in pursuing slow paying clients until their dues are met. He has never had to resort to court action or the threat of strong-arm tactics, and has got results by a thoroughly professional approach. Over the years he has become calmer due in no small part to the staid influence of Emerson who helped him considerably during the difficult period after boxing.

* * *

Despite the massive changes in his life, Dave never lost

contact with boxing. More importantly, people within the sport never forgot him. Consequently, over many years, he has remained in demand to attend functions as guest of honour, and to present awards at amateur club shows. Ever appreciative of the opportunities the sport gave him, he has rarely refused such invitations, and genuinely enjoys supporting and advising youngsters of all levels.

Dave also maintained contact with Sugar Ray Leonard after the American visited him in 1982. He travelled to Las Vegas during the late 1980's for Sugar Ray's fights with Marvin Hagler, Donny LaLonde and Thomas Hearns, and received five-star treatment on each occasion.

"He was the best fighter I ever met, and in my opinion one of the best of all time," Green told a *Cambridgeshire Times* reporter in 1987. "I phoned him the other day to ask about his comeback fight against Marvin Hagler, and he told me how he is training. He doesn't need the money – it is just a question of pride. He feels he never fulfilled his potential, and that bugs him."

Tremendous mutual respect has always existed between Green and Leonard, and the American superstar insisted that whenever the Chatteris man was planning a trip to the States, he let him know in advance. Sugar Ray then always ensured that ringside seats were made available for him, and that he was well looked after.

Wherever Leonard was, Dave and his travelling companions were invited. They attended training sessions, weigh ins, press conferences and post-fight parties. The bond which existed between the two was never more apparent than one afternoon in 1988, prior to Sugar Ray's fight with LaLonde. As soon as he realised Dave was at his gym in Las Vegas, Leonard immediately stopped training, walked over to his former opponent and threw his arms around him.

For the Hagler fight in 1987, Dave sat immediately behind Sugar Ray's wife. A group of disabled children in wheelchairs were nearby, and he was extremely moved by the attention she gave them. The fight was the greatest he had ever seen, and the atmosphere electric. He was convinced that Leonard got the decision because Hagler left his big effort too late. "It was a very close fight," he recalled, "but the game is all about opinions."

Although they lost touch when Leonard divorced and moved to California, contact has been renewed. A reunion was planned in March 2003 when the former world champion was due to travel to Britain with his fighter, Vince Phillips, who was challenging Ricky Hatton for the WBU light-welter-weight title. Unfortunately, business commitments prevented Sugar Ray from making the trip.

Since retiring from the ring both have taken up golf, Green playing off a handicap of 12 and Leonard off 16. It was planned for them to meet over 18 holes, and promoter, Frank Warren, promised to put up £5,000 for the winner to donate to a charity of his choice.

"I had no chance of beating Ray in the ring, but I'm confident when I meet him on the golf course, I'll bash the hell out of him," Dave told Colin Hart of *The Sun*. "Knowing how competitive he is, he won't be able to resist this challenge."

Dave was extremely disappointed when Leonard's trip failed to materialise, but challenging him on the golf course in the future remains one of his ambitions.

Green also maintained contact with Carlos Palomino, and met him on two occasions whilst on holiday in the United States. The first was in Las Vegas, and then in 1997 on a visit to California with Kay and the twins, Dave telephoned and invited him to dinner. They met the former champion and his daughter at a restaurant just outside Los Angeles, and after the meal Dave insisted on paying the bill. "You beat me fair and square, so it's the least I can do," he remarked.

A measure of the respect people in boxing have for Green was highlighted in the late 1980's when Rob Smith visited Palomino's old gym at Westminster, California. Amongst the people there were the former world champion's Mexican trainer, Noe Cruz, and manager, Jackie McCoy. During a conversation with Rob, Cruz said that Green had the biggest heart he had ever seen in a fighter. "He had the heart of a lion," he remarked. On the wall of the gym was a signed photo of Dave which he had sent to Palomino a few years earlier.

✦ 19 ✦

CHARITY, GOLF AND GOOD LIFE

Despite his busy work and sporting schedules, Dave has for many years been a tireless worker for charity. Directly and indirectly, it is estimated that he has helped raise hundreds of thousands of pounds at events throughout the United Kingdom. These include golf, darts, football and snooker matches, personal appearances, as well as countless visits to pubs throughout East Anglia to crack open whisky bottles containing customers loose change. His attendance is usually free of charge and at his own expense.

His involvement in charity work began shortly after he turned professional, often in the company of Andy Smith and Joe Bugner. As soon as he began to make a name for himself, however, personal invitations came flooding in to attend events throughout the Fenland region. He was determined to do what he could for people in need, and in 1976 donated a darts trophy to be played for in aid of a cancer scanner appeal. He even helped circulate entry forms to pubs and clubs in the Cambridge area.

In February 1977, Dave played in a darts match against world star, Alan Evans, and England ladies international, Maureen Flowers, as part of a charity function at Cambridge City Football Supporters Club. The event raised £400 to help pay for two infusion pumps in the children's ward of Addenbrookes Hospital.

The match of the evening featured Green against Evans in which the darts expert won with a double-four, double-nine finish. Afterwards he politely declined Green's offer of a fight. "We are different weights," said the large Welshman to the amusement of the audience, "it wouldn't be fair."

Dave has played in many other charity darts matches at Fenland venues with top class players including Eric Bristow, Bobby George and John Lowe. Being the local celebrity, organisers saw it as an added attraction if he played in one of the games.

At snooker, he faced South African star Peter Francisco in a match at Peterborough. He was present when Alex 'Hurricane' Higgins played at Chatteris Working Mens Club one Friday evening. The following morning the two of them opened a sports shop at Whittlesey. Green considers Alex to be one of the finest players the game has ever seen because he was so exciting to watch.

Other fund raising events he has attended include a raft race on the river Nene at Peterborough, and a scanner appeal dinner in Manchester where he was joint guest of honour with former England football captain, Brian Robson. Dave has massive respect for men like Robson and Higgins because their attitude to their chosen sport was the same as his own. They were exciting, entertaining players.

For several years, Dave has also attended events organised by former world flyweight champion, Charlie Magri. Most are at his pub at Mile End in the east end of London to raise funds for people, especially children, with special needs. Dave's former opponent, John H. Stracey often provides a musical cabaret, and other regulars include former world champions, John Conteh and Alan Minter.

Charity golf events, however, are where Dave devotes much of his time, and he attends on average one such event most weeks throughout the year. They range from large functions at prestigious courses such as Wentworth,

Sunningdale, Sandwich, Royal Lytham and Gleneagles, to smaller events for local charities at courses generally in the Midland, Eastern and Southern counties.

He took up the sport in 1975, and joined Ely Golf Club before moving to Ramsey. When the Warley Park Club near Brentwood, Essex, opened in 1979, he was made an honorary member, and has remained there ever since.

Invitations to attend major charity events started shortly after Dave first went into business. As a high profile sporting personality, organisers from different walks of life saw him as a major attraction likely to boost their fund raising efforts.

Large events he supports include the English Blind Golf Society day at Wentworth, the Barnardo's Classic at Chigwell, which he has attended for about 14 years, and the Dan Maskell Tennis Trust celebrity golf challenge at Wentworth which he has supported for five years. The major part of funds raised at this event help fund wheelchair tennis in which leading participants play to such a high standard that an average club player would have great difficulty beating them. Dave supports the event totally, and in 2003 successfully bid a substantial amount in the auction for a pair of tickets for the men's final of the all-England tennis championships at Wimbledon.

Green's calendar of engagements is substantial, and other charity golf days he attends include those organised by Essex Boys Clubs, Licensed Victuallers Associations and football clubs. Travel is no object, and he plays at Moor Park, Gosforth Lakes, Haverhill, Warley, Mottram Hall, Cheshire, Brockett Hall and many other courses throughout the UK. He particularly likes supporting events which raise money for needy children, and for many years has attended those organised by the Variety Club of Great Britain. He is also a regular supporter of an annual event at Potton staged by Cambridgeshire charity, 'Wheels for Martin's Friends', to raise funds for people needing wheelchairs.

The charity events have enabled him to meet and play golf with many celebrities from other sports particularly football.

They include Sir Geoff Hurst, Bobby Moore, Martin Peters, Jimmy Hill, and Frank McLintock, with whom he operated a cash converter business between 1995 and 2000.

In 1996, Green became a celebrity member of registered Cambridgeshire charity, The Pidley Mountain Rescue Team. Since then he has made a massive commitment, including organising two celebrity golf classic events to raise funds for the charity and Somersham Football Club of which he is President. Proceeds are divided equally, and those donated to the football club are used for the development of youngsters to replace existing team members as they retire or move on.

The events are well organised, with invitations being extended to celebrities, particularly those within sport and show business. Many items are donated for auction, and more than £6,000 has been raised at each event. As Chairman of the golf day committee, Dave arranged for a Harrier from RAF Wittering to do a fly-past to start the 2003 event at 10am.

The Pidley Mountain Rescue Club is a world famous charity formed in 1968. It operates from the village of Pidley, the highest point of the notoriously flat county of Cambridgeshire, just 68 feet above sea level. It was formed after a local man, Bob Johnson, was rescued by a group of American servicemen based in the area, after his car broke down near Somersham. They pushed him all the way up a hill, after which he light-heartedly remarked that it was a mountain rescue, and suggested setting up a charity. All of the rescuers joined, as did many other servicemen and local residents.

The club currently has a membership of over 600, and is increasing all the time. Everyone on the 10-strong committee is involved because they want to be, whilst others who don't take an active part make regular donations. The purpose of the charity is to raise funds exclusively each month, to provide a piece of equipment desperately needed by a disabled person in the County of Cambridgeshire, to improve their respective quality of life.

Celebrity members include Sir Ranulph Fiennes, Sir Brian Mawhinney MP, Lord David Renton, Dame Norma and John

297

Major, as well as many people from the world of sport and entertainment. Life membership is £10, and every penny raised goes towards the nominated projects. There are no overheads such as telephone bills or postage because they are sponsored.

Since becoming involved with the charity, Dave has shown a willingness to do anything to help. In November 2003, the 22nd anniversary of his last professional fight, a tribute night was held for him at Burgess Hall, St Ives. A raffle and auction raised over £600 which he insisted was donated to the Pidley charity. The event was organised by Dominic Shepherd, a life-long boxing fan who had hero-worshipped Dave since he was a boy. His grandparents, Bertha and Barry Hadder, owned a farm at Manea, and were neighbours and friends of Ken and Mary Green.

When Dave was in his prime, Dominic's mother got him a signed photograph of the Chatteris fighter. Years later Shepherd became involved in charity work by taking part in 'white-collar' boxing. When he was about to have his first contest, Green telephoned him and wished him luck. He travelled to London for his next fight and worked in his corner. As Dominic began showing nerves just before the first bell, Dave said: "Remember one thing, you've never lost with me in your corner."

"But you've never been in my corner before," replied Shepherd.

Dominic won his fight, the friendship with Dave developed, and now he stages tribute nights to his former idol, with proceeds going to charity.

Dave also gives tremendous support to the Chairman of Pidley Mountain Rescue Team, Gil Boyd, who telephones him most weeks to discuss a needy case. Whatever his commitments, the former boxer usually makes himself available.

He has made numerous local radio and TV appeals because many of the people in need live in or around the Fens. On one such occasion during 2003, just after Dave had taken delivery of a new top-of-the-range Mercedes, he and Boyd went to BBC Radio Cambridge for an interview to promote his celebrity golf day. As he turned into the car park, he had an accident which caused substantial damage to the front of the car. Yet when he walked into the studio about 15 minutes late, he made no mention of it. He was relaxed and composed throughout the interview, and only when it was over did he talk about the accident. Although he was upset, the most important thing to him was promoting the charity event.

It was so typical of Green, a thoughtful, caring man who always puts other people before himself. His willingness to devote time to worthy causes stems from the fact that he realises his own good fortune at having been born without any of the distressing deformities suffered by so many others.

The Pidley charity receives notification from the NHS about adults and children in Cambridgeshire with individual needs. Through people, including Gil Boyd, there have been countless occasions when Dave has learned about such cases, and regardless of where they live, he has gone to see them. One involved a two year old blind boy from Somersham who had serious problems. On discovering where he lived, Green visited him, and was very emotional when he returned home.

Another important aspect of the charity work is to supply disabled people with four-wheel buggies sponsored by a Mobility Centre at Peterborough. Dave makes every effort to be present when deliveries are made because he hates letting people down. On one occasion involving a lady recovering from a fractured spine, he had booked a holiday abroad, but was so disappointed at the thought of not being there that he offered to cancel it.

Being well connected with celebrities in other sports, Green is a real asset to the Pidley charity. In 2002, a seriously ill little boy had a dying wish to receive a Newcastle United football shirt signed by the players. Through his friendship with Nottinghamshire County cricketer, Basher Hussein, he got a contact at Newcastle, and a shirt was obtained. It was a measure of Dave's attitude that if he is unable to do something himself he will endeavour to find somebody who can. There have been many instances where he has obtained help from other celebrities because they know he will always be willing to reciprocate.

Apart from competing in charity events, golf is very much Dave's main form of relaxation, playing on average two or three times a week, most months of the year. He frequently played with Andy Smith, and his partner at ex-boxer events is usually his close friend and former sparring partner, Jimmy Harrington, who lives at Biggleswade.

Whilst Dave takes the game very seriously, it has provided many moments of amusement. Each year, he has a golfing holiday in Spain with his son and a group of friends. In mid-March 2002, they had booked to play a course near Marbella on what turned out to be the first really hot day since they arrived. The sun was beating down, but as they reached the car park, one of the group suddenly realised he had forgotten the sun tan lotion. "That's okay, I've got some in my bag," said Green to everyone's relief, because being up in the mountains they knew it would be impossible to buy any.

"Can I borrow your sun tan lotion dad?" said David junior as they unloaded the clubs from their vehicle. Green took a bottle from his golfing bag and threw it to his son who couldn't believe his eyes when he saw the name 'Wella' on the label. Being a hairdresser by profession, he knew it was a hairdressing product.

"Dad, this is a bottle of shampoo," he said to everyone's amusement. It transpired that the sun tan lotion was in the bathroom of their apartment, and Dave had been putting it on his hair for three days. "You know, I thought something was wrong," he chuckled, "because it would never lather up."

After the round of golf, the group went to the clubhouse to get some tea. While the others went to buy some souvenirs, Dave set about organising their refreshment. As he walked into the restaurant, a man approached him and said: "I know you, you're a boxer."

"Yes," said Green as he carried on getting checked in.

"Don't tell me your name," continued the stranger, "let me get it."

Meanwhile, the man was joined by several of his mates interested to know who he was talking to. "I've got it," he said suddenly, "you're 'the Bomber'."

"No," said Dave, not offering any clues as to his identity.

"Yes, you're Herol 'Bomber' Graham," said the stranger excitedly.

"Sorry mate, wrong colour," retorted Green. "He's a black man."

The man was extremely embarrassed as everyone burst into laughter. Dave politely explained who he was, shook his hand and gave him a autograph.

A few years earlier, Green and Andy Smith were playing in an ex-boxers golf tournament at a course in Kent. During the game Dave hit his ball out of bounds into a wooded area alongside some private gardens. He casually walked off to retrieve it, but hurriedly returned a couple of minutes later looking somewhat ashen-faced. "What's up Dave?" enquired one of his playing partners.

"There's a geezer in there who says he's fed up with us golfers," said Green. "The trouble is, he's got two bloody great rotweillers."

A few minutes later, Andy Smith's ball flew into the same clump of trees. Unperturbed by Dave's remark, he set about retrieving it, and within a few minutes returned to the course clutching his ball. "How on earth did you get it?" asked Green. "I chinned the geezer, knocked out the dogs, got my ball and walked out," replied Smith without a glimmer of a smile. "And you're supposed to be the boxer."

Later that evening, Dave was playing snooker in the club-house with boxing referee, Marcus McDonnell, for a small side-stake. With only the blue, pink and black remaining, he was a long way behind and couldn't possibly win. Suddenly, the light above the table went out, whereupon Green said: "That's it then, call it a draw."

Although he has been totally committed throughout his

boxing career and subsequent business enterprise, Dave still manages to devote a tremendous amount of time to his family. They have always been a close unit, doing everything together. The children were brought up to be polite and disciplined, but had regular birthday parties, treats and holidays. He fully supported their leisure and sporting pursuits and helped them with their training.

When Suzanne and Emma were about 13, they were picked for Cromwell School cross-country team, and went on to represent Cambridgeshire. To ensure that they were fully prepared, Dave woke them at 6.30am each morning and took them running before they went to school. At the end of every session he insisted they did a sprint finish just as he had when he was in training.

The two girls were also extremely good at netball, both being regular members of the school and county teams. When they were about 12, they started a netball club at Ely. It was not well funded, so whenever money was needed for new kit, travel and entry to tournaments, Dave invariably donated it personally or through his company by way of sponsorship. He provided a lump sum at the start of each season in order that the club could have good equipment, and adopted the same policy when his daughters started a similar club at Chatteris.

After leaving Cromwell School at the age of 16, Suzanne went to Long Road Sixth Form College, Cambridge, where she studied 'A' levels for two years. She was then admitted to De Montford University, Bedford, to study for a sports degree to enable her to become a physical training teacher. She remains a successful and enthusiastic netball player, and in 2003 was picked for the England Universities team. She is also a member of the development squad for the England ladies team.

Emma attended the College of West Anglia at King's Lynn after leaving Cromwell School, and studied childcare. She qualified as a nursery nurse and has a job looking after babies to the age of two years.

Like his father, David attended Burnsfield Infants School

before going to King Edward and then Cromwell. As soon as he was big enough, he started playing football. Dave attended all of his school matches and took him to Sunday games when he played for Chatteris Tigers between the ages of 11 to 18.

They have a wonderful relationship because always wanting his son to have the same discipline and principles that he did, Dave has never been let down. After doing a hairdressing course at college, young David worked at a saloon at St Ives before moving to a better position as a ladies and gents hairdresser at Ely. "If you like, he's my Andy Smith," remarked David junior. "He still watches me play football, and always tells me if I played well or badly."

By watching his son play for Jewson league side, Somersham Town, Green got to know all the Directors. Bob Emerson had been Chairman some years earlier, so the club already had a long connection with Renoak Limited whose sponsor boards are displayed around the pitch. When the previous President resigned, Dave was invited to fill the position. Since doing so, he has put a lot of personal and company money into maintaining and developing the club, as well as the donations from his charity golf days.

The former fighter has loved family life, and done everything a father could for his children. Two days after Suzanne and Emma passed their driving tests, two brand new Peugeot motor cars were on the drive when they arrived home. Each had a huge bouquet of flowers on the back seat from 'Mum and Dad'. Both later got personalised index plates.

David, Suzanne and Emma appreciate the benefits of having caring parents. Their hard working father's astute business brain has ensured that since they were small children they have enjoyed holidays abroad every year to Spain, Portugal and America, where they visited Disneyland on several occasions. They have also spent many short breaks and weekends at various parts of the United Kingdom.

The family made many trips to Javea, a resort on the Costa Brava which they first visited in 1982 after their friends Rodney and Sheila Marriner bought a property there. It had a

303

genial atmosphere, the people were friendly, and the beach safe for the children to play on. The weather and food were good, and they enjoyed their first visit so much that they returned regularly, often twice a year.

Dave got to know a lot of people in Javea, and became extremely popular. He often visited the local boxing club which Rod Marriner had formed, gave interviews for the regional newspaper, and opened a night-club owned by a Yorkshireman. At one stage he considered buying a property there.

During one holiday to America when Suzanne and Emma were about six, they visited a large waterpark in Florida. During the day they took a ride on small inflatable dinghies on 'The Lazy River', a one mile long, fast-flowing lagoon which travelled through rapids and waterfalls. Whilst Emma stayed with Kay, Suzanne chose to go with Dave and her brother, but soon got left behind as they got competitive. Instead of laying flat on the dinghies, they stood up and were trying to race one another. When they reached the end of the course, Kay asked where Suzanne was.

Meanwhile, Suzanne had got off at an earlier stopping point and told somebody she had lost her dad. She was taken to an official who took her to a large stand overlooking the lagoon to see if she could see them, but to no avail. Messages were then broadcast over loudspeakers asking if anyone had lost a child, and within a few minutes the others came and found her.

Throughout their childhood David, Suzanne and Emma saw plenty of evidence of their father's generosity and competitiveness. During a holiday in England, Dave went into an amusement arcade and began playing on a fruit machine. At one stage, he hit lucky, and as coins rattled out, a small group of 13-14 year old lads stood and watched him.

He carried on for a while, chatting to them as he fed the coins back into the machine. Suddenly, Suzanne and Emma tried to drag him away because they wanted to go elsewhere. "Just let me have one more go and I'll be with you," said

Green pushing another coin into the slot. About £10 spilled out, but instead of putting it into his pocket, he divided it up, gave it to the lads who were watching and told them to enjoy themselves.

Dave's competitive spirit, however, almost caused problems one Sunday afternoon at the Metropolitan Police sports ground, Chigwell, at an event organised to raise funds for the family of a murdered policewoman. There were a variety of team events including a pillow fight on a greasy pole. Competitors went in order of height, and Green was on third against a female.

Knowing what his father was likely to do, young David told him to take it easy, hoping he would let the woman hit him a couple of times first. As soon as the order to commence was given, however, he clouted the woman as hard as he could and knocked her off the pole. David, Suzanne, Emma and other members of the team were very embarrassed, and there was some hostility from a few spectators. The woman, however, got up laughing and there was no bad feeling.

Things became more intense, however, during a netball match against the Met Police. Green and his three children were playing for a Chatteris team, and although it was intended to be a fun game, he took it very seriously. He was extremely competitive, argued with the referee, and when a fight nearly developed the match was abandoned.

* * *

Success in business has ensured that Dave has a wonderful lifestyle. A Manchester United supporter since he was a boy, he went to a lot of matches some years ago, often taking local people as a treat or to give them a lift after enduring a difficult time.

He has been friends with Brian Robson for a long time, having first met him at a function at Old Trafford. When he arrived, Robson was carrying a Manchester United shirt, but at the end of the evening gave it to Green for his son.

305

When Dave had his 50th birthday celebration at Pidley Golf Club in 2003, Brian was a surprise guest. Kay had contacted ex-Cambridge United player, Graham Smith, who telephoned the former England captain and he immediately agreed to attend the event because of his respect for the former boxer.

Dave is also close friends with Harry Carpenter who covered most of his fights for BBC television. For many years they played a round of golf at Dulwich, and afterwards joined their wives for dinner.

Gifted with a good sense of humour, he is frequently asked to do after-dinner speaking, often at events unconnected with boxing. In 1994, clips of some of his speeches were included on a video entitled 'Sporting Comedy – Boxing'.

Dave is often called upon to speak on local radio regarding special events connected with boxing and football. When the BBC television programme Superstars was re-launched in 2003, he was asked to report to a studio at Peterborough by 8am on the day of the first programme. In October the same year, he was a guest in Newcastle at a talk-in with Pele and Sir Bobby Robson.

He loves playing dominoes, and represents his local pub, 'Walk The Dog', in the Chatteris league on Monday evenings, and March league on Wednesdays. Despite his success in life, Green loves mixing in the local environment because it allows him to maintain contact with many people he has met over the years.

Although he has always had a busy life, Dave has never forgotten Andy Smith. Throughout the years following his retirement, he remained in close contact with him and his family. In the early 1990's, he took his former manager to Darlington to meet Brian Curvis whom Andy had not seen for many years. He and Green had identical professional records of 37 victories against four defeats.

When Smith suffered ill health during 2000, Dave visited him every week and often took him for a drive. The illness progressed to such an extent that Andy was eventually admitted to hospital, but Dave kept up the visits. On

Christmas morning 2002, he was at his bedside for over two hours. When he was transferred to a care home at Eastrea near Whittlesey, Green still visited him on a regular basis despite his heavy business commitments. At the request of the family, Dave and Kay took Andy from the home to his wife's funeral in August 2003. To guarantee his comfort they also took a nurse and a chair.

If Dave has a weakness, it is his tendency towards fast driving, and whilst he is a law abiding citizen, he has occasionally attracted the attention of cops or caused speed cameras to flash. He was even caught by cameras twice the same day within the space of half an hour. The first was on the A1 at Sandy, and later on the A141 towards March.

During a holiday in America in the 1990's, Dave was pulled up for speeding while driving a shooting brake type vehicle from Orlando towards West Palm Beach. When asked where he came from, the cop snapped: "I knew you were from England. Why do you come all this way on holiday and then tear about all over the place?" He was then asked to produce his driving licence and confirm his name and address.

"Do you know why I call my house 'Ringside'?" asked Green.

"Why?" enquired the cop. "Are you a fighter?"

"Yes," replied Dave, "I fought the great Sugar Ray Leonard."

"Gee, you fought Sugar Ray Leonard. Well you slow down. If you do about 75, you'll be alright."

Dave escaped a ticket for speeding, but had to produce his licence at a police station and pay $15 administration fee.

In September 2003, he left home one morning at about 4.30am to go to Stansted Airport to catch a flight to Ireland where he was due to play golf. As he sped through the country lanes towards Sutton doing about 85mph, he became aware that another vehicle was behind him. When it eventually flashed him down he realised it was a police car. "Oh, I'm glad it's you Dave," said the officer when he got out. "For a moment we thought somebody had pinched your car." After an exchange of pleasantries he was allowed to continue his journey without getting a ticket.

✦ 20 ✦

REFLECTIONS

When Andy Smith pulled Dave out of his fight with Reg Ford in November 1981, it was sad that such a brave and talented fighter should end his glorious career on his stool with tears and blood trickling down his cheeks. Yet from that sadness grew tremendous respect from the fact that both manager and boxer could end it with dignity. "It was a big shock to me," Green remarked later, "but I will never question Mr Smith's judgement."

There can have been few closer relationships within sport than that which has existed between Green and Smith. It was also totally professional from start to finish. For 30 years they have been closer in many ways than a father and son, enjoying a wonderful friendship, and above all mutual respect.

Dave has always expressed his gratitude for the support and guidance given to him by Smith, and never hesitates to say so whenever called upon to give a talk about his ring career. He readily admits that without that guidance there would have been no Dave 'Boy' Green, the world class fighter who thrilled followers of the sport for so long. His quality of life and success in business would never have reached the heights they have without the continued advice of 'Mr Smith'.

Throughout their years in boxing, they talked things out, but Andy always made the decisions and Dave respected them. Whilst there was some anger at the manager's decision to make a prompt and public declaration of Green's retirement, it was one he knew he had to make. It was also one of the most difficult yet one of the most important.

"I knew in the end I would have to make the decision – that I would have to face it – and that it would be effective only if I chose the right moment," Smith admitted in an interview some days later. "As I watched the fourth round against Reg Ford, I knew that moment had come. I knew how far David was from the glory he had known. And I knew he knew."

"David is an emotional man which is why he reacted the way he did," continued Andy, "but it was not long before he knew the decision was right."   .

Already financially well off, Green had no need to fight, and thanks to the compassion and foresight of his manager and close friend, he left the sport in good health and at a time when he still had a massive following. Consequently, he remains as popular in retirement as he was as a fighter.

With the passing of time, Dave has never ceased to appreciate the opportunities given to him by Andy Smith. There were no gaps in his life, and no time to brood over the good times. By the time he retired from the ring he was already established in a flourishing business.

The recent problems experienced by former world heavyweight champion, Frank Bruno, highlighted the difficulties experienced by high profile fighters when their ring careers come to an end. The rigours and routines of early morning roadwork, and the daily sessions in the gym, suddenly become a thing of the past. Depression and loneliness can then easily develop from inactivity if the mind is not right. Thanks to the foresight, love and professionalism of his manager, Dave 'Boy' Green had no such misfortune.

Smith was always confident of Dave's future because he knew him better than anyone. He recognised his determination to succeed in everything he did, and played on it. "His enthusiasm and dedication will always rub off on other people," he once enthused. "That is what he brought to boxing – that and courage, and it took him so much further than others more naturally gifted in skills. The same will happen in his business."

Smith was to British boxing what men like Sir Alf Ramsey, Brian Clough and Ron Greenwood were to football – an expert manager who knew his business inside out. When it came to looking after his boxers, he was as tough as any man in the ring, particularly when it came to purse money.

"He drives me crazy when he comes to my office to negotiate terms," promoter Harry Levene once remarked. "He's a very tough cookie. He's a Scot and I'm a Jew, so I don't know who wins. Usually we're both satisfied, so I suppose you could call it a draw."

Smith's formula for success was total dedication. "You have to be able to take liberties with your family life," he remarked emphatically in one interview. His dedication went as far as sharing his home with his boxers during the week before a big fight in order to keep a fatherly eye on them. Green, Joe Bugner, Des Morrison and others spent many nights at the bungalow called 'Valandra' in St Ives where Andy lived with his wife Valerie, sons Andrew, Alan, Robert, and daughter Marie.

Although his retirement from boxing was sudden and unexpected, Dave never had the desire to carry on just for the sake of extra cash. His sheer love of the sport was what motivated him, and in particular he loved winning. He was a crowd-pleaser of the highest quality, yet his style contributed to his four defeats all coming inside the distance. Going forward all the time, he was more open to a counter-punch than a stylish boxer who moves in all directions.

Despite Dave's bitter disappointment at leaving the sport he had served so well for 15 years as an amateur and professional, there was never any talk of a comeback. He was therefore puzzled and somewhat fearful when his friend,

Sugar Ray Leonard, embarked on a third comeback in 1997 at the age of 40. "I find it all very sad," he remarked when contacted by a national newspaper. "He made a lot of money out of boxing – more than $100 million, and achieved all he wanted. People watching this will forget just how good he was. Instead of being remembered as an all-time great, he could go down as a plodding grandad. That's no way for a man of his talent to go out."

Dave genuinely likes Leonard, and for more than 20 years has spoken about him with sincerity, respect and affection. "He's a really nice bloke – one of the nicest you'd wish to meet," he once told a local journalist.

Despite his devastating defeat, he has never regretted fighting Sugar Ray back in 1981. "The plan was to use the first round to see what he was like, and to stay with him," he recalled. "I was a pressure fighter, and relied on fitness and work-rate to wear my opponents down. But I knew the game was up when I went back to my corner. I couldn't get near him – he was too good."

"I haven't got Sugar Ray's ability," remarked Green in another interview several years later. "I got where I did through sheer hard work. If I'd trained for 25 years, I'd never have beaten him, but when I went over to fight him, I honestly believed I could. I wouldn't have gone otherwise."

Dave's concern about his former opponent very much reflected from his own good fortune. He had a wonderful lifestyle built initially from boxing, but once he was over the hill, had never questioned his manager's judgement. With the passing of time he realised that one fight too many could have made all the difference to his health and well-being. The same dangers faced Sugar Ray, and it saddened him.

Unlike many boxers, Green continued working full-time until he was well established as a professional. For about three years, he and Kay lived off his earnings from the farm, and banked everything else. "When you haven't got much money, you do try to save a little bit," he remarked when reflecting on his earlier life.

311

Having been taught at a young age to look after his money, Dave was very organised, and his shrewd business brain enabled him to purchase his luxury home which he appropriately named 'Ringside'. Over the years, he continued to develop it, having an outdoor swimming pool constructed in 1985. Six years later, he installed an indoor pool and a jacuzzi.

"With the money I made from boxing, I could have doddled along doing nothing for the rest of my life," he remarked, "but I am not that sort of person. I wanted to improve my life for the safety of my family. If I hadn't been a boxer, I would probably have still been a farm worker."

Dave has never forgotten the start in life given to him by his parents. They supported and encouraged him in everything he did, and although he bettered himself considerably over the years, he saw them regularly and never changed his attitude towards them. "David gives us everything we want from a son," Ken Green once remarked, "and that is pride and respect. Obviously in the case of an emergency, he would help us out, but we enjoy life as simple country folk, and don't want to change."

Even before travelling to London one day for a training session a few weeks before the Leonard fight, Dave called at his father's farm. "Hello dad," he said, "I'm just off to London to spar a few rounds with Kirkland Laing." It was in the days before mobile 'phones, and even though he was married he nearly always told his parents where he was going.

Ken Green idolised his sons, and attended all their football and cricket matches. He saw most of Dave's fights, both amateur and professional, and travelled with him to Denmark and America. He did, however, miss his second professional contest against Dave Coombs at the Anglo American Sporting Club because he didn't have a dinner suit. Being a man of simple tastes, he thought he would feel out of place if he turned up in ordinary clothes, so he decided not to go.

Dave was extremely disappointed, and told his father he was as good as everyone else. When he boxed Tommy Joyce at the same venue three months later he made sure Ken borrowed one and went along. From that day he never looked back, and whenever Dave attended a black-tie event, he usually took his father with him. He was always proud to say; "This is my dad." When he attended the Boxing Writers Club dinner to receive his 'Young Boxer of the Year' award, Ken was at his side. During the evening Dave introduced him to many of the top boxers present, including John Conteh and Alan Minter. It was one of Ken's proudest moments.

When Ken passed away on 30 October 1990, it was Dave's biggest regret that he had not been with him. At the time he was attending a business exhibition in London. When he telephoned during the morning his father had complained of feeling unwell. After having his lunch, he sat in his chair and died peacefully in his sleep the same afternoon. Kay telephoned Dave and broke the news, and as soon as he returned to Chatteris, he went to see his father at the Chapel of Rest. He visited him again before the funeral the following week.

Ken and his wife had never moved from Tithe Road, and he was still working the farm at the time of his death. They lived quiet, but contented lives, and during the 1970s became successful members of Chatteris Bowls Club. Ken won a mens' singles championship, and Mary a ladies' pairs. Mary passed away on 20 January 1998, having been admitted to hospital with breathing difficulties the previous day. They are buried in the same grave at Chatteris Cemetery, New Road, which Dave visits frequently, usually alone.

Being part of a close family unit was of considerable benefit to Dave. He was given every opportunity by his parents, and this was something he developed when he eventually had his own family. There was togetherness and support for each other just as it had been when he was a youngster. He and his brother were both in the school football teams, played cricket and did cross-country running together. Although Michael didn't like boxing, he became a karate enthusiast. He also ran three London marathons, in 1982, '83 and '86, completing the 26 mile course in times of 2 hours 57 minutes (twice) and 3 hours 01 minutes.

In 1979, while Dave was still boxing, they entered a 10 mile charity run at Whittlesey. Taking the event very seriously, Dave completed the course in 57 minutes, about a mile ahead of Michael who took five minutes longer. Dave has always regretted not having taken part in the London marathon which he is convinced he could have completed inside three hours. Despite his application for 2004 being rejected, it remains one of his unfulfilled ambitions.

Although life now moves along at a more gentle pace, Green often reflects on his boxing career because he knows that without it, he could still be working on a farm. "I feel I have been very fortunate because boxing stood me in good stead for the future," he once remarked. "I was also lucky because it never really changed my life. I'm still one of the boys, and it's nice that people don't treat me any differently."

Coming from the same town as Eric Boon, Dave felt he had something to live up to, and constantly reminds people that the old champion was his inspiration. There was massive respect between the two, and they were often jointly invited to attend functions. Together with Isle of Ely MP, Clement Freud, they took part in a darts match to raise funds to help Chatteris Boxing Club purchase their gymnasium. On 23 April 1976, just ahead of Dave's fight with Herbie McLean, they appeared together on a BBC television documentary-style chat programme, 'Generations Apart', hosted by Harry Carpenter. In March 1978, Green was a guest at a testimonial dinner for Boon at the World Sporting Club in London.

Chatteris was the only amateur club Dave boxed for, and his exciting style earned him a lot of local fans. "I was always proud to be billed from there," he remarked, "because it has always been my home."

When his old trainer, Jim Moore, retired from his duties with the club in October 1977, Green was quick to show his appreciation. "If it hadn't been for you, the club would have folded long ago," he remarked as he presented Jim with an inscribed cup. "You played a big part in my career, and

314

without your encouragement, the club might not have kept going and I might not have kept going."

Dave has always been appreciative of people who helped him during the early years of his life. In particular, he maintained contact with his old headmaster, Dennis Hall, who always insisted that he was the finest footballer ever to go through King Edward School. He also believed Green was good enough to have become a professional footballer, top cross-country runner or distance athlete.

Although he never believed Dave could become a world famous boxer, Hall followed his career closely, and attended several big fights in London including those against Piedvache, Stracey and Palomino. Following the defeat by the world champion, the schoolmaster had a feeling of great pride rather than sadness.

Dave still attends functions at the school, where for many years, a large framed photograph of him has been displayed in a prominent position in the entrance hall. Similar pictures hang in the P.E. department of Cromwell School and at the Chatteris Conservative Club. They are a reminder of what was a fantastic time for people living in the Fenland region. There was no big time football, and they were desperate for a big sporting hero. When Dave came along, he captured public imagination in a massive way.

Everything took off after he had beaten Billy Waith in what was the most dramatic sporting event for local people since the days of Eric Boon. It was the first time most of them had been to the Royal Albert Hall, and they returned with many others for the fight against Joey Singleton. By the time Dave won the European title, his following had snowballed to areas beyond Peterborough and Cambridge. He was so big that in the Fens his appeal was likened to big names such as George Best and Bobby Charlton.

Despite the passing of time, everyone in Chatteris still knows Dave and remembers the good times. During a short trip along the High Street, he frequently acknowledges or speaks to a dozen or so people of all ages. His rapid rise to fame never lost him any of the friends he grew up with. In fact, he gained many, but they were not the spongers or hangers-on who so often attach themselves to successful fighters. They were genuine local folk who gave him things rather than took them.

Some boxing fans were particularly generous, none more so than Nicky Dixon from Carlisle who went to all of Dave's fights. One night, after a bout in London, he presented the Chatteris man with a one ounce gold nugget, and another of half an ounce for Kay.

Another ardent fan to attend most of Green's fights was Norman Forester, also from Carlisle. He later opened a steak and fish restaurant with a boxing theme which he appropriately called Dempsey's. Photographs of famous boxers decorate the walls, but the show-piece is Dave's tiger-skin dressing-gown and a pair of his trunks which are displayed in a glass case.

Members of his Supporters Club Committee got tremendous pleasure from being involved because he was a credit to the town and an example to young children. When the committee folded in February 1985, monies left over were donated to Oxfam at Dave's request. An acknowledgement from the charity stated that the welcome gift had been allocated to relief work being carried out in Ethiopia and Sudan.

One of the finest sportsmen ever to come from East Anglia, Green's popularity is incredible. Although people supported him as a fighter because he was exciting, there was much more to it than that. He was a cheerful, resilient, salt-of-the-earth Fenlander who was never affected by success, or attracted by the bright lights of the big cities. Chatteris is his home, and that is where he has lived for his entire life. Around him, there is nothing he has not earned through sheer hard work and unlimited courage.

Once he started moving up the professional ladder, Dave received countless invitations to dinners around the country, requests to present trophies at amateur boxing clubs, and a wide range of other functions unassociated with boxing. They included opening new branch offices of Leicester and

Gateway Building Societies at March and Chatteris, school fetes, village bazaars, a putting green at Ramsey, and a sports shop owned by his close friend, England international table tennis star, Paul Day.

After Chatteris Cricket Club pavilion was burned down in 2000, Dave was invited to open the new one once the building was complete. He even attended a prize-giving at a local homing pigeon society and opened steam engine fairs in East Anglia.

When he opened a bazaar at March Adult Training Centre in 1980, he was presented with a toy train made by a pupil, and a Dave 'Boy' Green rag doll in boxing gear for his baby son. Once the event was underway, he volunteered to help out on a stall selling homemade toys. His attendance helped raise a total of £875 for Wisbech & District Society for Mentally Handicapped Children and Adults.

Making personal appearances is a trend which has continued ever since Dave retired from the ring. He is still as well-known as he was when he was fighting, and loves the glossy activity because it goes with the business he was in. "When people ask you, and boys keep coming up for your autograph, you know you are getting on," he remarked. "I loved it. You work for the fame, and I think you should get some sort of reward. I think it helped Kay and me too, we are both less reserved."

More than 20 years on from his fighting days, Green is still a massive attraction whenever he attends amateur shows. Totally unaffected by his fame, he has time for everyone, and never refuses to sign the array of objects thrust at him during the course of an evening. He is in his element when he presents the trophies, and always has words of encouragement for every young boxer, especially the losers. "Look, don't you get upset," he told a distraught 11-year-old who had just lost a close decision in his first contest on a show at Biggleswade in February 2004. "I lost my first schoolboy fight and look where I got. Just keep up your training, keep on trying and you'll be alright."

The youngster's tears ceased almost immediately, and there was a bounce in his step as he walked away proudly clutching his trophy. He had met Dave 'Boy' Green for the first time, and half an hour later strode up to his table and politely asked him to sign a pair of miniature boxing gloves. "You're okay now aren't you?" enquired Green with a warm smile as he duly signed his name for the umpteenth time that evening.

It was a moving experience, but something which comes so naturally to Dave. "This is the ground roots of boxing," he stressed. "Without these kids, there's no future in the game, so it's up to us to do our bit to encourage them."

Although he no longer holds a position with the British Boxing Board of Control, Green is sometimes called upon to assess the ability of applicant professional boxers living in the East Anglia region. Before a licence is granted, the Board have to be satisfied that a boxer can look after himself. Dave is well qualified to make such an assessment, but if he feels a lad is unsuitable, he will say so.

Dave is extremely proud to have been a boxer, and has video tapes of every one of his professional fights. He has a meticulous record of all his amateur contests logged in an exercise book. His array of scrapbooks bulge with cuttings from local and national newspapers, and he has a complete collection of programmes from the professional shows he boxed on, and most of the amateur ones as well. Cabinets in his snooker room are crammed with trophies, and a gallery of framed black and white photographs adorn the walls.

He staunchly defends the sport against criticism. In many interviews since he retired, has always said that given the chance he would do it all over again. "I have no regrets," he once remarked. "I did better than I ever thought I could, so I was well pleased."

Dave had no professional aspirations until he met Andy Smith, and even when he started boxing for pay would have been happy just to have won a Southern Area championship. He never did win that title, but only because he didn't fight for it. Yet his rise to stardom was amazing, and by far exceeding his expectation was so typical of the Dave Green everyone knows. Whatever the challenge, he has always wanted to be the best, whether it be in sport, business or raising money for charity. He has long held the view that the more a person puts into something, the more they get back. That was always his philosophy as a fighter, and he has carried it on through all other aspects of his life.

Despite the fact that he continued working full-time for some years, Green always accepted boxing as a 24 hour-a-day job, 365 days a year. Although many other fighters set aside a couple of months to train before a contest, he went running every day no matter whether he was on holiday or had a fight coming up. Even after his retirement from the ring, he continued to run at least two or three times a week. His level of fitness was incredible, and meticulously kept diaries confirmed that he ran 1,084 miles and sparred 266 rounds during 1980, a year in which he had only two fights.

Dave has always considered the greatest moment of his career was standing in the ring at Wembley as the national anthem played before the Palomino fight. He then listened proudly as Master of Ceremonies, Nat Basso, announced; "My lords, ladies and gentlemen, this is the main event of the evening – a contest over 15 three-minute rounds for the welterweight championship of the world."

Basso, one of the finest MC's of all time, had real atmosphere in his voice, and the professionalism to make an occasion very special. "I thought, bloody hell, what am I doing here?" recalled Green. It had all happened so quickly for him.

Although he failed to lift a world title, Dave was already a champion in terms of public popularity and respect. As a tremendous crowd-pleaser, he was a throw-back to the tougher times when men fought to escape difficulties caused by social problems. He created incredible atmosphere wherever he fought. The tiger-skin dressing-gown, snarling aggression and baring of the gumshield, all added to the excitement, as did the bugle calls from the galleries and the antics of his ardent fans who poured into the London arenas on fight nights. It was claimed that at least half of those people had never been to a boxing arena until he came along.

When Green retired from the ring, British boxing lost one of its most colourful exponents. His career had taken him from the simple life in a Cambridgeshire farming environment to the brink of a world championship. A role-model for sport, highly successful businessman and tireless worker for charity, it is amazing that he has not received recognition in the form of an award in the New Year or Queen's Birthday Honours. He is an extremely deserving case, and such an honour would be just reward for his commitment to sport and society.

Dave has time for everyone, and even when busy makes himself available, especially for people in need. Many have benefited from his efforts thanks largely to the fact that he has always appreciated his own good fortune, and is committed to putting something back. Success in no way changed him, and his quiet polite manner has endeared him to people throughout the United Kingdon. Fight fans paid good money to watch him as a professional, and he repaid their support with seven years of sheer excitement and courage. Tough battles failed to quell his appetite for the hardest of all sports.

When Dave said from the ring the night he retired that he had loved every minute of it, he meant it from the bottom of his heart. He was a born fighter who trained all the time and reached an incredible level of fitness built up, not just over months, but many years.

"People don't realise the depth of Dave Green's desire," Andy Smith once remarked at a press conference. "He's a model professional who puts 100 per cent into everything he does."

Nobody could have devoted more to his sport than Green did, but he acknowledges the tremendous support he received from his loyal and loving wife Kay. Whilst monitoring his diets, suffering his moods as a fight approached, she maintained a good home in which he could relax. She continued that support throughout his business life, and after 30 years of marriage they remain a close family unit.

Rarely is a bad word ever spoken about Dave Green. He has never caused any controversy regarding the way he conducts himself, and his story would be ideal for a 'This is Your Life' programme. He is a credit to himself, his family and the people of Chatteris. Those who know him and share his company are privileged.

APPENDIX

Dave 'Boy' Green's Junior Amateur Fighting Record 1966-1970

Date	Opponent	Result	Venue
1967			
Mar 31	M. Stango (Bedford)	L Pts 3	Cambridge
Apr 14	C. Thompson (St Ives)	W Pts 3	St Ives
Apr 22	T. Mantle (Boston)	W KO 1	Boston
Apr 24	F. Green (Leicester)	W RSC 2	Leicester
Apr 28	R. McLean (Lynn)	W RSC 1	Chatteris
May 1	K. Kelly (Coventry Irish)	L Pts 3	Kettering
May 19	K. Kelly (Coventry Irish)	W Pts 3	Overstone
May 26	A. Cunningham (Birmingham)	L Pts 3	Chatteris
Oct 20	K. Kelly (Coventry Irish)	W Pts 3	Chatteris
Oct 27	F. Wagstaff (Bedford)	W Pts 3	Ely
Nov 9	C. Loveland (Northampton)	W RSC 3	Northampton
Dec 7	F. Wagstaff (Bedford)	W Pts 3	Huntingdon
1968			
Feb 17	T. Bines (Colchester)	L Pts 3	Dereham
Feb 21	F. Wagstaff (Bedford)	W Pts 3	Littleport
Mar 9	D. O'Connor (Birmingham)	W Pts 3	Overstone
Mar 16	M. Maloney (Apethorpe)	W RSC 1	Somersham
Mar 23	J. Chapman (West Ham)	L Pts 3	Littleport
Apr 29	G. Hills (Five Stars, London)	L Pts 3	Harold Hill
Nov 16	D. Sayell (Aylesbury)	L Pts 3	Stevenage
Dec 7	O. Ourso (Lowestoft)	W RSC 3	Lowestoft
1969			
Jan 17	D. Sorrell (HMS Ganges)	W RSC 2	Ely
Feb 14	D. Sayell (Aylesbury)	W Pts 3	Chatteris
Feb 22	D. Sayell (Aylesbury)	L Pts 3	Aylesbury
Mar 7	M. Lowton (Phoenix)	W RSC 1	Market Harborough
Mar 31	P. Norton (Dereham)	W RSC 1	Swonton Morley

Apr 17	J. Chapman (West Ham)	L Pts 3	Bethnal Green
	(N.E. London Junior championships Class A semi-final)		
Apr 18	D. Sayell (Aylesbury)	W RSC 2	Chatteris
May 24	P. Cowley (St Pancras)	W RSC 2	Hitchin
Oct 10	G. Evans (Fitzroy Lodge)	L Pts 3	Ely
Nov 17	G. Evans (Fitzroy Lodge)	L Pts 3	Walworth
Nov 20	K. Laing (Union Steward)	W Pts 3	Corby

1970

Feb 7	J. Scott (Somersham)	W Pts 3	Somersham
Feb 12	K. Davies (Clifton)	W Pts 3	Corby
Apr 28	S. Sloane (Garden City)	W RSC 2	Bethnal Green
	(N.E. London Junior championships Class B semi-final)		
May 9	K. Hussey (Battersea)	L Pts 3	Finchley
	(London Junior ABA semi-final)		

Junior Amateur Summary

Bouts Taken:	35
Won	23 (12 inside the distance)
Lost	12

Dave 'Boy' Green's Senior Amateur Fighting Record 1970-1974

Date	Opponent	Result	Venue
1970			
Oct 1	D. Smith (Eltham)	W Pts 3	Norwich
Oct 30	J. Scott (Somersham)	W RSC 2	Chatteris
Nov 4	I. Ramage (Newmarket)	W Pts 3	Rushden
Dec 1	I. Ramage (Newmarket)	L Pts 3	King's Lynn
Dec 14	F. Wagstaff (Bedford)	W Pts 3	Bedford
1971			
Jan 16	S. Crickmore (Lowestoft)	W Pts 3	Beccles
Feb 5	M. Stango (Bedford)	L RSC 1	Chatteris
Feb 9	P. Gaffney (London)	W Pts 3	Watford
	D. Swann (Ollerton)	W RSC 1	Thruston
Mar 11	B. Taylor (Repton)	L RSC 2	Bethnal Green
	(London N.E. Divs. bantamweight semi-final)		
Mar 15	F. Wagstaff (Bedford)	W Pts 3	Dereham
Mar 19	H. Humrick (Germany)	W RSC 1	Beccles
Mar 25	H. Stroh (Germany)	W RSC 1	Hunstanton
Mar 26	D. Waldock (Luton Irish)	W Pts 3	Newmarket
Apr 6	R. Eady (Wellingborough)	W Pts 3	Billing
Apr 17	A. Merry (Royal Oak)	W RSC 2	Boston
May 18	M. Spencer (Fitzroy Lodge)	L Pts 3	Belhus Park
June 5	P. Senni (Norwich)	W Pts 3	Beccles
July 3	P. Sutcliffe (Chatham)	W RSC 3	Ipswich
Sept 10	S. Markham (Southend)	W Pts 3	Cambridge
Sept	T. Glienke (Bremen)	L Pts 3	Bremen, Germany
Oct 8	B. Cassidy (Waltham Forest)	W RSC 2	Beccles
Oct 16	R. Mather (Hitchin)	W Pts 3	Peterborough
Oct 29	T. Wallace (Ely)	L Pts 3	Chatteris
Nov 1	M. Barton (Southall)	L Pts 3	Hemel Hempstead
Nov 9	S. Polak (Clifton)	L Pts 3	Watford
1972			
Jan 27	T. Wallace (Ely)	L Pts 3	Norwich
Feb 9	D. Waldock (Luton)	W RSC 1	Dunstable
Feb 15	J. Wylie (Watford)	W RSC 2	Watford
Feb 16	C. Mikellides (Met. Police)	W KO 3	Watton
Feb 28	F. Williams (Ruddington)	W Pts 3	Northampton
Mar 9	D. Hollyoak (Repton)	L Pts 3	Bethnal Green
	(London N.E. Divs. lightweight semi-final)		
Mar 16	P. Fitzgerald (Eltham)	W Pts 3	Ipswich
Apr 14	L. Wagner (Germany)	W RSC 1	Peterborough

Apr 28	P. Fitzgerald (Eltham)	L Pts 3	Yarmouth
May 6	L. Bruce (Stifford Cliffs)	W RSC 2	Beccles
May 11	M. Heyden (Germany)	W RSC 3	Cambridge
July 1	D. Allen (Chatham)	L Pts 3	Ipswich
Sept 28	M. Spencer (Fitzroy Lodge)	W Pts 3	Norwich
Oct 7	D. Allen (Chatham)	W Pts 3	Beccles
Oct 16	M. Ryce (Abingdon)	W Pts 3	Northampton
Oct 30	D. Gwilliam (Wechell's)	L Pts 3	Kettering
Nov 9	P. Turrell (Beccles)	W Pts 3	Cambridge
Nov 13	A. Meakin (RAF)	L Pts 3	Abingdon
Nov 22	P. Carson (Belfast)	W Pts 3	Bournemouth
Nov 30	H. Watson (Huthwaite)	L Pts 3	Thurmaston
Dec 8	R. Ruloss (Wesel, W. Germany)	W KO 1	Wesel, West Germany

1973

Jan 26	J. Zeraschi (Alexandra)	W Pts 3	Boreham Wood
Feb 2	P. Turrell (Beccles)	W Pts 3	Chatteris
Feb 11	H. Christensen (Randers)	W Pts 3	Randers, Denmark
Mar 1	J. Kelly (Peterborough) (Eastern Counties light-welterweight final)	W RSC 3	Ipswich
Mar 17	B. Finnegan (Golden Gloves, Birmingham) (ABA quarter-finals)	L Pts 3	Beccles
Mar 29	K. Laing (Clifton)	L Pts 3	Cambridge
May 21	G. Fowler (South Oxley)	W RSC 3	Northampton
May 22	D. Loveland (Kettering)	W Pts 3	Overstone
Oct 18	H. Watson (Huthwaite)	L Pts 3	Thurmaston
Oct 23	G. McManus (Epsom & Ewell)	W Pts 3	Hemel Hempstead
Oct 29	M. Kelly (Cheltenham)	W Pts 3	Cambridge
Nov 6	M. Ryce (Abingdon)	W Pts 3	Watford
Nov 16	A. Braidwood (Robert Browning)	W RSC 2	Luton
Nov 24	H. Madsen (Denmark) (Eastern Counties v Jutland)	W RSC 1	Beccles
Nov 29	K. Laing (Clifton)	W RSC 1	Thurmaston
Dec 10	A. Hillman (Orpington)	W RSC 2	Northampton

1974

Feb 7	M. Hooker (Westree)	W RSC 1	Bethnal Green
Mar 2	R. Duffy (Ipswich) (Eastern Counties welterweight final)	W RSC 1	Beccles

Mar 12	M. Ryce (Abingdon) (Zone Finals)	W Pts 3	Luton
Mar 23	K. Laing (Clifton) (ABA quarter-final)	W Pts 3	Birmingham
Apr 10	A. Barnes (Warrington) (English ABA semi-final)	W Pts 3	Hull
Apr 17	T. Waller (Lynn) (ABA welterweight semi-final)	L Pts 3	Manchester
Apr 22	A. Meakin (RAF)	W Pts 3	Northampton

Senior Amateur Summary

Bouts Taken:	70
Won	51 (21 inside the distance)
Lost	19

Dave 'Boy' Green's Professional Fighting Record 1974-1981

Date	Opponent	Result	Venue
1974			
Dec 10	Yotham Kunda	W KO 2	Nottingham
1975			
Jan 20	Dave Coombs	W KO 2	Hilton Hotel, London
Feb 12	Derek Simpson	W Ret 7	Cambridge
Mar 11	Barton McAllister	W RSC 2	Wembley
Apr 8	George Salmon	W Pts 8	Cambridge
May 12	Tommy Joyce	W KO 3	Hilton Hotel, London
June 3	Angus McMillan	W Pts 8	Royal Albert Hall
Oct 14	Al Stewart	W RSC 2	Royal Albert Hall
Nov 10	Brian Jones	W KO 2	Cambridge
Nov 25	Alan Salter	W RSC 1	Royal Albert Hall
1976			
Jan 20	George McGurk	W KO 2	Royal Albert Hall
Mar 2	Billy Waith	W RSF 11	Royal Albert Hall
	(final eliminator for British light-welterweight title)		
Mar 20	Giuseppe Minotti	W RSF 4	Wembley
Apr 6	Jim Montague	W Pts 8	Royal Albert Hall
Apr 27	Herbie McLean	W Ret 4	Royal Albert Hall
June 1	Joey Singleton	W Ret 6	Royal Albert Hall
	(British light-welterweight title)		
June 22	Ernesto Bergamesco	W RSC 5	Wembley
Sept 14	Jean-Pierre Younsi	W RSC 1	Royal Albert Hall
Oct 12	Ugo Di Pietro	W RSC 1	Wembley
Oct 26	Ramiro 'Clay' Bolanos	W RSC 4	Royal Albert Hall
Nov 9	Jimmy Heair	W Pts 10	Wembley
Dec 7	Jean-Baptiste Piedvache	W Ret 9	Royal Albert Hall
	(vacant European light-welterweight title)		
1977			
Feb 22	Mario Guilloti	W Pts 10	Royal Albert Hall
Mar 29	John H. Stracey	W RSC 10	Wembley
	(final eliminator for WBC welterweight title)		
June 14	Carlos Palomino	L KO 11	Wembley
	(WBC welterweight title)		
Sept 27	Andy Price	W Pts 10	Wembley

1978

Feb 21	Roy Johnson	W KO 4	Royal Albert Hall
Nov 7	Aundra Love	W RSC 8	Wembley
Dec 5	Sammy Masias	W RSC 1	Royal Albert Hall

1979

Jan 23	Henry Rhiney	W RSC 5	Royal Albert Hall
	(European welterweight title)		
May 1	Lawrence Hafey	W RSC 5	Wembley
May 15	Rafael Rodriguez	W RSC 8	Wembley CC
June 28	Jorgen Hansen	L KO 3	Randers, Denmark
	(European welterweight title)		
Sept 25	Steve Michelarya	W RSC 3	Wembley
Dec 4	Dick Ecklund	W Pts 10	Wembley

1980

Mar 31	Sugar Ray Leonard	L KO 4	Landover, USA
	(WBC welterweight title)		
Oct 14	Mario Mendez	W RSC 2	Royal Albert Hall

1981

Jan 27	Gary Holmgren	W RSC 6	Royal Albert Hall
Feb 24	Jose Ramon Gomez Fouz	W Pts 8	Royal Albert Hall
June 2	Danny Long	W RSC 2	Royal Albert Hall
Nov 3	Reg Ford	L Ret 5	Royal Albert Hall

Career Summary

Bouts Taken:	41
Won	37 (29 inside the distance)
Lost	4